# The Leadership Game

## The fast and fun way to transform silo mentality into a matrix culture of high-performance teams

Ian Robson

D1714859

## Dedication

This book is dedicated to my wife, without whose support it could never have been written.

Edition 1

Copyright © 2019 Ian Robson

ISBN 9781075211898

Published by Perception Dynamics Ltd

# Contents

# Chapter 1

## The fun way to improve performance

There are two ways we can transform organizational performance and culture. The first is slow, difficult and frustrating. The second is fast, fun and easy. Nevertheless, the slow and difficult way is still the most common approach. This is where managers try to motivate subordinates to change, using traditional top-down methods. The problem is that trying to directly change and align other people's behaviour is often like trying to herd cats.

The fast and fun way to achieve change and performance improvement is based on the Leadership Game. The Leadership Game transforms unmanageable complexity into coordinated simplicity. The Game creates the motivation to both collaborate and achieve rapid change, using any performance improvement technique. In fact, we will see that:

*The Leadership Game provides a simple and effective way to engage individuals, groups, or organizations in consistently meeting any or all critical service standards*

So, if it is that easy, it would seem odd that managers often find it difficult to achieve fast change. After all, there is no shortage of different ideas. There are thousands of management books. There are hundreds of thousands of management articles. Many such articles cover various forms of leadership, which should motivate people to collaborate and help their organization to achieve its goals. Many books go into great detail of how teams can use different performance improvement techniques to improve quality or reduce waste. The problem is that even the most conscientious manager can soon become overwhelmed by the sheer volume and range of material.

Much of the literature focuses either on leadership or specific techniques to analyse and improve performance. Yet most managers are aware that trying to engage people, to use a new performance technique, is not as simple as showing them the technique. As the saying goes, "You can lead a horse to water, but you can't make him drink". So just focusing on leadership to try to motivate people to collaborate, without a structured, problem-solving approach, can be equally futile. Clearly, rapid success needs both the method and motive.

However, there are also many case studies of rapid change. Unfortunately, these often describe completely different types of organizations with different cultures. To understand and combine the different approaches, a manager would need the brains of Einstein and the powers of Superman.

Even if managers find a case study that mirrors their own circumstances, and describes both the leadership and performance techniques used, there is still a problem. Just trying to copy what we see in a case study is like trying to copy a magician pulling a rabbit out of an empty hat. We cannot repeat the magician's trick just by mimicking the actions we see. The magician's success is based, not on what their audience believe they can see, but what they cannot see. So, no matter how often they watch the trick, the audience remains obliviously blind to what is blindingly obvious to the magician.

The same applies to case studies. We will find it difficult to repeat other people's success unless we first understand the invisible, psychological states that cause the change. Yet, until now, there has not been a simple approach that is based on sound psychological principles. Nor has there been an approach that can easily and rapidly be proven in practice at any scale, in almost any circumstances.

## A different view of the organization

If we are going to understand the psychological principles behind rapid change, we first need to develop a different view of organizations. Most people understand the vertical management structure. This is the hierarchy that progressively sub-divides the organization into more specialist functions. This vertical, top-down hierarchy is the most widely used and successful of all management ideas.

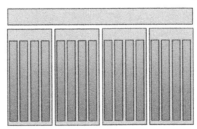

It is simple, structural and powerful. So it would be foolhardy to even think about replacing it. In the simplest form, managers are responsible for the effective coordination of the resources in their control. Those resources include their subordinates' working time. So managers delegate operational responsibilities and trigger the actions as needed. Managers may also set personal performance targets. Yet the vertical structure, when used by itself, has several inherent disadvantages.

**One of the most serious disadvantages of relying solely on the vertical structure is that it encourages a state called Silo Mentality.**

In simple terms, silo mentality is the state where most people only show interest in their own local area of responsibility. They have little interest in collaborating with peers and colleagues to improve the overall effectiveness of the organization. They see no reason to make changes in their area, just to solve other people's problems. So they often resist change. Silo mentality occurs where people consider it is always their manager's responsibility to coordinate the actions of subordinates.

"So this is what silo mentality looks like!"

Thus, people's area of responsibility becomes smaller and smaller, progressing down the hierarchy. To see how we can overcome these problems, we need to understand that the vertical structure is only half of the picture. The missing part is the complementary, but equally powerful, structure needed to continually develop the organization.

To explain the complementary structure, I repeatedly use the analogy of the relay team. Relay teams are great examples of how two complementary structures work together. The first is the traditional, vertical, top-down management hierarchy. So a team will have a team manager as part of their vertical structure. In this role, the manager coordinates the resources needed for the team to take part in the races. So managers select who will be in their team. They organize training for the teams. They ensure their teams get to and from the competitions.

### Performance systems

However, relay teams also have a horizontal structure of *performance systems*. Once the race has started, the team of peers collaborate to coordinate their actions in the most effective way. In effect, we can view this structure as based on the horizontal pathway of the baton. The runners have to get the baton from the hand of the starting runner to the hand of the final runner. However, their focus is to arrive at the finishing line before the competition. So the time set by the external competition is the standard of excellence or benchmark the team needs to beat.

The team members collectively coordinate their actions to pass the baton as effectively as a single person could pass it from one hand to the other. So the team's views of their individual responsibilities are not restricted to the silos of "running with the baton". They have a clear picture of the complete baton pathway, as well as the external groups or competitors who are setting the benchmarks.

However, the horizontal performance systems are not just active during each race. The manager and team members will have previously been collaborating to improve the team's performance. During this time, the manager takes a leadership role, to engage the team in progressively improving their overall capability to meet the benchmark standard. Therefore, vertical and horizontal structures do not work in isolation in the relay team. They complement each other in achieving the best possible result. So, in a relay team, we can say that:

*The vertical management structure coordinates the resources needed to achieve operational outcomes*

*The horizontal performance structure controls the capability to achieve benchmark standards*

However, in the relay team, the team captain may also be taking a leadership role. So we can also say that:

*Performance systems consist of a set of leadership and high-performance team roles*

Organizations also have horizontal pathways. These take the inputs to the organization, through various processes or stages, as they transform into the outputs that deliver services. In a supermarket, those service or process pathways could represent the flow of products for sale. That would start with the delivery from producers. It would finish with the purchase and removal by customers. Alternatively, a pathway could represent the route of patients through the different stages, as they pass through a hospital for an operation. Those stages could include registration, waiting on the ward, the operation, and recovery, to name but a few. So we can also say:

**_Service pathways typically involve a sequence of stages or processes needed to create an outcome, to the standards needed to achieve a purpose_**

In simple terms, we can map these service pathways onto the vertical management structure. The pathways appear as horizontal lines, passing through the various vertical, specialised functions. These horizontal pathways are like the pathway of the baton in a relay race. So the service pathways form the basic structure in which performance systems exist.

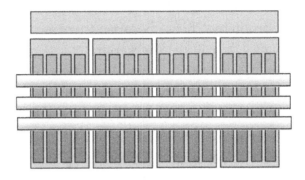

Unfortunately, people often assume the horizontal structure automatically represents another layer of management. However, if we are to discover the secrets of the magician's illusions, we need to view service pathways as the complementary structure for performance systems.

We have seen that, in the vertical structure, it is the managers who are technically responsible for the coordination between subordinates. However, our metaphorical runners are often responsible to different managers. In turn, each manager is only responsible for the individual performance of their own section. So, with the vertical structure, none of the individuals, controlling the separate parts of the pathway, are responsible for the effectiveness of the "baton" passes. Nor are they responsible for the overall pathway performance.

However, the successes of real relay teams are dependent on both these aspects, not just the individual performances of the runners. For the same reasons, the success of organizations is equally dependent on the overall effectiveness of its service pathways. Even so, few organizations have formal methods for engaging the people, who control the processes in a pathway, to collaborate in transforming the effectiveness of the pathway flows.

Even if we add an extra layer of matrix or service management to coordinate the pathway flows, it does not solve the basic problem. This is because there would still be a set of individuals controlling the separate actions along the service pathway. None of them would have any responsibility for the overall performance of the metaphorical relay race. Nor would any of them be responsible for the effectiveness of the connections or baton passes. They are still likely to view these aspects as the responsibility of the project or service manager. So they are unlikely to have any ownership or motivation to improve either. This means that while we view these horizontal pathways from a management perspective, we will always struggle to achieve rapid change and performance improvement. So, we will start by assuming that:

***Every service pathway has an associated pathway of performance systems***

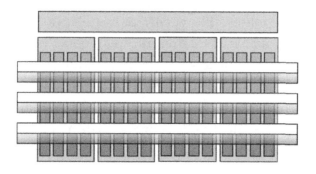

### Service development and delivery pathways

So, we are going to split the service pathways into two component pathways. The first is the service *delivery* pathway, which includes all the various processes and activities needed to deliver the service. The second is the service *development* pathway, which includes all the relevant performance systems in the pathway. However, we cannot create performance systems unless we find a robust way of reproducing the psychological conditions of relay races along service pathways. Without performance systems, there is likely to be a repetitious stream of issues between the various roles along the pathways. Those issues are caused by one person, not passing an outcome to the standard needed by the recipient. These issues might include a report delivered later than promised, or a quality problem. In other words, issues occur when the standards delivered at pathway connections do not meet the standards required.

*So, using the relay analogy, we can map such organizational issues as gaps or "dropped batons" at the connections between specialist stages in the horizontal service pathways.*

We have seen the vertical structure can easily remove the responsibility for effective collaboration along the pathway. So, we need to understand how we can recreate the psychological conditions of high-performance teams. Once we can do that, we will always be able to use the fast and fun way of change and performance improvement.

Indeed, throughout the following chapters, we will see how the Leadership Game uses a set of simple principles to develop high-performance, silo-busting cultures. We will see the Game is simple enough for small groups to solve local problems quickly. We will also see that it is powerful enough to transform the culture and performance of whole organizations. That makes the Leadership Game a game-changer.

This is not a wild or unsubstantiated claim. You will find that this book is full of case studies showing how the Game has achieved rapid culture change and performance improvement in real-life situations. However, these examples are not used as templates to copy. They are used to help us understand how people develop new mental models that result in such rapid change. Many of these are examples where I, or my colleagues, have directly facilitated managers to use the Leadership Game. However, thousands of managers have also attended my master classes on rapid cultural change. So several of the case studies are examples where such managers have quickly achieved success on their own. They achieved this simply by applying the principles of the Leadership Game, which they learnt in those master classes. However, it is worth repeating that you will not succeed by trying to copy a technique. You will achieve success by applying the principles highlighted in each example.

To show this point, the first case study we will consider was one launched by one manager soon after attending one of my master classes. In all the case studies I describe in this book, I have changed the names and some details to protect the confidentiality of clients. However, all the case studies are real examples of the ease and speed with which anyone can achieve change and performance improvements.

This first example only involves a few people. However, that makes it a good starting point to understand the basic principles of the Leadership Game. Then, as we progress through the chapters, we can build on those basic principles, until it becomes obvious how we can achieve rapid transformations across whole organizations. This is because the approach of the Game allows us to first prove the success on a small scale. Then prove a small-scale rollout of that success. Then we prove the success of the full rollout. We will see how this approach to organizational change is much faster and effective than traditional top-down approaches.

## The legal case study

In this example, Trevor was an operations manager in a public service regulatory institution. The regulator's role was to ensure that all organizations in their sector met the defined legal requirements. The regulator offered various services, including advice, training, and inspection to help organizations meet the legal standards. It also had a small legal group who took the necessary legal steps in cases where organizations were not progressing satisfactorily.

After attending one of my master classes, Trevor identified how he could quickly test the power of the Leadership Game in his current role. Although he was responsible for all operations, his primary problem was the legal section. This section consisted of five qualified legal solicitors. Once a case had been referred to the legal group, they began a series of standard legal procedures. These included the final stage of taking an organization to court, if necessary, to get a legally-binding programme to achieve the required outcome.

The legal team had an IT system to log the progress of each case. However, the members of the legal section often neglected to update the system. Trevor kept trying to encourage the members of the group to keep the IT system up-to-date and to track the time taken to complete cases. The legal officers often politely acknowledged the requests and then ignored them. Alternatively, they simply replied that they had to follow the agreed legal process, so there was no way of speeding up. Similarly, they explained the more time they spent updating the IT system, the more the backlog would increase. They considered the only way to reduce the backlog of cases was to employ more legal staff.

Trevor felt the group had the potential to work together more effectively to address the backlog without more resources. Although this may seem like a special example, most managers can identify similar scenarios. To start the process, Trevor had a short session with the members of the legal section. He started by reiterating the purpose of the whole department was to ensure external organizations in their sector were compliant with legislation. He explained that it was essential that everyone in the department was aligned with that purpose. Even when they sent legal correspondence, they needed to view the processes from that perspective. The aim of such stages should be to encourage the client organization to become compliant. He then wrote the key fact at the top of the flipchart: "Help ensure organizations are compliant with the legislation."

On its own, this introduction is not likely to change anything. However, as we will see, it does help to ensure that everyone focused on the common context in which they needed to operate. Trevor then asked the team to identify the legal processes they would need to complete in the worst possible case. He used a flipchart to draw a series of circles, putting the relevant names of processes in each circle. He then asked the group to assess the stages from the perspective of trying to ensure the organizations complied with the legal standards as quickly as possible. He drew rectangles between the processes to represent the delay between each stage.

He explained that, with any pathway, it was important to define the benchmark standards between each stage. So, he asked the group what they thought would be the most effective period between each stage for encouraging organizations to achieve the necessary standards. So the group collectively agreed on the number of days that would have the best effect between each process. Trevor then wrote the information on the flipchart. In effect, this was a map of a service pathway, with the benchmark standards needed at the connections, to ensure the pathway was as effective as possible.

Trevor then explained that it was important for every section in the department to ensure that it was coordinating its actions in the most effective way. So it was important to monitor whether they were becoming better or worse at keeping to the most effective standards. He explained that he would set up a special report in the IT system that would use the benchmark standards set by the team. The report would print the total combined number of days over the standard for all the current cases. For example, if ten cases were all ten days overdue, then the total number of overdue days would be one-hundred. It would also show the number of overdue cases at each stage.

Trevor now explained that he would put a large, blank graph on the flipchart sheet and put the sheet on the wall of the team area. This would provide evidence that the new system was working better than the old system. So he asked the five team members to each take it in turns to run the report at the end of each day. It would only take a couple of minutes each day. That meant it was only a few minutes of extra work each week for each member of the group. Once the team member had run the report, they should put it on the wall and manually enter the current number of overdue days on the graph. By looking at the trend over time, it would be clear if the organization was getting better or worse at keeping to the benchmark standards the team had set.

Trevor explained that as long as the group could show that they had the process under control, he would not need to become involved. However, he asked that the person who had updated the graph should take the lead in ensuring there was a brief group meeting at the beginning of the next day. That session would allow them all to view the graph, review progress, and discuss any ideas for reducing any backlog.

The team agreed to the new method because it was a minimal amount of work. They also agreed who would be the lead in arranging the meeting and updating the information on which day. This list was added to the flipchart sheet.

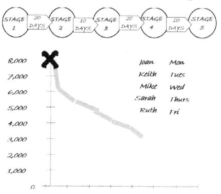

Trevor had an office off the open plan area where the legal team and other departmental staff were located. The graph was on the wall of the open plan office, near to the door to Trevor's office. The next day, the group were interested to see what the figure was. However, when they plotted the first figure, every member of the team was shocked to see the total was 8,000 days. Immediately, the legal team agreed the figure was ridiculous. They felt it must be because the computer system was out of date. Indeed, Trevor could hear many of the comments of disbelief. When Trevor passed the graph the next day, he saw that it had magically come down to just under 6,000 days. The team explained that this was simply because the computer was reporting incorrect information. They almost implied that this was the fault of the IT system. However, they had now corrected the system. They also explained that they were looking at ways to improve the figure further.

The team continued to take it in turns to update the chart daily. Rapidly, the number of overdue days started falling substantially, without Trevor becoming involved. However, on one particular day, two members of the team were away on holiday. Joan, the team member who was due to run the report, had a reputation for being something of a loner and not a genuine part of the team. Although she worked at a reasonable pace throughout the day, she was inflexible. Even when she arrived late to work, she never stayed a minute past five o'clock.

On this particular day, Joan pressed the button to print the report from the IT system. While she was waiting for the report, she put on her coat. However, when she started to update the graph, she immediately saw that if she updated the graph, it would break its unbroken downward trend. Trevor heard her exclaim, "Oh! It hasn't gone down!" In principle, this was not an issue. Daily variations in circumstances would always mean there could be variation around any trend. However, she did not want to be the member of the team who updated the graph when it was breaking its downward trend. So she took off her coat. For the first time in her career, Joan stayed an extra twenty minutes to process two other cases. She then re-ran the report and updated the graph. As she did so, she said, "There, that is better!"

On the face of it, this sudden change in behaviour does not make sense. Yet it is similar to the point where the team first plotted the total number of overdue days. Then, their assessment suddenly motivated the team to update the IT system with all the old information. Both situations caused a sudden change in the previously established behaviours of those involved. So, as we progress, we will need to fully understand the psychological reasons that triggered such dramatic changes.

The downward trend in the graph continued for some time. Then it started to flatten off. A few days after this, the team asked to have a meeting with Trevor. In that meeting, the team explained the problem was that they only had a limited allocation of slots with the local court. So they asked Trevor if they could arrange with the courts to twin-track the number of cases for the next month to reduce the backlog. They felt that they could convince the courts to do this because they would explain that reducing the backlog of cases would lead to fewer court hearings in the future. Trevor happily agreed to this – it was something he had suggested some months earlier. Then, the group had rejected the idea. Now, they were trying to get his buy-in to increase their own workload to meet the new schedule!

The downward trend of the graph continued over the next four months until there was not a single overdue case. Shortly after this, Trevor left the organization. However, two years later, he returned for a meeting. While in the building, he happened to meet a member of the legal team. He asked Trevor to come and have a look at their graph. He then took great pride in showing his ex-manager there was still not a single overdue case.

## Replicating the success

This transformation seems so simple that you might think it would be simple to copy in different scenarios. Indeed, the following chapters will show exactly how to reproduce similar successes with both small groups and whole organizations. However, as I explained earlier, believing we can achieve this type of success, just by copying what we think we have seen, is like the magician's trick – an illusion. We will never see the real causes while we are viewing the case study from the vertical management perspective. From this view, we might describe the causes of success in standard, textbook explanations.

For example, we might consider this as an example of a manager showing great leadership qualities. Yet it is difficult to identify any such qualities from this case study. Equally, we could try to explain it as just an example of a manager giving a group of people a measurable target. However, no target was given or even suggested. Alternatively, some may describe it as 'what gets measured gets done'. Nevertheless, most experienced managers will know that just asking a group to measure performance is unlikely to change the group culture to that of a high-performance team. So these simplistic explanations are not going to help us to reproduce this success.

Another interpretation is the group became a team through ownership and empowerment. Again, most experienced managers will be well aware that just asking a group to work as a team and sort out the performance issues is not a robust way of changing culture. Ownership and empowerment are natural consequences of the Leadership Game. However, they were not strategies used by the manager to create a high-performance team. So, no amount of explanation of the manager's involvement with the group can completely explain the rapid change and performance improvement that occurred. There were other psychological forces at work in this case study. These were the forces that were able to rapidly transform the group with silo mentality into a high-performance team.

In fact, there is no simple factor responsible for the success in this case study. Indeed, many factors combine to create the necessary psychological conditions. It was those conditions that made this a fast and easy transformation. However, these factors seem invisible when we look at the details from a vertical, management perspective. Nevertheless, they are obvious once we start viewing the story from the perspective of horizontal challenges.

Fortunately, the Leadership Game inherently creates the complete set of conditions needed to ensure that successful change can be fast and fun. So, to understand those conditions, we need to start by looking at the role of the wall chart.

### Performance boards – Evidence of success

Managers in most organizations use performance information from various documents, such as graphs, spreadsheets and charts, to make everyday decisions. It would be easy to consider the wall chart, map or board used by the legal team as just another example of a useful tool. However, the map was not just a useful tool. In fact, we will see that:

*Consistent accountability for the performance board is the central lynchpin of the fast and fun way to achieve change and performance improvement*

We will also see that:

*Without that lynchpin, change is likely to be painful and slow*

The performance board is analogous to the board of any board game. You cannot play the game without the right board for that game. The board, in this case, served a different purpose to the way information is used in many organizations. For example, the measure was not the typical type of measure used in vertical structures. In this example, it appeared the group were only measuring outstanding days. However, as we will see, psychologically:

*They were using a performance board to collectively account for their success in improving the capability of their service to meet the benchmarks of excellence*

In comparison, the typical vertical approach would be to measure the number of cases completed by each individual. Motivation might be created by paying bonuses based on individual performance against arbitrary targets. Neither of those approaches was used in this case study. Similarly, the typical vertical approach might be for a central department to produce information and graphs. The department would then distribute it to managers for them to communicate to their staff. Again, this is not what happened in this example. So what did cause the rapid change?

To help understand the role of the performance board, I often ask executives in my master classes about their own experiences. I ask if any of them have visited organizations renowned for their performance-focused cultures, such as a focus on product quality or customer service. Then I ask those delegates, who have made such visits, whether there were any publicly displayed performance maps or charts on the walls. I also ask if it was the local teams using those maps, rather than their managers.

It soon becomes clear that many such organizations do have many public performance maps owned by local teams. So visitors often assume that it is the organizational culture that ensures teams consistently update performance maps. However, this assumption is wrong. *The cause and effect is the other way round.* The boards or charts are evidence of the teams' successes in finding and removing the pathway performance gaps. Those gaps are the difference between the current capability and that needed to meet the benchmark standards of excellence. In other words, it is not that groups in such cultures start to use public performance maps as one of their tools. It is that these organizations have used the principle that:

*Organizational cultures rapidly transform when the groups, who control the pathway processes collectively account for the maps of their pathway performance gaps.*

So, to understand how to apply this principle in our own organizations, we first need to understand the principles that will enable us to solve two complex problems. The first solution we need is a simple way of analysing pathways to optimise their performance. The second solution we need is to understand the psychological conditions that engage groups in collaborating to use the first solution. This is because the Leadership Game brings these two solutions together to create the fast and fun way of improving performance.

### Reality can be more complex

Although I have represented the organizational flows as a

small set of horizontal pathways, the detail of such pathways is far more complex. Indeed, there is a complex network of flows of information, people, goods, resources and services in organizations. These are the metaphorical batons. Therefore, it is easy to assume that pathways and standards in some organizations are too complex, vague or intangible to map. Such complexity often makes it difficult to know where to start mapping pathways, or identifying the gaps or dropped batons. So to develop a structured approach, which addresses all these issues, we are going to use a problem-solving technique called *Systems Thinking*.

## Thinking in Systems

Systems thinking is an approach that allows us to see the bigger picture as a set of interconnected systems. This allows us to easily home in on critical details. Systems thinking has only been regarded as a separate discipline within the last fifty years or so. However, people have used the principles for much longer. Indeed, many of the transformations, from mystic arts to respected sciences, have come about by applying systems thinking. A classic example is the science of medicine. Up to a few hundred years ago, medicine had advanced relatively little from the types of practices used by witch doctors. However, medicine rapidly developed into a science, once specialists started to view the complexity of the human body as connected systems. For example, it is now common language to talk about the respiratory system, the central nervous system, the circulatory system, the digestive system, to name but a few.

In this book, we are going to use the systems approach to help us understand the complexities of organizations. So, we are going to use the approach to help in understanding both components of the Leadership Game. These are the visual mapping of the pathways, and the psychological conditions that ensure people automatically collaborate to improve pathway performance.

*We define a system as a coordinated set of resources within a boundary, acting as a whole that is greater than the sum of its parts.*

Indeed, we can see almost anything as a system. So a relay race, a football match or the central heating in our houses can all be considered as systems. When we draw a system, we are creating a map, model or representation of a real-world system. However, when we start to use systems to understand organizations, then the approach becomes even more powerful. An organization is a system. So we can also represent an organization by a simple boundary. However, organizations do not work in isolation. They are interconnected with external systems such as customers, clients, suppliers and regulators, to name just a few. They also comprise of internal systems for producing the goods and services they supply. There will also be other internal systems to obtain the goods and services needed to operate. Organizations will have systems to recruit and train staff. They have systems to keep track of orders, payments and salaries, to name but a few. So we already view organizations as comprising of many component systems. However, it is essential to remember that such systems involve people coordinating the necessary actions.

### The power of conceptual boundaries

The power of systems thinking is that it allows us to map conceptual boundaries around systems, even when there is no clear boundary in the real world. For example, we have already identified a few of the internal "systems" of the human body, such as the digestive or nervous systems. These are so interconnected that it would be impossible to physically separate them to see how they worked in isolation. Using conceptual boundaries to define systems allows us to better understand what is happening inside each system. It also allows us to see how each system connects with various other systems.

This contrasts sharply with the more usual problem-solving technique of pure analysis or reduction. Analysis simply breaks down a problem into component parts. That allows us to study each part separately. However, systems thinking allows us to do more than understand the internal workings of the separate systems. It also allows us to see how the various systems connect with one another, to build up into a whole that is greater than the sum of its parts.

### Internal and external views of pathways

So, we can represent or map any system by drawing a boundary, such as a square or a circle. Once we have the system boundary, we have a choice. We can start mapping all the component systems *inside* that boundary. Alternatively, we can ignore all the internal detail of the system. We can just map how that system *externally* connects to other systems to create even bigger systems. For example, we can use the systems approach to identify potential gaps in something as complex as a national postal system. Any national postal service is likely to be complex inside the organization. However, from outside, the system is simple. It takes the letter, which we posted into a letterbox, and delivers it through the house letterbox of its destination address, within a specific timescale. This pathway is easy to map. In effect, this is a "helicopter" view of the pathway.

However, now consider looking inside the national mail system. Consider trying to map the connections between all the internal organizational systems needed to move letters from the box to destination. That map could soon become very complex. Yet, from outside, it is easy to map the pathway, including the benchmark standards and any potential performance gaps at the pathway connections. For example, the benchmark standards for the delivery of letters are that they will be delivered, undamaged, within the defined timescale and at the agreed cost to the stated address. From this perspective, if the letter is not delivered within the defined timescale, there is a performance gap in the service pathway. So, from the external perspective, benchmark standards, pathway flows, connections and performance gaps in the service pathways are easy to identify.

Similarly, consider a mail system, which is delivering millions of letters each day. If it performs at 99% of on-time delivery of letters, this may sound reasonable from inside the system. This is a typical internal measure of the capability of a system. Yet with that performance, it could potentially upset tens of thousands of recipients each day, because they did not receive their letters or parcels on time.

So, we can see that:

*Inside the system, people focus on carrying out the actions needed to produce an output*

However:

*Outside the system, people are concerned about the output meeting their standards*

So from this external view, we can assess whether the capability of the system is improving or not. We can say that our ideal future would be our helicopter view of the system, working in a way that created zero upset customers. If the total number of "upset customers" is reducing, then the capability of the system is improving. We will look at this in more detail in later chapters. However, when we start to use this form of measurement, we call it "assessing the system capability as an external assessor". So we can easily develop a map that shows the current helicopter view of the pathway system, as well as the benchmarks that define what the pathway needs to look like in the future. When we combine the current helicopter view with the benchmarks that need to be achieved, we call it the *performance view* of the pathway. In effect, the performance view shows the gap between the current pathway and the future pathway capability, which is capable of meeting those benchmarks.

In fact, all team sports and games are constructed around the psychological conditions created by the performance view. For example, consider the relay race. Inside the system, the runners collectively move the baton, from the input of the pathway to its output. We have seen the success or benchmark standard is the standard set by the competition. The judge, or external assessor, will assess which team, or subsystem, achieves the critical standard needed to win the race. So, the runners coordinate their actions as effectively as possible. This is because they are assessing the performance in the same way as the external assessor at the finishing line. This may seem an odd way to describe a relay race. Yet, this principle applies to any situation that inherently transforms a group into a higher performance team. So, we can say that a critical aspect of the fast and fun way is to ensure:

*Everyone who is working inside a system is also consistently using the performance view to assess the system capability, through the eyes of the external assessors*

It is the combination of the internal and external views that are critical to the complete picture of the pathway. It is difficult to overemphasise the power of ensuring people become accountable for this performance view. It is the principle at the heart of most successful transformations. Indeed, in the legal case study, there was a clear point when the group started to plot the total number of overdue days. This was the point when the people inside the legal system started to assess the system capability as external assessors. That was the point where the groups used the performance view of the pathway to start becoming a high-performance team. So we need to understand how we can more generally apply such a simple principle to complex problems. To do this, we need to see how the principles of systems can help us better understand the psychology behind human behaviour.

## Understanding the psychology of behaviour

We often assume that it is difficult to change people's behaviour. Yet, people continually change their behaviour to suit different contexts. For example, a person's behaviour immediately changes, if they change from playing football to cricket. Equally, their behaviour will again immediately change if they stop playing cricket and start playing cards. So we are going to use the principles of systems to help us understand how people naturally change their behaviour to adapt to different situations.

For a person to coordinate their actions, their brain has to process all the various information it is receiving from outside. In effect, the brain achieves this by creating an internal mental model, which represents the external context the person faces. It does this by using what psychologists call the executive part of the brain. So to make that process as effective as possible, the first mental stage is to retrieve just the information needed to react to the external circumstances. Therefore, the executive brain first groups just the information relevant to the current context. It starts building this context from the external information that it is receiving through the person's senses. It then groups this information with the internal memories and developed skills it needs to mentally model the current context.

## Thought bubbles

Obviously, we cannot see what is happening inside the brain. So we are going to imagine that everyone has a thought bubble coming from the top of their heads.

We are going to assume the picture or model that they build to represent their current situation is visible in their thought bubble. Therefore, if they were running in a relay race, they would have a picture or model of a relay race in their thought bubble. If they were playing baseball, then that would be the model visible in the bubble.

However, we are going to consider every situation as a system. So we view different situations as different systems. This means that when someone is playing baseball or running a relay race, their thought bubble contains just the information that is relevant to that system.

This means we can say that when people enter a situation that they are familiar with, they call up that system information into their thought bubble. They can then relate it to the current information from their senses.

## Two levels of systems

So we can now consider two levels of systems. There are the real world systems and a mental model of those systems. For example, the real world system for a game of football would be the physical activity taking place on the pitch between the two teams. However, at the level of mental model systems, each player would have their own mental model, showing in their thought bubble, of their own view of the real, physical game.

## System protocols

We can define the internal working of any system as its protocol. A protocol can consist of several pieces of information, such as the rules of the game, a set of instructions, a recipe or route. Different types of systems will have different protocols. So football matches will have different rules of the game to rules used for tennis. The protocol for each system defines the set of internal subsystems. Each subsystem has a role in the main system. Each role will have a related set of actions or responsibilities. So the protocol will also define the allowable and disallowable actions of each role.

When people enter a system, it is analogous to actors taking roles in a play. In effect, the actors have to become those characters. They behave in the way that their roles need to behave, rather than the way that they would act when not performing in the play.

Subsystems or roles within the system, waiting to be filled

In the same way, when people take up roles involving work, play or family life, they will change their behaviour according to their internal version of the protocol of their current role. In effect, although we are not consciously aware of it, we are continually adapting our behaviour. We will change from playing one character or role in one system to being a different character or role in a different system.

This means that when people enter a football match, they will use the mental protocol for the role they are playing in that system. If they play a game of rugby, they will use the rugby protocol. If they enter a tennis system, they will play by the tennis protocol. In each case, their behaviour will be different. With this simple mental method, people can respond rapidly to changing contexts.

So the key to understanding what changes a person's behaviour is the fact that:

**_A person's behaviour is likely to change automatically and naturally as soon as they change their perception of the system they are in or the role that they are taking in that system_**

## The protocol of the Leadership Game

Therefore, people's behaviour is dependent on the protocol they are currently using. In the next chapter, we will see that although it is difficult to change an existing mental protocol, it is easy to engage people in learning and using a new protocol. This is what happened in the legal example. There, the group were asked to use a protocol for what, in effect, was a new "game". That was to account for the performance of the service pathway and have daily meetings to agree on their plan of action. Although this was trivial, it ensured they were consistently accounting for the documentary evidence of their success in removing the pathway performance gaps. Yet, in this case, this was enough to transform the culture and the performance of the group's pathway.

It is important to remember that at no point did the manager try to change people's behaviour in terms of the way they carried out the legal processes. However, as we will see in the following chapters, the seemingly trivial stages of engaging the group to "play" a new game, with its own rules, is the most critical step in the whole process. It is the failure to complete this step successfully, which makes so many change programmes slow, painful and prone to failure. Yet, the critical nature of such steps is almost invisible from just reading the case study.

## Summary

In this chapter, we have seen there is a second, complementary structure in organizations. This is the performance structure, which is based on the horizontal service pathways. We have seen that it is difficult to make groups directly responsible for the overall performance of horizontal pathways. However, it is possible to ensure relevant groups are responsible for maintaining and accounting for the performance boards for those pathways. These are the boards that show the map of the pathway gaps. We have also seen that high-performance teams naturally form when the people who are in control of a service pathway become responsible for accounting for their performance board. This is the simple basis of the fast and fun way to achieve change.

So we have seen that on the one hand, we have a performance board, showing the capability of a service pathway to meet the benchmark standards. On the other hand, we have a group of individuals who work on the processes inside the pathway. We bring those two aspects together with the Leadership Game. This ensures the group, who can collectively control the performance, become accountable for the performance board. When that happens, the group naturally becomes a high-performance team. So combining the vertical management structure with the horizontal leadership structure creates a matrix culture of high performance.

Over the following chapters, we will continue to develop this principle further. We will use our knowledge of systems to create a powerful approach of analysing pathway performance. So it should not be surprising that, as we develop it, the result will inherently combine many other well-known and proven techniques. We will also see how this basic approach is expanded to transform whole organizations. In fact, no matter what the size of the transformation, the same principles will apply. So, in the following chapters, we will progressively identify the principles and protocols of the Leadership Game. These are the principles that will ensure change and performance improvement is fast and fun.

# Chapter 2

## The perceptions of control

### Review and Overview

In chapter one, we saw how we could use systems thinking to help understand the fast and fun way of achieving change and performance improvement. We saw that relay teams have two coordinating systems. The first is the vertical management system. The second is the horizontal peer group performance system. Almost all organizations have clear vertical systems. Yet few have a formal structure of horizontal, challenge-team systems.

In this chapter, we are going to look more closely at the psychological switches involved. In particular, we will look at the switches that allow the Leadership Game to engage groups in collaborating to create high-performance teams. We will again use a case study to explain the point. We are also going to see how the Leadership Game expands the mental boundary of control. We will see how the boundary of perceived control is a critical aspect of human behaviour. Finally, we will briefly look at the other psychological triggers that are also critical to rapid change.

### Protocols

#### Small changes

When managers have only experienced the difficult, top-down approach to change, they often consider the Leadership

Game is too easy to be true. Executives often say to me that they have tried "something like that, but it doesn't work". To which I explain that the psychology behind the Game is such that seemingly small differences can have disproportionate effects. Often, managers try to view the Game as a useful, top-down technique for managers to engage staff. Managers who view it from that perspective often consider that there is no difference between this approach and the methods they have used unsuccessfully in the past. So, we will use the legal case study, described in the first chapter, to assess the effect that apparently small changes would have on its success.

When I do this in my master classes, I ask delegates whether they think any of the following changes would have affected the outcome:

- The manager running the report every day himself, as well as updating the wall chart himself

- Not having the first session, where the group developed the overall context and collectively agreed on the benchmark standards at the connections

- Not having an agreed rota that ensured every member of the team took turns in being the lead, who both updated the chart and ensured there was a brief review meeting each morning

Most delegates intuitively consider that any of these changes would have a harmful effect on the outcome. However, if we are to be able to consistently achieve rapid transformation, we need more than just intuition to guide us. This is because achieving change and performance improvement is always fast and simple, as long as we create the correct conditions. This means we need to look in more detail at the model of human behaviour described in the previous chapter. The model of thought bubbles and system protocols will help us understand the psychological effect of the Game board.

### Mental and mapped Protocols

In chapter one, we saw that systems such as football or tennis have a clearly defined protocol. Indeed, there may be documented or mapped rules for different system protocols. However, that does not mean that everyone's mental protocols are the same, even when they are all inside the same system. For example, the written protocols, or rules of the game, for football define that players should not foul each other. However, some players may interpret this as meaning that they can foul, as long as they are not caught. This would be their personal version of the rules; their own mental protocol of the written protocol of the football system.

So it is important to remember that it is a person's own mental protocol of the current system that affects their behaviour. This is the protocol in their thought bubble. It is not their manager's or anyone else's perception of the correct protocol. It is not necessarily the protocol that someone has told the person to use. It is not what they should know, nor is it what seems obvious to anyone else. Nor is it common sense. It is not even the documented protocol. People develop, store and use their own mental versions of the system protocols. Their behaviour is a consequence of their own versions of those system protocols.

For example, there may be a stated rule at work that people should not use computers for accessing social media sites. Some people will interpret this to mean that they need to make sure that no one sees them using computers for social messaging. Others will accept that they must not access social media sites under any circumstance. So if a person appears be behaving inappropriately, we can now start to see why. It is because the protocol, which they have retrieved into their thought bubble, is inappropriate. So we are going to call the mental protocol, currently being used by someone, their *protocol-in-use.*

### Protocols in everyday life

So, a system may have a clearly defined protocol. However, if we are not aware of that protocol, we will not be able to act correctly. For example, I occasionally hire cars when travelling. On one occasion, I found that I could not find how to open the fuel cap cover. I had to go and ask the assistant in the garage shop. She explained to me that on the car model that I was using, I had to pull a lever at the base of the driver's seat inside the car. In effect, the system protocol was simple. My problem was that I did not have a mental version for the protocol of that system. However, once I learnt the new protocol, I could use it every time I needed it while driving the hire car.

Most of us have had similar experiences. They can be embarrassing. We cannot complete the simplest challenge if we do not know the system protocol. Many of my delegates mention that even getting coffee out of a new coffee machine can be a challenge if you do not know the protocol! So, we cannot even make a cup of coffee or open a petrol cap without knowing an effective protocol. This means we have little chance of bringing about change, without an effective protocol.

### Vertical management protocols

We can even start to better understand intangible concepts,

such as management style, by looking at their protocols and how they affect people's thought bubbles. For example, as I briefly mentioned in the first chapter, we can say that managers start by creating the bigger picture in their thought bubble. They then split that picture into manageable processes. This enables managers to assign responsibility to the subordinates to carry out the separate processes.

The problem with this approach is that it can leave pathways and thought bubbles disconnected.

In other words, this vertical protocol inherently creates many horizontal gaps for which there is no clear responsibility. In effect, this is silo mentality.

### *Resistance to change*

So we can say that every system or situation has its own protocol. Once people consistently use that protocol, the protocol-in-use becomes progressively more difficult to change. Yet, when we rely solely on the vertical hierarchy, managers are expected to identify the required changes and then get their subordinates' "buy-in" to bring about those changes. This can be difficult because it is analogous to trying to get someone, who is currently playing tennis, to agree to new rules, where they need to use a baseball bat rather than a tennis racquet. Not surprisingly, people resist such changes. This is why it can be difficult to convince people to change their existing protocols-in-use.

As I briefly mentioned in the first chapter, although it is difficult to change existing protocols, it is relatively easy to engage people in learning new protocols. People do this when they find themselves in new circumstances. In such cases, they have no established mental protocols to change. When managers engage groups in collectively mapping the horizontal pathways of their services, it is a new situation with new rules of the "game". So it is much easier to ensure the group use those new rules. In this game, they collectively map the service pathway, together with the relevant benchmark standards and the gaps at the connections. This is the start of developing the bigger picture of the pathway they collectively control. It is the picture that shows both the external and internal views of a pathway. It is the view that we have called the performance view of the pathway.

This process begins to change and align the group's mental models of their roles in those service pathways. The more they account for the map of the gaps in meeting the benchmark standards, the more their behaviour in the real world will naturally change and become more effective. We will see the

Leadership Game rules are that the team have to get the manager's "buy-in" for any changes they need to implement. Further, the rules of the Game are that those proposals have to meet strict criteria. This is a reversal of the normal, top-down approach. So, the Leadership Game can be viewed as a team-building board game, focused on continually accounting for the map of the improving performance of their service pathways.

## The Game-board level

### *The chess analogy*

To help us understand why that approach of using a map is so powerful, we will start by considering the analogy of two people playing a game of chess. In a world with such a wide range of different computer games, many people may never have played chess on a chessboard. However, most know a little about the game. Although there are a fairly small number of chess pieces, there are many possible choices for each move.

The protocol for chess is that two players compete to win the contest by exceeding the standard set by the other. Of course, just knowing the protocol of chess or the rules of the game does not help a player to decide which move to make. To do that, the player needs a method of solving problems. In effect, the players develop a mental model of the chess game in their thought bubble. They use their mental model to mentally make possible moves and predict the likely effects of those moves.

## The initial two levels

So, at this stage, the players are playing chess at two levels. The players are physically moving the chess pieces in the real world. However, they make their decisions about the game in their thought bubbles.

## The huge chess pitch

Now let us now consider a variation of the normal chess game. Imagine two average players are playing chess on a giant chessboard. That chessboard is larger than several football pitches. The chess pieces are huge. They are many times the height of the players. They are so large that they need rollers to allow the players to move the pieces. Nevertheless, it still takes much effort to move each piece.

Not being able to see the whole board makes it more difficult to make the best decision for the next move. However, let's imagine that one of the players is using a personal mini chess set. This chess set acts as a physical or visual model of the pieces in the real game on the pitch. Every time the player wants to make a move, he uses his small chess set to decide the move to make. He then goes to the large chess pitch and moves the relevant piece. Also, when his opponent makes a move, the player, with his own model of the game, updates his personal chess set. The other player does not have a personal chess set. He is trying to keep track of the moves by looking around at the big pieces and their position on the giant board.

In this scenario, which player would you predict has an advantage? If there is an advantage, why? Would it be a small, large or huge advantage?

When I describe this scenario to managers at my master classes, most predict the player with a personal chess set would have an advantage. When I ask what degree of advantage the mini chess set gives, most people consider that it will provide a large or huge advantage. They consider the player with the personal chess set has this advantage because that player can see the big picture.

## *A living map or model*

Now, we can consider the chess game board as the map of the real-world system. It contains all the information about the current state of play of the real operations on the playing pitch. To many people, the advantage of the chess board seems too obvious to mention. Nevertheless, again, it is far more profound than it may appear. It suggests that whenever complex changes occur, out of direct sight, anyone can gain a large advantage by using an accurate model of the system.

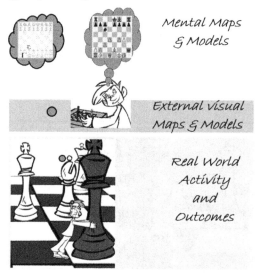

Mental Maps & Models

External Visual Maps & Models

Real World Activity and Outcomes

However, it is essential that this model is an accurate representation of the current state of play. If it is not an accurate representation, decisions made from the game board could be worse than decisions made on the pitch. Now imagine that both players started using the same mini chess set. In this scenario, both players would have the same advantage of having a helicopter view of the model of the chess pitch. So neither player has an advantage over the other. Technically, the contest is still on the chess pitch, or in the 'real world'.

*Yet, in practice, all the protocols, models and decisions are being applied to the chess model, rather than the giant chessboard.*

However, as we noted earlier, the chess example involves two players competing. This is clearly different from the collaborative efforts of the legal team. Therefore, we need to alter the analogy to one that develops teams.

### Protocols define collaboration or competition

It is the system protocols that define the relationships between roles in the system. So they also define whether the people taking those roles collaborate, compete or disengage. For example, if two people took up roles in the same team of a football match, they would collaborate. If they entered roles on opposing teams, they would compete. If they took up roles in teams that were playing different matches, they would disengage from each other's activities. So, to better reflect what happened in the legal case study, we need to change our chess set analogy to a board game with a protocol that ensures collaboration.

### Team Scrabble

To achieve this, we could replace the giant chessboard with a huge Scrabble© pitch.

In principle, a small Scrabble© set could provide the same advantages as the mini chess set. Similarly, two players could compete using that same small model of the real-world Scrabble© pitch.

However, the difference between chess and Scrabble© is that we can change the rules or protocol for Scrabble© to become team Scrabble©. Then, the game is played by teams, rather than individuals. Teams can consist of two, three or four people collaborating.

In this scenario, a small Scrabble© board would also make it much easier for the team members to collaborate in planning their actions, before moving the huge pieces. This is because the teams are using the small Scrabble© board to see the big picture and decide what actions they should take. So it is the protocol used on the small board game, at the map level, which defines whether a group work as individuals or collaborate as teams.

### Changing the psychological state

In effect, by ensuring the rules or protocol of the map-level board game needed collaboration, we have ensured that players coordinate their actions in the bottom, real-world level. That is exactly what happened with the legal team. The board-game protocol ensured the group of individuals had to work together. They had to collectively plan how best to coordinate their actions to maximise service pathway performance.

*In effect, as they played the game, they developed a single, collective thought bubble, focused on achieving the common purpose.*

So pathway maps are the intermediate level between the real-world systems and the mental models. This is the level that consists of visual models or maps of the performance of real-world pathways. The pathway maps are, in effect, the "game board" of the Leadership Game. The game board provides the documented evidence of the capability change at the real-world level.

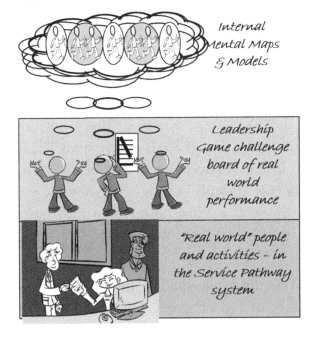

We are going to investigate this pathway map level in much more detail over the following chapters. This is because this is the level at which mental models, and thus behaviours, are changed. It is the level at which groups play the Leadership Game in a way that develops a performance view of the pathway. It is the level that transforms silo mentality into a culture of high-performance teams.

### The meaning of accountability

As we will see, understanding the concept of "accountability" is critical to the success of the Leadership Game. However, it is important to realise the meaning of "accountability" in the Leadership Game is very different to the common understanding of the term from the vertical perspective. From that view, when people ask "Who is accountable?" they often mean who is to blame for something that has already gone wrong. That is almost the opposite of the meaning of accountability in the Leadership Game. Here, the word "accountable" means responsible for keeping account of, and accounting to others for, the map of the pathway standards and gaps. In the next chapter, we will see that this is not the same as other responsibilities. Although it is the responsibility for a relatively trivial task, it is nevertheless a "time critical" responsibility. As we will see, this is because it is part of the fail-safe system. So, if the rules of the Game do not create this accountability, then the game will probably not rapidly change behaviours and overall performance. In such circumstances, it would be the system rules that are the problem, not the people.

Thus, the rules for updating the graph and the morning legal sessions ensured everyone in the group was accountable for the evidence of the progress. The sessions were short, to the point, and achieved clear performance improvements, as shown by the graph trend. So, it is useful for us to ask ourselves how many organizational meetings have we attended that could match that level of effectiveness. In organizations that solely rely on the vertical structure, meetings are often long, painful and unproductive.

## Bakery case study

To help understand the rules of the Leadership Game, we are going to look at a case study involving a commercial bakery. This organization had several factory units producing bread for supermarkets. One of the units was operating at a level where its costs were 10% higher than comparable units. Harry, the general manager, had asked me to help because he could not engage his senior management team in achieving the necessary decrease in costs.

His management team considered that they had done as much as they could to reduce costs within their individual departments. Below the top senior management team, there were several section managers. Harry had tried cascading performance targets down to section managers. However, these section managers often complained that they could not meet their own targets because of a lack of cooperation from other sections. In any case, each section manager felt that their own sections were performing as efficiently as possible, under the circumstances.

I discussed this with Harry. I described how the Leadership Game worked. I explained that it developed the horizontal performance system structure of the organization. I further explained how the first stage was to engage the relevant group to see they were entering a different system, with different rules. I explained this was a critical first stage of the Leadership Game. If the group did not comprehend this difference, their behaviour would not change. The second stage was to engage them in playing the Game by the new rules. These rules ensured they were all accountable for the maps of the performance gaps.

Harry decided to engage the section managers in leading a set of cross-functional, cost-reduction projects. He agreed, with the members of the senior management team, for them to act as project facilitators. Harry decided to use his personal style to ensure the section managers clearly understood they were in a different system. So he set up a session with the section managers. The meeting was in a small meeting room, permanently set out with tables in a "U" shape. He started the session, outlining the basic information that the unit had operating costs of over 10% more than comparable units. This meant there needed to be a set of projects focused on reducing costs by at least that amount.

Although the group already knew this, he was grouping the relevant information to "set the context" of the performance view in everyone's thought bubble. He then made sure everyone realised the scale of the total challenge by asking them all to do the calculation, as to how much 10% was in hard currency. The calculation was not difficult, and they all reluctantly agreed it was £500,000. Harry asked for one of the group to write that figure on the flipchart. Again, there was a degree of reluctance, until one of the section managers stood up and wrote the total on the flipchart.

Harry then explained that he needed to ensure that everyone in the room understood what everyone else's primary responsibility was. So he asked everyone to write the description of their primary job on the top sheet of their A4 pads. Somewhat bemused, they each wrote the relevant descriptions. These included descriptions such as "Oven

Department Manager", "Dispatch Manager" and "Maintenance Manager". Harry then asked them to use some Blu Tack© to stick the sheets on the walls behind them. Harry then looked at the descriptions. Then, after a few moments of silence, he said that he found their descriptions very interesting. He continued to explain that they were very interesting because they were all wrong. These descriptions were simply titles in the vertical management structure. He expected, as experienced managers, they should have their sections almost running themselves.

He explained their most critical job was to collaborate in helping the organization achieve its aims. Currently, the most urgent aim was to reduce costs. They needed to reduce those costs to the level where the unit operated at least £500,000 a year less than current performance. So Harry expected the managers to provide him with the evidence of their progress in collaborating on cross-functional or horizontal projects, which would collectively achieve that aim.

Although this is not an approach I would normally suggest, it did have a dramatic effect. It ensured that the section managers started to realise they were in a different system. In this system, they had to assess the capability gap as an external assessor of the whole unit, rather than just their own sections. In other words, they had to start developing the performance view of their pathways. The next stage was to get the section managers to "map the pathway gaps".

So now, Harry asked the section managers to assume that they had the full cooperation of all the other managers in the room. He then asked them to use separate A4 sheets to list each possible cross-functional project that could reduce their operational costs. He also asked them to both list the other sections they would need to involve, as well as the potential savings achieved by each project. Then, to remove any duplication, he asked one of the section managers to list each project on the flipchart, while each section manager shouted out their list. Against each project was the potential savings. When they added all savings of the projects on the flipchart, the total was more than the needed £500,000.

Harry then explained that, in future, there were going to be weekly sessions for the section managers. In these sessions, the managers for each project would present on the progress of their projects. He accepted the information on the flipchart was currently only a rough list of estimates. So, the first session would be in ten days to give them all time to work with their colleagues to draft their first plans for each of the best projects. After that, he would expect them all to give a brief, joint, weekly presentation for each project, based on the information on a standard A4 project review document.

He handed out a copy of a sample project template. It was based on a formatted sheet of an Excel workbook. It contained areas for the project name, the names of the managers, and the predicted savings. There was space for a brief description. Each row on the sheet represented each week of the project. In each row, there was also a colour-coded cell. Green meant the project was on track to meet its predictions. Amber meant that it was currently behind schedule, but should still be completed on time. Red meant the project was in trouble and needed support. In the cell in the final column of the spreadsheet was the current estimated savings of the project.

Harry explained that each project sheet represented the pathway of the project from start to successful completion. All the project sheets would be linked to a master spreadsheet. So each week, the master sheet would list each project on a single line with the latest information for that week. At the bottom of the sheet was the total projected savings of all projects. If any project sheet had not been updated on the computer for that week, the master sheet would show a blank line.

Harry explained the managers had to take turns in taking the lead for being the overall system assessor. Their job was to make sure all the lines on the master sheet had the relevant information. The lead for that week had to circulate the master sheet to the managers before that week's meeting. At the beginning of the meeting, the lead would present the information on all the projects. Then each group would briefly outline their progress. Where projects had amber or red coding, the group would outline the help they needed from other managers to complete the project on time.

After that first meeting, Harry was well aware that some of the managers would need some cajoling to make sure they would be ready for their first presentations. So he made a point of dropping in to see each manager over the next few days, to enquire how they were progressing. Some managers made excuses that they had not yet had time to arrange any project meetings. In these cases, Harry would invite them to call the relevant colleague while Harry was in the office. He also made it clear that this was not an optional exercise.

Although I was not present at the presentations, Harry described the first presentations as "very amateurish". However, after two or three weeks, the sessions became far more professional. Each group would briefly outline the progress so far, together with their proposed next steps. They also identified any issues where they needed help. Other managers seemed open in offering their support. After four weeks of presentations, Harry was confident the unit would reach the necessary performance within the time limit. His confidence proved justified. Total costs fell even further than predicted. This was not just because of the projects. Even during normal operations, managers focused on minimising costs and naturally collaborated to achieve that aim.

It is important to understand that these Game presentations were again much more effective than typical meetings. Often, in organizations that solely rely on vertical coordination, the senior manager chairs such meetings. In this context, subordinates often sit around a table having long discussions, but rarely feel accountable for the collaboration needed to ensure successful results. So we now need to look more closely into the psychological difference between Game presentations and traditional meetings. To help understand these differences, we first need to consider the perception of control.

## Perceived Control – the basis of behaviour

Many psychologists consider the key factor that affects human behaviour is the motivation to preserve *perceived control*. As we obviously cannot control everything, in effect, we define a boundary within our thought bubble. Within that boundary are the items for which we perceive we are responsible, and we can control. Outside that boundary are the issues, which we perceive others control.

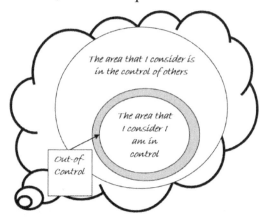

Between those two areas is the area of out-of-control. This is the stressful area for which we feel responsible, but which we are not in complete control. Because this area causes stress, our brain has two choices to remove that stress. It can just consider the current context as being in the control of others. Alternatively, we can move out of our comfort zone and put in the extra effort to bring the situation under control. If the current context is only slightly beyond the current boundary of control, our brain is more likely to take the latter course. Indeed, as we will see in the next chapter, this is the psychological mechanism that motivates people to keep playing video games. Every time someone achieves something, which was previously beyond their boundary of control, their area of perceived control expands. In other words, they are motivated by continual achievement. Again, we will see that this is a key element of the design of Leadership Games.

However, the opposite is also true. The more people consider an outcome is the responsibility of others, the more the perceived area of control is likely to shrink, and the less likely people are to take action outside that area. This principle is useful in helping to understand silo mentality. This occurs when someone perceives the boundary of the system, for which they are responsible, only includes their set of processes or activities. In this state, they do not feel responsible for any of the external consequences of those actions.

### The Milgram experiment

At first glance, the boundaries of control may not seem very relevant to organizational behaviour. However, as far back as the 1960s, psychologists realised the potential seriousness of the boundary of perceived control in the context of vertical hierarchies. Then, a psychologist called Professor Milgram carried out a set of experiments. Those experiments became some of the most controversial psychological experiments of all time. The original purpose of the experiment was to try and understand the power of conscience over obedience to authority. In effect, authority is an integral part of vertical structures. However, Professor Milgram was trying to uncover the psychological triggers that enabled many Germans in the Second World War to carry out such terrible acts against other human beings. He was trying to understand why they seemingly did not have any conscience for the consequences of their actions. They simply considered that they had no choice but to carry out the orders they were given.

Before attempting to run the experiment in Germany, Milgram tested the experiment in the United States. His team placed adverts in local newspapers for volunteers to help in a study of learning, taking around one hour. Each volunteer attended the university at different times. The experimenter, who was a stern character in a lab coat, greeted each volunteer as they arrived. He would introduce the volunteer to a somewhat overweight accountant who had seemingly also volunteered for the experiment. In reality, the 'accountant' was a member of the psychologist's team.

### The purpose of the experiment

The experimenter then explained to both volunteers that the purpose of the experiment was to understand the effect of punishment on learning. This was not the true purpose of the experiment, but this is what the real volunteer was led to believe. The experimenter explained that one of the volunteers would need to act as a learner and the other to take the role of the teacher. The learner had to learn a series of paired words.

The teacher would ask questions to test the learner's memory of paired words and give punishments for wrong answers.

By use of a rigged draw, the real volunteer would always take the role of teacher, giving the punishments, while the plant accountant would always be the learner, who was seemingly receiving the punishments.

The experimenter took both the volunteers into a small, adjoining room. He explained that every time the learner made a mistake, the teacher had to give an electric shock as punishment. In the adjoining room, both the volunteers used the electrodes in the room to experience what a 45-volt shock felt like. It was unpleasant but bearable. The accountant then sat down and was strapped into a chair, where the electrodes were attached to his wrists. Then the experimenter and the real volunteer started to move back into the adjoining control room. However, before they shut the door of the small room, the accountant explained that he had a heart condition. He asked whether the experiment would have any effect on his health.

The experimenter, in front of the real volunteer, assured the accountant the experiment was safe and would not have any ill effect on the accountant's health. The experimenter and the volunteer then left the small room and closed the door behind them. Communications between the real volunteer, in the control room, and the accountant in the adjoining room, were through a microphone and loudspeaker.

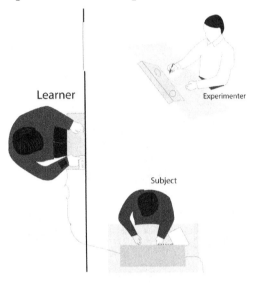

The volunteer then sat in front of a control panel, which had a row of buttons.

The experimenter then explained to the volunteer that whenever the learner gave a wrong answer, the voltage of the electric shock should be increased by 15 volts. The control panel in front of the volunteer clearly showed the progression of the increasing electric shocks. The buttons started at 15 volts and progressed through 30 volts, 45 volts, all the way up to 450 volts. The buttons were all clearly marked. As well as the voltage, there was also a clear sign of the level of shock.

| Voltage | Label |
|---------|-------|
| 15 - 60 | Slight |
| 75 - 120 | Moderate |
| 135 - 180 | Strong |
| 195 - 240 | Very Strong |
| 255 - 300 | Intense |
| 315-360 | Extreme Intensity |
| 375 - 420 | DANGER |
| 435 - 450 | XXX |

### The real purpose of the experiment

As previously explained, the real purpose of the experiment was to understand the relationship between conscience and obedience. The aim was to identify how far people would continue increasing the voltage of the shock simply because they were told to. Milgram was going to measure this by recording the point at which the volunteer's conscience would take over and make them refuse to continue giving shocks to the learner.

In fact, the buttons on the control panel were not connected to the electrodes attached to the accountant. Instead, each button would trigger a tape recording of the apparent response of the accountant to each level of shock. To all appearances, these recorded messages would be coming directly from the accountant in the room next door. At first, when the accountant seemingly received a low voltage shock, there would be no audible response. As the voltage increased to 75 volts, the volunteer would hear grunts and moans. As the voltage increased further, the accountant would seem to kick on the wall and shout that he could no longer stand the pain.

| Voltage | Label | Response |
|---------|-------|----------|
| 15 - 60 | Slight | None |
| 75 - 120 | Moderate | Grunts and moans |
| 135 - 180 | Strong | 150 – Asks to leave <br> 180 – Can't stand the pain |
| 195 - 240 | Very Strong | Can't stand the pain |
| 255 - 300 | Intense | 300 – Pounds on the wall <br> Insists on being freed |
| 315-360 | Extreme Intensity | No sound |
| 375 - 420 | DANGER | No sound |
| 435 - 450 | XXX | No sound |

The experimenter told the volunteer to treat silence as a wrong answer and continue the experiment by increasing the voltage of the shock. If the volunteer pressed buttons over 300 volts, which were all marked as extreme intensity, danger and XXX, there would be no response at all from the adjoining room. There would be complete silence.

### The psychologists failed to predict the results

Before the first experiment, Milgram asked forty psychologists to predict how many US citizens would continue with the experiment all the way through to 450 volts. They predicted that less than one per cent of the volunteers would ignore their conscience and continue to comply with the instructions of the experimenter. It thus came as a chilling surprise to find that 65% of the volunteers completed the full experiment, all the way up to 450 volts. Indeed, most volunteers continued with the experiment past 300 volts before pulling out of the experiment.

When the experimenters debriefed the volunteers after the experiment, they were reintroduced to the accountant to show that they had, in fact, not caused any harm. However, they were asked if they had believed the experiment was for real. Almost all of them believed it was a real experiment. They genuinely believed the shocks were being inflicted on the accountant. Many believed the accountant had been seriously harmed or even died during the experiment. When asked why they continued with the experiment, even when they realised they were harming the accountant, their response was almost always the same type of response.

*The volunteers kept giving higher and higher levels of electric shock because they thought they were not in control of the decision to stop the experiment*

This experiment became so notorious that it was eventually banned. This was for fear there may be lasting psychological damage to the volunteers. However, some have argued the real reason for the ban was because so many people found the results unpalatable.

### The organizational problem

The experiment is often only considered as showing that obedience can overwhelm the force of conscience. However, in his book, Professor Milgram suggested that this mechanism was, in fact, the one that allowed human beings to create organizational hierarchies. He considered there had probably been important evolutionary advantages to a trigger that allowed the creation of hierarchical organizations. The mechanism that evolved to enable this coordinated behaviour was obedience to perceived authority. Thus, it seemed unavoidable that people lower in an organizational hierarchy would, in effect, switch off any concern about the consequences of their actions when they were carrying out the instructions of their superiors.

Milgram suggested that humans have an internal psychological switch. When the switch creates one psychological state, people make their own assessments of the external world to make their own decisions. In the other psychological state, people cede control to a higher authority and obediently carry out the instructions of that authority, without any thought of the consequences to other parties. When a person is in this latter state, Milgram pointed out that "the individual no longer views himself as responsible for his own actions. He or she defines themselves as an instrument for carrying out the wishes of others." Milgram also concluded that the people in the experiment were not people like you and me. In effect, they **were** you and me.

"I think he has taken the Milgram experiment too literally!'

There have been many other psychological experiments

that confirm the principle that obedience to authority switches off the part of the brain that assesses the consequences of our actions. One example of this state was given to me by one of my delegates, who was an air-accident investigator. In one case, one of the aircraft engines failed, but the captain switched off the fuel to the remaining engine that was still working. The co-pilot knew the pilot had made a mistake but said nothing. Without any engine power, the plane crashed and killed many of those on board.

Indeed, this same psychological state was a major factor in NASA's Challenger space shuttle disaster. That craft exploded on take-off on January 28, 1986, seventy-three seconds into its flight. The explosion caused the deaths of all seven of its crew members. The following investigation found that NASA's organizational culture and decision-making processes had been a key contributing cause to the accident. Engineers had predicted the low temperatures predicted that morning would mean there was a high risk the craft would explode on take-off. Yet at the final meeting the night before, after a long and heated discussion, the engineers complied with their manager's wishes to agree that the launch should go ahead. In fact, one engineer went home the night before the launch and told his wife that the launch was going to kill seven astronauts the next day.

### The perception of "others-in-control"

It is easy to think that this behaviour only happens in extreme scenarios. In fact, it is constantly visible in many organizations. For example, I often hear stories similar to the organization that gave its purchasing department a target to reduce the costs. These costs were mainly for parts and raw materials bought as the inputs for manufacturing. The purchasing department took on the challenge with great relish. However, many of the new purchases were of a lower quality than before. This caused a higher level of rejects in the manufacturing department. In turn, this increased the cost of the items produced to such an extent that overall costs increased, even though the cost of raw materials fell. Even worse, the lower quality meant products became more unreliable, leading to higher levels of customer returns and complaints. In turn, this meant that previously loyal customers went elsewhere.

Similarly, another organization tried to turn every section into a "profit centre". When any section operated below its cost budget, the difference was considered to be the profit made by that section. So, for example, there was a section responsible for recruitment. They placed the adverts and arranged the interviews for applicants for the job vacancies in the organization. Their strategy for maximising their nominal profit was to restrict and delay the adverts published for job vacancies. This meant that vacancies went unfilled for months. In turn, this meant other departments had to substantially increase the overtime paid, to fulfil the orders. So, overall costs increased. This was not a small organization. In fact, it was a well-known organization. In the previous year, the organization had made a profit of £500 million. Within two years of introducing profit centres across the organization, it was making a substantial loss.

These are not isolated incidents. Silo mentality means the people concerned do not feel responsible for the consequences of their actions, outside their system boundary. However, we should not necessarily see this psychological switch as something that is permanently on or off. Neither should we consider either state as inherently good or bad. In fact, for organizations to function, this switch is likely to continually trigger between one psychological state and the other. Indeed, we are all flipping this switch constantly.

For example, consider the scenario where you are driving your car. You may well consider yourself "in-control" of the situation. Then, suddenly, you see a person at the side of the road, with all the trappings of authority associated with a policeman's uniform. The person steps out and signals you to stop. Immediately, you switch into "others-in-control". You stop in the middle of the road, as directed because you believe you have to. You will probably not consider that you are responsible for the queue of traffic that builds up behind you. You are likely to consider the problem is the responsibility of the policeman who has signalled you to stop.

There is nothing necessarily inappropriate with your behaviour. Society could not work if people did not trigger others-in-control at suitable times. In fact, it is not just people with the trappings of authority that we defer to. If we are driving and the traffic lights turn red, we defer to the implied command of the traffic lights.

The other point that we need to remember is that people want to stay "in-control" of their silos. This is the reason they will typically resist external change that tries to change the way they currently control their silos. Some people enjoy taking on challenges and putting themselves temporarily in the stress of being out of control. However, the higher the perceived consequence of failure, the less likely people are to stretch themselves in that way. So at first, we will assume that most people do not naturally put themselves in that state, in traditional top-down organizations. Indeed, the Milgram experiment suggests that even the presence of someone in authority, such as a manager, encourages people to stay inside their comfort zones without considering the consequences to others outside that boundary.

In fact, managers often unwittingly create these conditions whenever they chair a meeting of subordinates. By definition, it is the manager who is taking control of the meeting. So people will talk about issues, but when they leave the meeting, their boundaries of control remain the same. So little changes. This means that managers often feel as though they are in a Catch-22 situation. If they use authority to ensure people carry out specific duties, then potentially, those people will not feel responsible for any consequences of their actions. Yet, as we identified in the first chapter, individuals cannot legitimately be held directly responsible for collaborating more effectively.

However, as we have seen, people can be held collectively responsible for accounting for the map of the pathway performance gaps that they collectively control. The more they account for the map of the pathway gaps that they collectively control, the more they develop a mental model of the map of the gaps. They also develop mental models of how to address those gaps. The more they develop the mental models of how to address those gaps, the more the gaps become within their circle of control. The more they perceive those gaps as entering their circle of control, the more likely they are to apply the solution protocols in the real world.

For example, in the legal case study, the group originally considered the performance of their legal work as outside their control. The manager first asked them to identify the benchmark standards that would ensure the system was as effective as possible. This started to build the pathway performance view in their thought bubbles. They were then given the responsibility of documenting the evidence of the gap between the current standard and the benchmark standards they had identified. In other words, they became accountable for the map of the gaps. Once they started plotting the current capability of the system they controlled, it was difficult to stay in the state of others-in-control.

At first, this was stressful. They tried to relieve that stress by blaming the computer system. This was because they were trying to stay others-in-control. However, once they could see there was a direct relationship between the decisions they made and the capability of their system, they became motivated to continue controlling that performance. In other words, as soon as they saw the graph coming down, they saw the performance standard was within their boundary of control. Then, they started feeling responsible for addressing the gap. They started to own the gaps on the map. So the psychological switch of in-control and others-in-control helps us understand organizational behaviour.

### Other psychological switches

However, there are other psychological switches that I will briefly mention. Combined, these switches give an even more powerful view of behaviour. The first switch we need to consider is one that psychologists call cognitive dissonance. Often, when the facts presented to people are in conflict with their established beliefs, those people simply ignore the information. To reassure themselves that it is reasonable to ignore the information, they label it as "fake news". If the information is in line with their beliefs, they will consider it as factual. So, for simplicity, we will call this the "fake-factual news switch".

The fake news switch is closely related to another psychological trigger. That is the in-group / out-group switch. The in-out group switch means that people tend to form into groups of "like-minded" people. They preserve cohesion in their own group by believing their own group to be superior to other groups. So, individuals align their views with the collective views of their in-group. This means the group will treat any information that suggests their group is superior as a fact. They will treat any information that is threatening to their collective view as fake news. Also, anyone who presents information inconsistent with the group view is likely to meet the response "Whose side are you on?" irrespective of the validity of their information.

However, when one group faces the challenge of having to gain another group's "buy-in" to succeed, it creates a collective challenge. The external group can no longer just be considered as "out-group", providing fake news. Similarly, when a group is accountable for publicising performance data they have collected themselves, the group cannot ignore that information as fake news.

Finally, there is the rational/emotional switch. This is variously referred to as the head/heart switch, the left and right brain switch, or the system-two, system-one switch. In simple terms, human brains have distinctive left and right hemispheres. These two hemispheres loosely relate to the two different modes of processing information. We can use the term "left-brain" as a metaphor for the slower, rational and analytical thinking. We will use the term "right-brain" as a metaphor for the faster, intuitive and holistic thinking. Different scenarios will trigger one or other side to be the dominant thinking mode.

For example, when we are under pressure to provide a quick answer or solution, the right-brain will be dominant. It will immediately come up with a simple, intuitive answer. In effect, the left-brain then acts as the subservient part of the brain. So if needed, the left brain can produce a seemingly logical justification for the emotional answer. However, when not under immediate time pressure, the left-brain will "mull things over" and create a more rational solution.

Throughout the following chapters, we will see that, collectively, this small set of switches help explain many of the behaviours we see in organizations. They help further explain resistance to change when that change is set up by the top-down approach of the vertical structure. However, we will also see how the Leadership Game inherently aligns those switches. That alignment ensures everyone is working collaboratively. In that mode, they can develop rational solutions to achieve the common goal of improving the effectiveness of the horizontal pathways.

## Summary

In this chapter, we have seen how the vertical structure creates the mental boundaries of control that define Silo Mentality. We have started to see how collective accountability for the map of the gaps in the Leadership Game overcomes the psychological limitations of the vertical hierarchy. It extends the perception of control in a way that automatically improves collaboration and performance. The Milgram experiment will help us better understand the difference between management and leadership. In the following chapters, we will see how this powerful principle can be applied more generally to the horizontal structure of the organization.

# Chapter 3

## The secret power of the G.A.M.E. loop

### Review and overview

In the previous chapters, we considered case studies in which groups changed rapidly, from being individuals with silo mentality, into high-performance teams. However, simply knowing the group used the Leadership Game does not explain why the process was so powerful. For example, in the legal case study, Joan broke the habit of a lifetime and stayed after five o'clock to work on some more case files. So we need to better understand the psychology behind that sudden behavioural change.

Of course, part of that understanding was the perception of control, which we looked at in the last chapter. However, in this chapter, we look at control in more detail. We see how we can consistently reproduce conditions capable of changing the habits of a lifetime. We use a case study to see how groups can use the same approach to control qualitative standards. We also look at fail-safe systems to ensure success.

### Coordination and feedback control

To fully understand how perceived control is relevant to pathway systems, we first need to understand the general principles of feedback control. Feedback control is like air. It is all around us. Such control systems are essential to life and everything that we do. However, like air, feedback control systems are largely invisible and overwhelmingly taken for granted.

An example of simple feedback control is the temperature control of our homes or offices. We can find even simpler feedback control in our fridges, ovens, computers and kettles. Our cars are full of an ever-increasing number of control systems. Indeed, our whole body is a mass of feedback control systems, regulating everything from our temperature to levels of oxygen, sugar and enzymes in our blood. In effect:

***A feedback control system is one that consistently coordinates sub-systems or processes, to address the external gap between the current standard and the standard required***

In fact, we can say that when a gap is not being addressed, it is a sign of the absence of an effective feedback control system. So, we need to start looking in more detail at the components of feedback control systems. Then we will be able to use that knowledge to understand how people take on the roles involved in feedback control systems within organizations.

As shown in the next diagram, feedback control systems consist of a set of sub-systems. These include coordination, control, and the processes in the service pathway. The coordination system first assesses the gap between the necessary standard and the current standard.

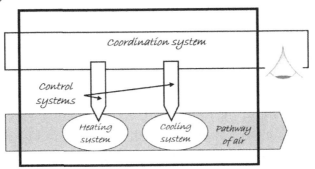

So for a room thermostat, this is the difference between the set temperature and the current temperature. The coordination system then "decides" which process it needs to trigger to close the gap. It then engages the relevant control system to switch the heating or cooling process on or off. That action will then bring about a progressive change in the temperature of the air. We can represent this by the pathway of the air changing its temperature through either the heating or cooling process. That pathway closes the gap.

At first sight, it may seem that people's behaviours in organizations are not related to room thermostats. Yet nothing could be further from the truth. People, both individually and collectively, are acting as feedback control systems in the organization. So the same feedback principles hold for organizations. For example, consider the legal case study. Before starting the Leadership Game, there was no feedback control for throughput time. The Leadership Game engaged the group to create an effective feedback system. In fact, such control systems are so fundamental to the workings of organizations, we can say:

***All actions, communications and information flows in an organization can be mapped as sets of interconnected, pathway control systems***

In other words, whenever we talk about "information" in organizations, that information is usually part of the control systems controlling pathway processes. Similarly, when we talk about organizational structures, we are describing the framework created by the connections of control systems. It is a lack of understanding of such control systems that will stop us from understanding the invisible causes of success in case studies. So it is essential that we fully understand how people use information to act as feedback control systems.

## Intelligent control

In the heating example, thermostats act as the coordination system or "brains" of the feedback control. These assess the external gaps and select how to respond. Our brains take similar roles so that we can preserve the perception of control. The difference is that when people act as control systems, our brains are constantly trying control situations by predicting the future.

For example, if you see a football rapidly coming towards your head, your brain will predict that, if no action is taken, the ball will hit you. That assessment triggers the brain to work out what actions it needs to take to avoid that undesirable future state. Once the brain has identified a solution, it will automatically engage the control of the sequence of actions that should avoid the collision.

Similarly, when we drive a car, we are acting as the coordination system for the car. However, our brains are much more complex than a thermostat. Such simple systems only address a current gap in a single standard. Our brains act as intelligent control systems. So they are capable of controlling many different actions to address a wide range of predicted gaps. Yet, at any particular time, our brain will focus on controlling just the most urgent and important gaps that we currently need to address.

## The G.A.M.E. cycle

Intelligent coordination is also based on continuous, high frequency, but basically simple feedback loops. So we need to understand how the intelligent coordination system works in practice. The coordination loop consists of four repeating stages. The four stages are *Group*, *Assess*, *Map* and *Engage*. Combined, they create the G.A.M.E. cycle.

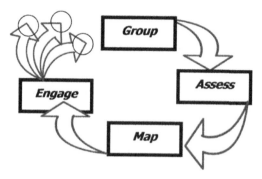

To understand these stages, we are first going to consider the scenario of a driver acting as the feedback control system of the car. We will assume the driver does not have a sat nav but has already planned her route. She is driving along a road, but will shortly need to turn off to follow her planned route. We need to understand how she knows what actions to take to keep control of her car. So, as she drives the car along the planned route, we are going to assume that we can look at the driver's thought bubble in ultra-slow motion. This will enable us to see how each mental stage works.

### Group

Our brains contain billions of neurons, which store a massive amount of information, scattered across the whole brain. However, as I briefly mentioned previously, to make suitable decisions, we only need a small subset of that information. So, because our driver knows she is driving a car, she will bring the system protocol for driving into the executive part of the brain. This will include the knowledge of the rules of the road, the knowledge on how to control the car, and knowledge of the route. She has to also continually update that information with the current picture of the road in front. So we can say the first stage for our driver is for her to *Group* just the information relevant to the car's current state into the executive part of the brain. This will create a picture of the context she needs to control. We represent that information by showing the mental image in her thought bubble.

She will know, for example, the rules of the road mean that she should normally drive in one lane. She will also know the capability of the systems she has to control the car. These will include the steering system to control the direction. It will include the acceleration and braking systems of the car to control the speed. So this information will also be in the group of relevant information. She will then predict where the car will be if she continues as she is. As she is moving along the road, she can predict the car will soon be past the turning on the left. The star in the following diagram shows her prediction of the future position of the car.

However, she also has the planned route on the image in her thought bubble. The planned route takes the turning on the left of the image. The cross in the following diagram shows where she needs to be.

The image in her thought bubble now shows both the point where she needs to be, as well as the point where she will be if she continues without taking action. In effect, the current view in her thought bubble has now grouped enough information to provide a context or mental model from which she can start to make decisions. We call this context the **frame, or frame of reference** against which she will be able to assess the information.

This completes the **Group** stage. In effect, this stage has grouped all the information necessary to create the equivalent of a helicopter view of the flow along the pathway. It includes information about how the internal controls of the car can be used. It also includes all the external information about the current position and route of the pathway. Her intelligent control system can now move to the next stage in the cycle.

## Assess the gap

Having completed the *Group* stage, her thought bubble uses that information to carry out the second stage. The second stage is to *Assess the most urgent and important gap*. This is analogous to the room thermostat assessing the gap between the set temperature and the current room temperature. In this case, the brain is assessing the gap between the two predicted states of where the car will be and where it needs to be. Now the driver assesses the gap to show that she urgently needs to act, to turn the car to the left.

However, before continuing, she also has to consider whether the driver-and-car system is capable of making the turn. In other words, she has to assess the certainty that she can develop a workable solution. If she has gone too far past the turning, she will realise that she needs a different course of action. Although, for the moment, we will assume that she assesses the system is capable of making the turn.

## Map the controllable gaps

Once the need to act has been assessed, it would be easy to think the next stage is to carry out the actions needed to close the gap. However, this would miss an important stage. Before we can address a complex high-level gap, we have to split it down into a set of lower-level, controllable gaps. In other words, the driver needs to *Map* the different gaps, which she needs to control to achieve the necessary result.

For example, the driver can control the system that changes the speed of the car. She can do this by adjusting the pressure on the brake or accelerator. Similarly, she can control the direction of the car by turning the steering wheel. So, both speed and direction are controllable gaps. In this example, she needs to reduce the car speed. Then, once the car is at the junction, she will need to change the direction of the car. Therefore, once she has assessed a high-level gap needs action, the next stage is to mentally map the gaps that need addressing. In this case, they are the speed and direction. Once she has identified the list of gaps, she can map how to coordinate the various systems that will remove the gaps in speed and direction.

### Engage process control

Now the brain has identified a set of gaps, with the suitable specialist systems or brain areas that can address each gap. The GAME loop now needs to **Engage** the control systems to trigger the lower level processes. In effect, these are the set of processes to address the gap. In this example, the lower level systems include the steering, braking and accelerating. However, the brain has areas specialised in working the braking and steering using arms and legs. So, once signalled, those specialised areas again keep going through the GAME loop to progressively split down the requirements. This keeps occurring until they reach the lowest level of triggering the various muscles in the driver's arms and legs.

### An example

To help understand how this relates to organizations, imagine the brain acts as a management hierarchy in a traditional organization. The top level, or chief executive, form the big picture needed to identify the most urgent gap. This is the **Group** stage. He then estimates the organization needs to reduce costs by £100,000 a year. This is the **Assess** stage. He has three subordinates, who each control specialist departments. So, if the chief executive was using vertical control, he might split down the overall £100,000 into a reduction in costs for each of the departments. This could be £50,000 for department A, £30,000 for department B, and

£20,000 for department C. Now he has mapped the controllable gaps. So this is the **Map** stage. The chief executive does not need to plan how to address each of the departmental gaps. He just has to pass the targets to the managers of the lower level systems. This is the **Engage** stage. In simple terms, the subordinates then carry out the processes to meet the benchmark standards.

If we looked inside those lower level systems, each department manager would then use the GAME cycle to divide their total reductions into another set of controllable gaps. They would then engage the control of their own sub-systems by giving each of their section managers a target to reduce costs by the specified amount. Finally, all the lowest level systems should have a simple plan, which they could put into action to reduce the overall costs of the organization by the £100,000. So whether it is a car driver or a set of organizational managers, the same GAME control cycle is used. It coordinates all the necessary low-level systems and actions needed to address a high-level gap.

### Cycle

Returning to the car driving example, we will see the GAME sequence is a continuous cycle. Having engaged the subsystems, it again cycles through the GAME loop to see if it needs to trigger further action. Of course, when driving, each cycle happens in a tiny fraction of a second. However, in the cost reduction example, the cycle may take weeks or months.

### The right sequence

So, the GAME cycle is the general coordination cycle that we use to coordinate purposeful actions. Understanding this cycle is essential because it has a direct impact on the protocols for the Leadership Game. The GAME cycle shows us the *sequence* in which people need to process information. For example, the driver could only engage the lower level control systems in the car *after* she had mentally mapped the necessary coordination of those subsystems. She only became motivated to start problem-solving mapping *after* she had assessed a gap between the needed standard and the standard predicted with no action. Similarly, she could only assess that gap *after* she had grouped information about both the current state and planned states. So, understanding this sequence of events is essential if we are to be able to engage individuals and groups in bringing about change.

### Relating the loop to a team

The same sequence also applies to collective behaviour. A group of individuals are only likely to engage their coordinated actions if they have previously mapped and agreed on the necessary coordination. They can only collectively map that coordination if they have all previously assessed the gaps they need to address. They can only do that if they have each previously been able to group all the information, including the required benchmarks needed to make the same assessment.

### Implications for leadership and communication

So the GAME loop has important implications for the way leaders and facilitators communicate with groups. Analysis, of the way successful leaders and facilitators communicate, often shows that they follow this sequence, even with the simplest of communications. For example, they may want a set of individuals to collaborate in mapping the pathway and its gaps. In principle, the group could just be asked to do that. However, often, skilled leaders and facilitators will first group the relevant information and then involve the group in assessing as the external assessor. This could be achieved in a few sentences. For example, a facilitator may ask a group, "Imagine you were a customer. Imagine you had just paid a considerable amount of money for one of our products. Imagine you then found it did not work when you went to use it. How would you feel?" In other words, the facilitator ensured the individuals all grouped the information that would enable the group of individuals to all assess as an external assessor. After answering that question, as external assessors, the group is likely to be far more motivated to map the gaps in the pathway they control. So The GAME loop is a powerful guide to improving communications.

### Assessing subjective or qualitative gaps

For example, in the legal example, Trevor started the first session by grouping the relevant information, before asking the team to assess the benchmark standards for the pathway. Once they had identified the standards, the team became part of the feedback control system for throughput time. That was clearly a quantifiable measure of system performance. However, often, we need to check the ability of a system to meet a subjective or qualitative standard. How can groups monitor and control those types of standards? To help clarify this issue, we are now going to look at another case study.

## The factory case study

One of my early assignments as a consultant was to help Mike, a factory manager, who felt he urgently needed to change the culture of those working in the factory. Mike explained that one particular customer accounted for over sixty per cent of the factory's output. That customer was currently looking to reduce the number of suppliers. The customer wanted a smaller number of more efficient suppliers, who shared the same values. To that end, the customer started to regularly send inspectors to check how the suppliers were operating. One of the key aspects that the inspector was assessing was the suppliers' level of cleanliness and safety within the factories.

Mike explained that the first inspection of the factory had resulted in a highly critical report on its housekeeping and safety levels. The inspector stated there was no sense of ownership in keeping the working environment clean and safe. For the factory to remain on the customer's preferred supplier list, it needed to improve these areas rapidly. The managers tried explaining to staff the importance of keeping the factory clean and safe, but their words made little difference. Mike explained the staff always blamed previous shifts for the state of the factory. They considered that keeping the factory to the required standard of cleanliness and safety was not their responsibility. They considered it was the managers' responsibility to ensure the other shifts meet those standards.

Mike explained to me the auditor used to give four weeks' notice of each inspection. So, just before inspections, managers would shut down the plant for the afternoon. Then everyone would clean the factory and remove hazards to ensure the factory passed its inspection. While this approach ensured they passed the inspection, it also increased their costs. However, Mike had just received a letter from the inspector. After the next scheduled inspection, the inspector would not be giving any prior notice of when the inspection would take place. In other words, after the next planned inspections, there would only be spot inspections. Mike was horrified. He felt certain that they would fail the first spot inspection. He could not instil the necessary sense of pride in the state and safety of the factory.

So, I explained how it was possible to change such

perceptions very quickly. I explained the principle of control systems. I explained that problems occur when there is no direct link between assessing the gap and the actions needed to address that gap. Under these circumstances, the people carrying out the actions do not feel it is their responsibility to ensure the critical standard is maintained. So, to address the cultural issue of a lack of interest in safety and housekeeping, two factors needed to change. The first was that everyone had to have the same perception of the standard being used by the external assessor. The second was that everyone had to be accountable for consistently and accurately assessing the capability of the factory to achieve the external assessor's standard.

I explained how the GAME loop helped to understand the changes needed. I explained that people, who were most directly in-control of the factory standards, needed to be the ones assessing the capability gap of the factory, in the same way as the external assessor. Once they naturally assessed the gap from that perspective, they would automatically work out the actions they needed to take to close the gap in their everyday activities in the service pathway. This would happen without anyone being told to pick up a broom. Mike was unconvinced by my explanation. So I asked him to compare it with the traditional top-down solution.

## *The traditional solution*

Traditionally, shift managers would have to spend their time checking whether the standards were being met. In other words, the managers would have to act as the coordination system of the feedback loop for safety standards. That meant the managers would do the assessing and then control subordinates by telling them what to clear up. This is the vertical command-and-control style of management. The problem is that people usually resent other people continually checking their work. Even worse, they become others-in-control of factory safety and housekeeping. Typically, it also creates low morale and lack of motivation. After all, if the manager's job is to assess standards and take actions to remove gaps, then by definition, it is the responsibility of the manager and not the manager's subordinates. This solution only encourages silo mentality. In other words, the managers would assess from the perspective of the external assessor and then try to change the behaviour of all the individuals in the factory service pathways. So Mike said that he could see the principle, but how could people have the same subjective standard the inspector had. Everyone had a different view of what was acceptable. It was a subjective assessment, so it was not measurable.

### *Temperature*

I explained that what was needed was a common frame of reference. Temperature is a good example. We take for granted that temperature is quantifiable and we can measure and compare it. We typically forget that it used to be a qualitative or subjective assessment. Before scientists created a temperature scale to act as a frame of reference, there was no quantifiable way to assess temperature. People would just make subjective assessments of whether something was warm, cold or hot.

The way we quantify such experiences is to set two definable reference points. With temperature, these are freezing and boiling water. We can then create a graduation scale between the two reference points (such as 0 to 10, -10 to +10, or 0 to 100).

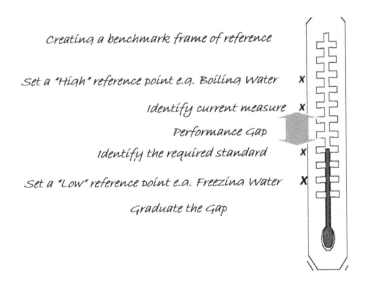

Creating a benchmark frame of reference

Set a "High" reference point e.g. Boiling Water    X

Identify current measure    X

Performance Gap

Identify the required standard    X

Set a "Low" reference point e.g. Freezing Water    X

Graduate the Gap

Once we have a graduated scale, we can use that quantifiable graduation scale to identify the relative measures of the current standard and the desired standard. Once we have identified those two points on the graduated scale, we can assess the gap between them. So for example, we may know that a person's normal body temperature should be 37 degrees Celsius, where 0 is freezing water, and 100 is boiling water. So if we measure a person's temperature and find it is 39 degrees Celsius, there is a gap of two degrees. So we know they have a fever. We can apply the same principle when creating a common frame of reference for anything that needs assessing. In this case, 37C was the benchmark. So, for ease of reading, I will often just use the term benchmark to mean the standard and its related frame of reference.

### Hell and utopia points of reference

The two extreme reference points, which we will use for the frame, are "hell" and "utopia". If we engage a group in agreeing what such benchmark standards look like, they can develop a common frame of reference for almost any issue.

Such points can be used as reference points on a scale of, say, 0 to 10. We could agree on an example of the standard-from-hell and set that to 1 on our 0 to 10 hell-to-utopia scale. We could then agree an example of the utopian standard and give that a score of 9. We now have the equivalent of a temperature scale. Creating this frame of reference is the main purpose of the Group stage in the GAME loop.

I explained to Mike that the standard that the inspector was using was the state of the customer's factory. So that was the standard of excellence that everyone needed to be assessing against. The baton, which needed passing after every task, was a working area that was as clean as safe as the customer's factory. Once everyone was assessing the factory against that benchmark, their behaviour would change automatically.

This explanation seems counter-intuitive. Surely, everyone could "see" the factory was untidy and unsafe. However, the ability to see is psychologically different from being responsible, and being accountable to peers, for accurately assessing the performance gap as the external assessor. When people do not use a benchmark standard to assess against, the standard they use is the standard that they see around them every day. So, if the factory is much the same as it was yesterday, then there is no assessed gap and no motivation to act. In fact, if there is no clear benchmark standard, then no standard is too low.

I explained to Mike, to assess as the inspector, staff would need the training to ensure they could assess against the same benchmark standards as the inspector. They would also have to be accountable for regularly taking on the role of the external assessor. So Mike agreed I should show John, the training manager, how to develop a short training session for the managers and staff. These sessions were held for groups of between twenty and thirty people per session. Everyone working in the factory was going to be accountable for the housekeeping and safety map. So, before the first session took place, John obtained some photos of the customer's factory. They showed it was spotlessly clean. Similarly, he had walked around the factory, taking photographs of various areas. He placed the pictures on the walls of the training room. To attend sessions in this room, staff and managers had to walk through the factory.

I had explained to John about the principle of the GAME loop. So before anyone could make any assessments, they needed to all group the same relevant information to create a common frame of reference. Further, everyone needed to own the benchmark standard of excellence. So John created a set of slides as an introduction to each session.

One of the slides listed the main customers and the proportion of factory output taken by each customer. Another slide showed the main competitors. He explained that customers were spoilt for choice of suppliers. He explained the main customer, who was taking sixty per cent of the factory's output, would only keep suppliers who had clean and safe factories. He also explained that, after the next visit by the customer's inspector, future inspections would occur without advance notice. If the factory failed the random audits, they would lose their major customer, leaving the factory's future in doubt. In itself, this information would have little impact, because most people were already aware of these facts. It was simply grouping information for the first stage of the GAME loop.

John then showed the groups some photographs of the pristine factory of their main customer. He explained that they were going to score the pictures. He said he was going to give that picture a score of nine for safety and cleanliness – because it may be possible to find trivial areas that could be improved. He said he had gone around the factory and taken some photos of the worst situations he could find in their own factory. He explained that these would be scored at 1. John then asked staff and managers to go round the room, in groups of two or three, scoring the other four photographs on the wall and recording the score.

Once they had completed this task, he allowed some general discussion for the groups to roughly agree their scores. In effect, the groups now had the skill to make a common, quantitative assessment of the state of the factory. Once the group completed the photograph assessments, John asked them to briefly walk around the factory with scoring sheets and make their own assessment of each area.

Managers predicted staff would give a much better score for factory cleanliness than managers. In fact, when staff marked each area, there was a genuine sense of shock and disbelief that the factory was in such a poor state. They could not believe they had walked past the same areas less than an hour earlier, when they walked to the training room, without noticing any problem.

On their return to the training room, they compared all the results to create an average score. On average, the staff scored the factory slightly below four, while the managers scored the factory with an average of slightly above five. At this point in every session, the mood of each group changed. Previously, everyone had treated the session like any other training session. So there was an almost comical atmosphere. However, after they agreed on the average assessment, as external assessors, everyone had a common perception of the real gap or crisis. They all showed a genuine motivation to make the factory cleaner and safer.

John explained that they could only succeed if everyone took responsibility for always leaving the work area clean and safe to the benchmark standard, irrespective of the original state of that area. That was the new "rule". If for any reason that was not achievable, they needed to agree with their colleagues and manager how to address the problem. If they felt that other shifts were not meeting that standard, then they should seek a staff meeting between shifts to address the problem. John stressed that it was everyone's responsibility to help ensure the factory achieved and kept the necessary standard of safety and cleanliness. If anyone felt that people in their own shift were sabotaging the future of the factory, they needed to discuss and agree on the proposals to address the problem.

John then explained that although he considered the minimum standard the inspector would accept was around eight, they needed to aim for a higher standard to be sure of success. So, he gave them a few minutes to discuss if it was reasonable to have a minimum success standard on completing every task of at least eight, and ideally nine. After a few minutes' debate, each group agreed that it was possible to achieve close to nine.

John now explained the end-of-shift log sheets had been amended to include a column for this housekeeping and safety assessment. Everyone needed to take turns to be the end-of-shift inspector. That rota would be displayed outside the shift manager's office. Each shift inspector had to fill in their score for the factory on the log sheet at the end of every shift. The office would only accept completed log sheets. The office would enter the score on the large factory graph, sited just outside the washrooms. John explained that it was essential the score was accurate. No one would be reprimanded for assessing a low score. Their role was to be the inspector from outside the organization. The assessments needed to accurately reflect the score an external inspector would give. If anyone could not give an accurate assessment, then they could be given extra training. In other words, John made it clear there was no benefit in making excessively favourable assessments. This completed the training session, which took about an hour.

### Assessing as the external inspector

After all the sessions had been completed, the first chart score was four, which was the average assessment of all the training sessions. Then, at the end of each shift, the duty inspector would enter the score on the log sheet, which would then be entered on the large graph outside the washrooms.

Within a couple of weeks, the factory score was almost nine. The improvement occurred, even though managers never asked anyone to clean an area. The score remained at this level over the following years, and fortunately for all concerned, the factory consistently passed their inspections and kept their main customer.

### What made the difference?

Anyone watching the training sessions in the factory example may have considered them as typical training sessions, much like any other. However, the sessions, and the fact that everyone took turns as shift inspectors had a disproportionate effect on motivation and behaviour. In effect, the changes brought together collective control and accountability for the gaps in the standards for safety and housekeeping. The whole approach of the sessions was to initially group all the information necessary for all staff to start to see the factory safety from the performance system view. This was developed as they assessed the gap from the external assessor's standard.

### Test the principle

Again, the important factor to realise here is that small difference can be the difference between this approach succeeding or failing. To test this principle, we can imagine a different scenario and predict the effect that seemingly small changes would have. For example, imagine a scenario where only the shift managers were trained to assess factory safety and cleanliness. Imagine that only the shift managers made daily assessments, and the graph was kept in the shift manager's office. In principle, the same actions would take place and the same data recorded. Would you consider this solution would be effective enough to resolve the problem?

When I ask my master class delegates this question, most predict it would be far less effective. They consider it would destroy all sense of ownership of staff to keep the factory safe and clean. What would happen in this context is that we would have broken a critical connection in the feedback control system. That is the direct connection between assessment of the capacity of the factory pathway system for cleanliness and safety, and engaging the actions that ensured the factory was left clean and safe.

## *Is this relevant to other circumstances?*

It is easy to believe this example is only relevant to cleanliness and safety. In fact, we will see that it is relevant to every Leadership Game board. In the legal example, "utopia" was zero days overdue. The starting point was 8,000 days overdue, so we can assume that anything over 8,000 represented "hell". Often, these points are implicit. However, every Leadership Game board still relies on the principle of moving away from a hellish standard and towards a utopian one, to progressively achieve the success standard.

## Video game motivation

Although the concept of feedback control is useful, it does not explain the motivation created by the Leadership Game. To understand that feature, we need to return to our earlier example of someone driving a car.

### *Maximising the performance of the coordination*

In that example, we can say the driver was coordinating the system that would transport her along the service pathway. This is the pathway that would take her from her starting point to her destination. In other words, we have described a feedback control system, which the driver controlled at the real-world level. However, now imagine that our driver finishes her journey and then starts playing a video game based on racing cars. In principle, she will use a similar GAME loop to control her virtual car. Her route is simply to stay on the circular track.

However, she will not just coordinate the controls to drive the virtual racing car around the track. Now there is another motivating factor. Our video race driver has taken on a performance challenge to exceed the success standard set by an external competitor. In other words, rather than just coordinating the actions needed at the service delivery level:

**The video game player is also taking part in the higher level performance system, trying to achieve a challenging benchmark standard**

So, rather than just staying within her current ability and comfort zone, she will try to achieve the challenge in the fastest possible time. She will deliberately try to push her level of control to the limits, and beyond her current skill level. In other words, rather than just mapping the gaps, which are easily within her control, her brain is mapping the near "out-of-control" gaps.

## Performance systems

From this perspective, when playing the driving video game, our driver has changed from just being in the system of coordinating a car along a pathway. She is now simultaneously in the performance system for that pathway. When she is in the performance system, the more she wins, the more she extends her boundary of control. The more she extends that boundary, the more she is motivated to push and extend her current capabilities even further. Every time she achieves success, she gains a real sense of achievement. Indeed, if she starts winning too often, she is likely to turn up the difficulty level. In that scenario, the challenge again motivates her to extend her current abilities even further.

This analysis helps us understand why video games are so motivational. They keep taking people just into the state of "out-of-control", but to a level where they can keep bringing the situation back "in-control". In effect, the player is trying to close a gap. That gap is the difference between the capability of the external competitor's coordination system and her own coordination system. So, we can apply the same principles of the video game to understand why the Leadership Game is so motivational.

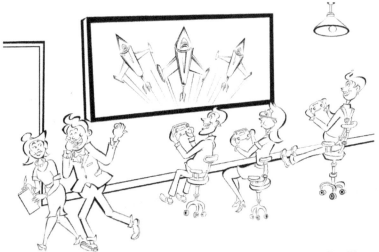

"I think they have taken the idea of video games too literally"

## Relating the video game to the Leadership Game system

In chapter one, I explained the advantage of mapping systems is that we can map visible boundaries that are not visible in the real world. Clearly, when the driver was playing the video game, there were no visible boundaries between the coordinating system and the performance system. In effect, the player was simultaneously in both systems. However, viewing the two systems separately allows us to define the different characteristics of each system.

## Relating the theory to the case study

There may not appear to be any relationship between the case studies and playing a racing video game. In fact, we will see the GAME cycle is relevant to all the case studies that we look at. For example, before starting the Leadership Game, everyone in the legal group would have been controlling their individual actions and processes in the same way the driver controlled her actions when driving along a planned route. In other words, they were acting as individuals in the service pathway system. The moment they started playing the Leadership Game, they moved to the performance system. In the first session, they collectively set the benchmark standards of excellence. That created the basis of a video game. In their morning meetings, they would plan how to assign their collective resources in a way that would achieve the biggest drop in the overdue days. In other words, there was now a challenging purpose for their planning. They would then use that plan when they left the meeting to carry out their normal daily actions.

However, this was not just an individual game. It was a team game. That means, when a member of the team gave a commitment in the morning, they would feel accountable to their peers to fulfil that commitment. So, they would still be pushing their own abilities, even when they were working on their own. Similarly, every day, the team saw an improvement in the graph. So they would see that they had achieved another success. This would motivate them to continue succeeding.

In that case study, Joan broke the habit of a lifetime. The graph had an unbroken downward trend that Joan was expecting to continue. Joan went to update the trend chart. Then her assessment of the entry, which she was about to make, showed there was a gap between the current performance and the level she was expecting. That meant that she had to make a choice. She could make the entry and go home. That would have meant that she would have ended the winning run of entries. Alternatively, she could take off her coat, enter two more cases, and then update the chart before going home. She chose the latter. That choice probably helped her be even more committed to ensuring the team kept winning in the future. In effect, she had psychologically moved into the performance system.

Although we cannot be certain, it seems unlikely that she would have acted in this way if one of the other team members had updated the chart on that day. Indeed, it is easy to imagine a scenario in which another member of the team started to update the graph and exclaimed that it had not gone down. In that scenario, what would you predict Joan's response would have been? I suspect she might well have thought, "That is your problem, not mine."

This is the reason the protocol of the Leadership Game is very specific. It requires that the people who collectively control a pathway gap must each take their turn in assessing as the external assessor and accounting for the gap. In effect, every time they made this assessment, they were in the performance system. The performance system is the system that has the performance view of the pathway coordination. In this case, the rota that showed who was updating the map each day ensured everyone took turns in the performance system. This means that in general, we can say that:

*The people in control of the pathway system need to be responsible for repeatedly taking the role of the assessor in the performance system*

### Removing the need to assess

We can use this understanding to look at the effect of other small changes. For example, in the Legal case study, would Joan have behaved any differently if she was able to just print the graph and pin it to a notice board? The theory tells us that her response depended on whether she assessed the gap. So if she just printed the graph without assessing it, then she probably would not have seen any reason to stay late. To overcome this problem, the sheet could have been designed to ensure an assessment. It could have had a question where the person had to circle one of two options: "better/worse". Small differences can have big consequences.

## Fail-safe control

Understanding feedback control and performance systems has helped to shine a light on some of the invisible aspects, which are behind the success of many case studies. However, before we move from the subject of control systems, we need to also understand the importance of fail-safe control. At the beginning of this chapter, I explained that control systems are all around us. Some of those control systems are fail-safe mechanisms. That is a mechanism that sends or stops a signal when the feedback control system is not working. For example, a gas central heating boiler has a range of fail-safe control systems. So, the control system that switches on the gas supply to the boiler can only switch on if another control system senses there is a flame to ignite incoming gas. This means we can say the central heating system is as safe and effective as the combined effectiveness of its control systems. We can also say that:

*A fail-safe control aims to prevent or signal a system failure, and to minimise adverse consequences*

Also:

*A fail-safe control is typically based on the default presumption that a critical or safe state has NOT been reached without evidence to the contrary*

### The ferry

In fact, missions of fail-safe control in the design of organizational systems can have disproportionate consequences. To understand how this can happen, consider the tragedy of the Herald of Free Enterprise. This was a car ferry between the UK and the mainland of Europe. This ferry, together with several sister ships, had a roll-on/roll-off design. That design had bow doors that could open to allow cars to drive straight in and out of the eight decks of the ferry. There were no watertight compartments. On the evening of March 6th, 1987, the ferry left the Belgian port of Zeebrugge with its bow doors still open. Within minutes, the seawater rushed in, flooding the decks and capsizing the ferry. One hundred and ninety-three passengers and crew lost their lives in the disaster.

The initial blame was put solely on the negligence of the assistant boatswain. He was asleep in his cabin when he should have been closing the bow doors. So the process of closing the bow doors never took place. However, a subsequent public enquiry blamed the culture of the ferry owners, Townsend Thoresen. There had been several previous minor incidents involving open bow doors on similar vessels. There had also been numerous requests for improvements. These included putting a light on the bridge to indicate the doors were closed and having a TV camera pointed at the bow doors. However, management had dismissed all such requests as unnecessary.

The official enquiry made numerous recommendations. These included putting warnings on the bridge of the state of the doors, improving procedures and training, and making the compartments watertight. However, the enquiry did not identify what was probably the most important question of all. How could the internal systems and procedures be designed in the first place, without a fail-safe system? That would be the system that ensured ferries could not leave dock unless the bow doors were closed. This may seem like being wise after the event. However, it is not. We will see that fail-safe control is fundamental to integrating the horizontal and vertical structures. So, we can say:

*Before designing any procedures, we should first identify the essential fail-safe and feedback control systems for the critical benchmark standards. Protocols should then be developed to ensure those control systems work effectively*

For example, consider the scenario where you were developing all the procedures related to the take-off of a passenger aircraft. Where would you start? The answer is that you should start with the checklist the pilot has to complete before take-off. This is a list of the benchmarks for the fail-safe system. Before take-off, the pilot has to create the documentary evidence, showing these have been accounted for. So this is where we need to start when designing operational protocols. For each fail-safe benchmark, we can then work back and identify the benchmark standards that need to be met. By progressing back in this way, the detailed procedures are the simple protocols needed to achieve each benchmark.

Similarly, in all the previous case studies, accountability for a performance board was the critical part of the fail-safe system. In the legal case study, if the graph was not filled in, or stopped its downward trend, it would have become immediately visible to the manager. Also, in the bakery example, the teams of section managers had to account weekly for their challenge information, showing progress in helping to achieve the benchmark standard. In the factory safety example, log sheets would not be accepted if the safety standard had not been recorded.

## *Performance boards as fail-safes*

So, we are starting to see how the performance boards serve several purposes simultaneously. We have previously seen how they create the conditions of a team board game, which ensures collaboration. We can now see that they also create a fail-safe system for each challenge. The advantage of this becomes clear when we realise that the typical vertical structure does not inherently include fail-safe systems. The problem faced by the ferry captain is the same sort of problem that managers face daily. The responsibility to close the bow doors had been delegated to the person who was able to carry out that process. Yet the captain or manager had to trust that the person had completed the process to the standard required. Often, the only way the manager finds out that a process has not been completed correctly is when the failure causes a problem.

In effect, a manager is others-in-control of delegated tasks, unless the manager directly supervises every action. Obviously, the recurring problems this creates in organizations are not usually as catastrophic as the ferry disaster. Yet it is happening all the time. It is the reason why many managers spend a high proportion of their time dealing with consequential problems.

## Summary

In this chapter, we have seen that we can consider the GAME control cycle as the basis of intelligent control. Understanding this cycle helps us ensure that people are able to process information in a specific sequence. This sequence defines the most effective way of engaging people to take control of a performance gap. We have seen that we can transform subjective, qualitative assessments into quantifiable measures by using a frame of reference graduated between hell and utopia. We have also seen that it is possible to align many people to a common benchmark standard, in a way that creates the conditions of a video game. Finally, we saw the performance board that can act as a fail-safe system. This is because it publicly shows if any one person is not "playing by the rules" and living up to their responsibilities.

# Chapter 4

## How mapping helps rapid culture change

### Review and overview

In the last chapter, we saw how a driver controls a car, using the GAME loop to follow a pre-mapped route. However, in this chapter, we are going to see how the driver would have also used the GAME loop to develop the mental map of the route before she even started driving towards her destination. We will see how our brains progressively use the GAME loop to split down high-level, complex maps of information into lower-level maps of more controllable pathway systems. We also see how we can use those maps to consistently align short-term goals with long-term goals. We then look at a case study to see how we can use the Leadership Game map to solve chronic problems such as two departments being "at war" with each other. Finally, we will look at the causes of the opposite state. This is when departments are completely disengaged from each other. We will look at the concept of holding units and their role in encouraging disengagement and silo mentality.

### The role of GAME loops in Mapping

#### Pathway units

To understand how we create pathway maps of smaller systems, we can return to the map of the baton pathway in relay races. There, we have seen the pathway is split into four running-with-the-baton process systems. Those systems connect with "passing-the-baton" connection systems. However, rather than just talking about systems, we are now going to use the term *units*.

### *Units are systems, which consist of a set of internal roles filled by resources that are coordinated for a purpose*

Those internal roles can be considered as the roles played by the coordinated sub-units within the unit. In other words, a unit becomes a system once all its roles have been filled by the appropriate resources. Each unit has a pathway. However, each pathway also has input and output connections to other units. This means that when we are planning any route, we can map it as sets of process and connection units.

### Using GAME loops

To understand how the driver would use the GAME loop to map the route as a set of units, let us again assume the driver did not have a sat nav. We will assume that she was trying to plan the route, or pathway, to drive between South London to Durham in the UK.

### Group

To solve this particular journey-planning problem, she starts to **Group** the relevant information, so she has the relevant information to assess the challenge.

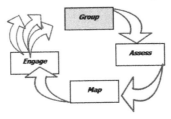

She would start with a map of the UK and then add the start and finish points to her map. She would also need to understand the scale of the map.

## Assess

This grouped information creates a high-level, big-picture map, which creates a frame of reference. That frame of reference will enable her to assess the gap. For example, the driver may look at a map of England and identify the distance between her home and her destination is about 250 miles. That assessment would trigger the next stage to plan a solution, which would potentially be within her control. However, she does not yet have a mental map of the route. In other words, she needs to break the overall gap into a set of smaller, controllable gaps.

## Map the controllable gaps

So the whole journey needs to be split into connected units, which can combine to create a complete solution. Each different road she takes will be a different unit. This is because each part of the journey will use a different resource. Most of the journey consists of using the M1 and A1 roads. So this is the most critical part of the planned journey. So this is the starting or central unit of the plan. We will assume the driver lives near to the A3 road and is going to connect to the M1 using the M25 motorway (the London orbital road). Therefore, she plans the route or pathway using those roads and their connections at various junctions. Although the driver plans the route in terms of roads and junctions, I will use the term "units" to show how we generalise this method of problem-solving. Therefore, she may plan the route as:

- From Home to A3 junction, use the A3 to A3/M25 junction

- From A3/M25 junction, use the M25 to the M25/M1 junction

- From the M25/M1 junction, use the M1 to the M1/A1 junction

- From the M1/A1 junction, use the A1 to the A1/Durham junction

In effect, she has mapped the overall pathway as a set of smaller, connected pathway units, as shown in the next diagram.

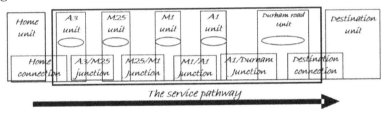

Each unit addresses a manageable gap. For example, the result needed when driving along the A3 is to arrive at the M25 junction. The junction is the connection unit between the A3 and M25 pathways. Similarly, the outcome needed for the M25 unit is to arrive at the M1 junction. From this perspective:

*The map of the pathway is a representation of the structure of the connection units between a set of component process units along the service pathways*

### Engage

Having mapped the coordination of the controllable gaps, our driver could then start her journey. She would do this by mentally passing that map to the GAME loop she uses to control the car processes, as described in the previous chapter.

## Proactive and active mapping

Therefore, the driver used the GAME loop to map the route or solution before the journey started. We call this *proactive* mapping. The driver then continuously applied the GAME loop to that map, to enable her to follow the route or pathway, which she had proactively developed. We call this *active* mapping. In other words, she was actively using the map that she had proactively developed.

## Short-term control for long-term goals

Because we carry out this type of planning all the time, it is easy to miss the power of the technique. When we drive a car, we continually focus on achieving short-term goals. For example, we will keep adjusting the steering to stay in the lane. This is just a lower-level GAME loop than the one we looked at in the previous chapter. However, once we have a map of the route to a longer-term goal, we can keep including that map in the group of information. This is the information we use to achieve short-term goals. This is exactly the example we looked at in the previous chapter. Therefore:

### Our map allows our continuous, short-term coordination to achieve long-term goals

It is easy to miss the importance of the previous statement. So imagine that developing a mental map of the route was analogous to painting a thick, luminous line in the middle of the roads we need to use. Imagine those lines also had a sequence of decreasing numbers every hundred metres. In this way, the starting point would be connected to the long-term destination by the line with numbers. As long as the driver focused on the short-term goal of following the line to the next number, he or she would be able to check their progress towards their arrival at their long-term goal. They would arrive at that long-term goal, even though they were only ever focused on achieving short-term goals.

The same applies when we try to align groups in achieving a long-term goal, no matter how far away the goal is. As long as they have a clear pathway to follow, with regular milestones then continually focusing on short-term goals will ultimately ensure everyone arrives at the long-term destination. This is a critical aspect of the performance view of pathways. However, the collective process of developing and using pathway maps is also a critical part of team building.

### Outward-bound team-building

To allow us to understand the role of the GAME loop and mapping in building teams, it is useful to consider the type of team-building course that uses maps. So, let us consider an outward-bound team-building course.

Often, this type of course involves taking groups to an unknown area. Each group has a map with coordinates of their current location and destination. The overall challenge is to reach the destination in the shortest possible time. There may be various challenges that the groups will face along the way, and there may be several groups competing for a nominal prize. This means the mapping involved is more than just planning a route to the destination; it needs to be the route that allows the group to undertake the journey in the most effective way. It creates the same sort of challenge as the video game. The map also serves the same purpose as the small chess set we considered in chapter two. The group will plan their strategy on the map to implement it in the real world.

When people work together, to proactively plan the most effective route, they often start to develop a team spirit. This is because they need to collaborate to agree on the route. In effect, collective planning helps the group develop a common, collective thought bubble. This part of the outward-bound course is similar to the planning that we saw when the legal team had their first session with the manager. In these circumstances:

*Collectively planning the most effective route on the map is a critical part of the team-building process*

## Using the map to review progress

In the outward-bound example, the teams are likely to continually and collectively review their physical map. This process helps to update their mental maps en route. So, this frequent reviewing of their progress against the plan on the map also helps in building team spirit. Every time the group collectively refer to the same map, they are aligning their thought bubbles. Put another way:

*When a group consistently review and update the planned route on a map, it develops and maintains the collective thought bubble of a team*

So consider the daily morning reviews around the map, which we saw in the legal case study. These are comparable to the frequent map review sessions of the outward-bound courses. They are also comparable to the weekly presentations of the section managers in the commercial bakery. Similarly, the Leadership Game has the same proactive and active mapping stages as the driver, when she developed and used a map. So we can start to see how mapping is much more than a useful technique. It is critical to the success of the case studies. Without an understanding of the power of mapping, we will only ever see the illusion of successful case studies.

### Small changes to the mapping protocol

We can also use the outward-bound example to help understand how small changes to the protocol could have disproportionate effects on the motivation of those involved. For example, imagine the course instructor appoints just one member of each group to be the 'map keeper'. In other words, the protocol is that only the map keeper can plan the route. Similarly, only the map keeper can use the map to check progress on the journey. Would you consider that this small change to the mapping protocol would have any significant effect on whether the group developed the collective thought bubble needed for teamwork?

When I ask my delegates this question, most predict that this change would destroy teamwork. They consider it would disenfranchise other group members, create conflict and blame, as well as creating hierarchical control. Interestingly, when they are explaining their views, delegates often use the term 'manager' when they are referring to the single map keeper.

However, not all of my delegates immediately accept that one map keeper would cause a problem. A few delegates respond that it could be more effective to have one person as the map keeper, with a set of specialists carrying out different tasks. In response, I remind them that my question was not about which approach would be more effective. I asked whether one map keeper would affect the development of the collective thought bubble needed for teamwork. Again, there may well be circumstances where a well-managed group of individuals would be more effective than developing a team. However, we need to first understand what stops high-performance teams from forming. To do that, all we need to ask ourselves is whether the conditions encourage or discourage the development of a collective thought bubble built from the performance view of the pathway. To confirm this point, we can apply the concept of a single map keeper to our analogy of the chess set. Consider the psychological difference if the person using the small chess set was shouting down instructions to a different person who was moving the chess pieces.

### Is this another case of common sense?

Again, some people consider these answers to be common sense. However, further thought suggests that this is more significant than might first appear. Again, it helps us understand how slight changes to the Leadership Game protocol can affect whether high-performance teams are encouraged or destroyed. The protocol that says, "Only one person is the map keeper" is likely to stop the formation of high-performance teams. The protocol that states, "Every team member is responsible for taking their turn in being map keeper and accounting for the map" is likely to encourage the formation of high-performance teams.

Therefore, we can start to understand the Leadership Game as first engaging the group in developing the map. Once they have been involved in developing the map, they need to be engaged in consistently using and updating the map. Even on first developing the map, they go through the GAME loop stages. So they initially group all the relevant information of the complex situation on a high-level map. That creates a frame of reference for them to assess the critical gap. Once they assess that gap, they can then create a lower-level map of the controllable gaps. Once they have proactively developed the map of controllable gaps, they can engage the second, active GAME loop. In that stage, they actively and often use the lower level pathway maps to guide their actions in the real world. We can apply this approach to any complex situation that needs collaboration.

This may seem an obvious principle. However, the simple fact is that in many organizations, those people in control of the actions inside a pathway have rarely, collectively mapped the gaps in their pathway. Even where they have identified issues, they are often not in a situation where they have ever been collectively accountable for addressing those gaps. Indeed, we can often track issues between groups to the fact that there have been no agreed protocols for the control of the connections between the groups. So our performance maps need to show where repeated issues are being created at the connection units by a lack of clear protocols. To help understand how mapping pathways in this way can address multiple issues, we are going to look at another case study.

## Departments at war

Often, organizations have departments that seem to be in constant conflict with each other. Most managers can identify at least one such example from their own experiences. Often, the problem has been in existence for many years. Typically, managers see it as insoluble because of the personalities involved. My master class delegates often raise their eyebrows when I explain that no matter how long the problem has existed, it is possible to solve it in a few weeks using the Leadership Game. Often, they find it difficult to accept that such long-standing and deep-seated problems can be addressed using a simple set of exercises. So I explain that they have already seen how small differences in the rules of the game can easily affect whether or not an exercise is successful. Thus, it is important to realise that many exercises, which superficially look similar, actually contain small differences that mean they will fail to create a high-performance, collaborative culture.

To show this to the delegates, I describe the various stages involved in a case study that involved two departments that were virtually at war with each other. If we were to try an approach to directly change people's behaviour, it would almost certainly fail. However, because this case study involved only two departments, controlling a single service pathway, it is a simple challenge for the Leadership Game. After describing each stage of the solution to my delegates, I ask them if they have any questions. This has proved to be a useful way for them to better understand the differences that affect the development of a high-performance culture. To reproduce that learning process, the following case study description includes questions often asked by my delegates, with the responses I give to these questions.

### The security company

The organization in question was one of the major cash-handling security companies in the UK. In effect, there were two different parts of the organization. One part consisted of a fleet of security vans that collected and delivered cash to various cash-dispensing machines, bank branches and retail outlets. There were depots across the country, which housed the security vans overnight. The other side of the organization consisted of a number of secure cash-counting depots. The security vans delivered the collected cash to these depots. Staff at the depots counted and repackaged the cash. Later, security vans delivered the cash to the cash-dispensing machines and retail outlets. Sometimes, a single site housed both the counting operations and van depots.

Previously, the company ran as two separate divisions. One board director was responsible for the security vans. A different director controlled the cash-counting depots. The company was restructuring to become area-based rather than functionally-based. There would be a service manager for each area, who would be responsible for both delivery and operations within the area. Unfortunately, over the years, the two divisions had developed different cultures. Worse still, they had no respect for each other. Much of the highest levels of hostility occurred on the small number of co-location sites. These housed both the security vans and the counting-house operations. At one co-location site, in particular, there was continual conflict between the two divisions that were resident on the site.

The directors decided to test the new area-based structure at this most problematic site. Customer satisfaction surveys showed it was providing one of the lowest levels of service of the whole organization. Peter, the new area manager, started to chair site meetings, involving managers from both divisions. Predictably, those meetings often degenerated into circular arguments. Both sides blamed the other for incompetence. This state continued for the first few weeks of the trial.

When I became involved, Peter explained that the situation was a nightmare. No matter what he tried, he could not get the two sides to act rationally to sort out their differences. I explained how the Leadership Game could resolve the issue. I explained the problems were caused by the 'dropped batons' between the departments.

I explained that we could use pathway maps to identify and resolve issues. I explained that pathways connect units. It is the connections between the units that we need to explore. I explained that, although there is no defined standard, we could represent these units by vertical rectangles. We could then represent the different processes or activities carried out by those units as circles within the rectangles. I explained that processes are analogous to the running-with-the-baton activity in a relay race. The process units are connected by connection units. I explained we could map these as horizontal rectangles.

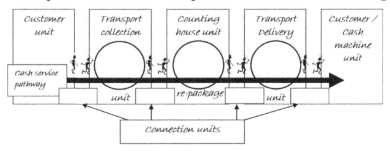

In this case, the map of the cash service pathway would look like the diagram above. However, there would also be more complex information pathways. For example, historically, customers made requests to the counting-house side of the business, for special deliveries of cash. Those requests would often cause conflict. The counting house would agree that they could provide the required level of cash, but the delivery side would refuse the request from the counting-house. Typically, this was because it would mean a detour for one of their drivers. Such refusals would create much frustration in the counting-house. Such frustration was made worse when they saw delivery drivers back at the depot more than an hour before the end of the shift.

This is a simple situation because the problem connections are between just two units or departments. So, in this case, we do not have to map the more complex information flows. We can just engage the two groups in collectively identifying and addressing the gaps between the two departmental units.

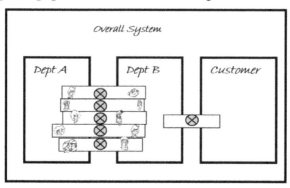

I explained to Peter that the main reason they were dropping batons was that there were no agreed protocols defining the roles and responsibilities at the connections. This problem would continue until there was clear, collective accountability for identifying and removing the gaps. It was true that the emotional hostility was preserving and aggravating the problem. This was a classic in-group/out-group situation. However, the solution was to put the two sides in an environment that created peer accountability for identifying and addressing the gaps in the connections between the two departments.

### The sticky note GAME

I described an exercise to Peter, which involved the groups using sticky notes. The technical name that describes this technique is Gap Accountability Mapping Exercise. However, as that also has the acronym of GAME, we will call it the sticky note GAME. So, Peter arranged a session involving the senior managers from the two departments, together with the managers who were their direct reports. This included about nine section managers from each of the two departments. The groups sat at separate tables, where each person had a pad of sticky notes and a felt-tip pen.

Peter explained the purpose of the reorganization was to give a higher level of service to their customers, by enabling the two divisions to work together more effectively. He explained that currently, this depot had a very low level of customer satisfaction. He went on to explain this first session was to identify issues that they needed to address to improve the level of service.

Peter then asked everyone to make their individual assessment of the effectiveness of the current relationship between the two departments. He asked them to assess it on a scale of minus 10 to plus 10. He explained that minus 10 represented an ineffective and hostile relationship, while plus 10 represented the highest possible level of effectiveness and collaboration. He then asked them to write their scores using a single sticky note per person. Peter then asked them to place their scores on a flipchart at the front of the room. He then arranged for the two departmental managers to agree on the overall average score and write it on the flipchart. The score was minus three. The groups greeted this with much hilarity. Once the laughter had subsided, Peter asked them if they agreed that the score showed there was not a professional relationship between the two departments. This question created an uncomfortable silence. The mood clearly changed as they began to see the gap. They started to perceive the crisis. Peter then explained that the purpose of the exercise was to find ways of rapidly improving that score.

### Questions and answers

Before continuing to describe this case study in my master classes, I ask delegates if they have any questions about this first stage. Below is a typical list of their questions and my answers.

*Question*: Why bother to quantify the problem when they know the relationship is terrible?

*Answer:* They are viewing the problem from a subjective, 'silo' and emotional perspective. Each department believes the other is causing all the problems. We need them to focus rationally and objectively on the same challenge of improving the effectiveness between the departments. In effect, they were being taken through the first two stages of the initial GAME loop: group the information and assess the gap. Psychologically, that put them in the state where they were more able and willing to map the gaps.

*Question:* Why start with the two groups on separate tables, rather than mixing them?

*Answer:* We need to accept the reality of the two groups at war. Trying to mix them at this stage would be artificial. In any case, as you will see, we are not trying to get the two groups to work together in this session.

### Map the connections and accountability

Returning to the case study, I had explained to Peter the aim of the next stage was to develop an agreed list of contributory connection gaps, which were causing the high-level conflict gap. As I explained earlier in the questions and answers, this first part of the meeting had started to follow the GAME sequence. The next stage was to involve the groups in starting to map the gaps. However, this mapping stage was split into three stages.

### Step A – Identify gaps at the connections

The first step was to engage everyone in identifying the

gaps in the connections between the two departments. So, Peter asked everyone to imagine the scenario where next week would be "the week from hell". (At this point, I explain to my master class delegates the "week from hell" could involve "the project from hell" or "the customer from hell", the "order from hell" or any similar issue that is appropriate.) Peter explained that in the week from hell, whatever could go wrong between the two departments would go wrong. He then asked that each person write one sticky note for each issue that they could identify.

### Questions and answers

*Question:* Why not ask for positive ideas for improvement?

*Answer:* We need to avoid identifying solutions before we define the problems, or 'gaps', between the groups. This is important and often where many similar types of techniques start to create the wrong psychological conditions. In such scenarios, each group would probably resist any solutions proposed by the other. Each group sees the other as the out-group, only capable of supplying fake news. Also, the aim of this mapping process is to identify the gaps at the connections and who will be collectively accountable for solving those issues. There should be no attempt to solve the issues until there is a full list of gaps and clear, peer accountability for each one. Once there is peer accountability, the groups can go away and start developing the solutions in small groups. It is difficult to over-emphasise the importance of not trying to identify solutions at this stage.

*Question:* Why ask about the imagined "week from hell" rather than focus on all the real issues that arose last week?

*Answer:* For several reasons: First, identifying past issues will be perceived as assigning blame. When blame is assigned, it creates a defensive response of story-telling, justification, or even aggressive verbal attacks, rather than problem-solving. This just exacerbates the problems of in-group/out-group, fake news and emotional reactions. However, no one can be blamed for imaginary issues because they have not happened yet. We also need a definitive list of ALL predictable gaps. Only some issues will have occurred last week.

*Question:* Why not let the manager write the issues on a flipchart?

*Answer:* Although it may seem bizarre at the moment, in such a situation, the psychological ownership of the issues would transfer to the person documenting the issues (i.e. the manager). That person becomes the map keeper. This is sometimes called 'passing the monkey' or 'hot potato'. So even at this early stage, small differences in the exercise can make big differences to the psychological conditions.

### Step B – Agree on the full set of gaps

Returning to the session, Peter started the next step. This step involved everyone in combining their views to agree on a definitive list of gaps. Peter had drawn a set of horizontal lines, roughly the depth of a sticky note, on the flipchart. He then asked for one person, in one of the teams, to place one of their sticky notes (containing the heading of one issue from his/her 'week from hell') at the left-hand side of the first row. They were then asked to give a brief verbal description of what was on the note. Before he started this, Peter explained to the group that there should be no discussion at this stage, unless anyone needed brief clarification. Once the first note was in place, Peter asked for anyone with similar notes to place them in the same row. The effect of this was to create a row of notes, all about the same issue.

Peter then asked a member of the other team to place one of their sticky notes in the left-hand side of the next row on the flipchart. Again, they gave a brief description without any further discussion. Similar notes were then placed in the same row. Peter alternated this between the two teams until they had displayed all of their notes.

**Potential Gaps**

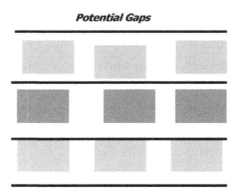

At this point in the session, there was a definitive list of potentially controllable gaps on the flipchart.

## Questions and answers

*Question:* Why ban discussions about each issue?

*Answer:* This is part of creating ownership of the maps of the gaps. Any discussion will potentially lead to arguments. This will substantially increase the time taken and create the wrong conditions.

*Question:* Why alternate?

*Answer:* Some of the issues will be identified by managers in both teams. However, often, specific issues will be a problem for just one team. We want a balanced process, to avoid frustration building up in one team. Also, we want each issue shown in a way that automatically creates a brief moment for reflection.

## Step C – Create accountability for the gaps

At this stage, the managers had mapped the gaps, because there was a set of potentially controllable gaps on the flipchart. However, those gaps only start to become controllable when we know who is accountable for each of the gaps. The teams who could address the gaps had not yet taken ownership of those gaps. In other words, at this stage, there was no accountability for addressing those gaps.

Peter now started the final step. This step was to create peer accountability for each of the gaps. Each gap needed a mini-team that would be accountable for identifying how to control the gap. The mini-team should include at least one person representing the unit or department on each side of the gap. The mini-team would need to account for how they could remove that gap in a way that was compatible with the overall solution.

So, Peter now asked everyone to put their names on two sticky notes. (The actual number of notes is the number of issues divided by the number of individuals in the smallest team.) He drew a vertical line near the right of the flipcharts. In effect, this created a box against each issue to identify the team members who would investigate the solution. He then asked everyone to put their first named sticky note in one of the team boxes against each issue. He explained that members could choose which issues they would work on. However, he also stated there had to be at least one name from each department, but no more than one name from each department at this stage. Also, everyone would have to place all of their named sticky notes against the issues. This ensured that everyone had to volunteer for roughly the same number of issues. Once everyone had put their first named note up, Peter asked them to put up their second note, to ensure that every issue had a team made up from both departments.

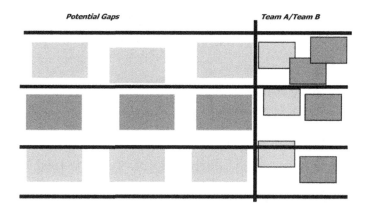

In principle, there was now peer accountability for every one of the low-level gaps. So Peter now explained that these mini-teams would need to look at each issue and present their solution the following week. The solutions would have to get everyone else's "buy-in", including his. He then agreed the date of the next meeting and ended the session. In effect, that ended the proactive mapping part of the Leadership Game. The group had mapped the complex high-level problem into a set of controllable gaps. Every gap had a team who would be responsible for accounting for the solutions.

### Questions and answers

*Question:* Why are the "rules" such that at least one person from each team has to put their name against each gap?

*Answer:* Most issues raised by one team will be a dropped baton, which they view as being caused by the other team. This means we need members of both teams to be accountable for the gaps in the maps and the solutions. That way, we should get joined-up solutions. It also creates both internal and external peer accountability. This ensures that both members of the team are viewing the issue as the external assessor. Each member of the team has to see the issue from the other person's perspective. Externally, the mini-teams are also all accountable to the manager and their peers in the other teams. This is because they need everyone's buy-in to their proposals.

*Question:* Why do the presentations of the mini-teams have to get everyone else's buy-in?

*Answer:* The final purpose of this simple exercise is to make sure everyone owns the collective solutions. The best way to get the group's buy-in is to ensure that they are each responsible for getting everybody else's buy-in.

*Question:* Why call the session to an end before they can develop solutions?

*Answer:* This is critical. This is the Engage stage. It is engaging the groups to cycle again through the GAME loop. Then each group will have to further break down each problem into a set of smaller, controllable solutions. This is the point at which we can create or destroy peer accountability. If we stop here, everyone knows who is accountable for presenting which solutions the following week. Everyone knows who is accountable for getting everyone else's buy-in to the solutions for each of the problems. It completes the proactive mapping use of the GAME cycle. If we allow general discussions now, all that could be lost. So we need to stop the session before that happens. We need to give everyone time to "mull things over" and be responsible for having to arrange meetings with their counterparts. This is often where seemingly similar exercises create the wrong psychological conditions. Trying to solve many issues with everyone in the room can be almost impossible, particularly when there is antagonism between groups. Under such conditions, there is no accountability; there are just many people giving their individual views. As described in chapter two, the presence of the manager can also aggravate the issue. This is because it encourages everyone to consider it is the manager's job to sort out the disagreements. Everyone else becomes "others-in-control" of developing solutions.

Also, we started with two groups who each considered the other group as the out-group. Once there are mini-teams, consisting of one person for each group, the two members have to become a single group, solving a simple challenge. The fail-safe mechanism here is that they know they have to find a solution that will get the buy-in of both groups. They will have the time for their rational problem-solving part of their brains to take the lead.

*Question:* Does this need groups of managers, or would it work with staff as well?

*Answer:* As we will see in later examples, it works at any level. However, it often works better with peer groups, rather than a mixture of staff and managers. What is interesting is that each level will often identify a different list of issues. So, the staff will have a different list to junior managers. Junior managers may have a different list to senior managers. This means, in principle, the approach can be run with different groups at different levels. In this case, Peter felt it would work best with the departmental managers and their immediate managers.

*Question:* Why set a date then for the next meeting?

*Answer:* We are creating the conditions of a set of time-limited, collective challenges. This is part of the fail-safe accountability. If there was no date for review, it is doubtful that the mini-teams would even arrange a time to solve their mini-challenges. With a date, each mini-team knows when they have to present solutions to senior managers and their colleagues. They become accountable for finding a solution within that timescale.

Returning to the case study, at the end of this session, the groups have broken down the ill-defined reasons for conflict into a set of manageable gaps. The map of the gaps shows all the component mini-challenges, with who is accountable for each gap. This is the end of the group proactive stage of mapping the gaps. Having developed the overall map, they will move onto the high-frequency reviews of their progress in removing the individual gaps.

### High-frequency, external reviews

The formal review sessions started the following week, as described. We can consider this stage as the active mapping stage of the Leadership Game. Each mini-team formally presented their proposals to remove the gaps at the pathway connections between the departments. The teams presented to all the managers involved. Each issue had its own flipchart sheet, listing the key points of their proposal for addressing the issue. When other managers had questions, which they felt were not fully answered, they had to write the issues on a sticky note. Each note was then placed on the relevant flipchart sheet. Peter had explained the mini-team involved should then come back the following week to present their update to those new concerns and issues. These weekly presentations would continue until the mini-teams had resolved all the issues to everyone's satisfaction.

At the end of the first presentation session, several proposed solutions had everyone's agreement. However, there were still some issues that needed resolutions from the mini-teams. So, they all agreed on the date for the next meeting. After three sessions, the teams had addressed all the issues. Just before the end of the third session, Peter repeated the first exercise. He asked all the managers for their individual assessment of the effectiveness of the interface between the two departments on a scale of 0 to 10. The average score had already risen from minus 2 to plus 6. Peter explained that the managers had to identify those issues that were still causing problems between the teams. They would repeat the process until they had resolved all predictable issues, and the score was at least 8, and preferably higher.

In later chapters, we will look in detail as to how these reviews sessions should function to create the right psychological conditions. In this example, the review sessions lasted four weeks, at which point all the managers reluctantly agreed the working relationship score had reached 9. This simple method transformed both the culture of the site and the service standards.

### *More than a temporary change*

Soon after this, Peter had a promotion, and a new manager took over the site. A month after taking the post, I asked the new manager how he was getting on. He replied that he had been worried about taking the job because, for years, this site had a terrible reputation. However, he now felt everyone worked well together. He considered it must be his style of management that had solved the problem!

This comment is interesting because, apart from the new manager, all the management and staff had been at the site for many years. The change, brought about by the Leadership Game, had remained intact, even though the bad reputation had remained. The new manager had no problems, not because of his style, but because the two sections had removed the gaps causing problems.

Although this case study may appear different from the previous case studies, it uses the same principles. At its heart, it is about using the rules of the Leadership Game to repeatedly create ownership and peer accountability for the maps of the controllable gaps.

However, this was a relatively simple example because it only involved two departmental units. In more complex scenarios, we will need a more formalised way of developing pathway maps. Nevertheless, we will see that we can use the principles of this sticky note GAME in many different circumstances.

### *Disengaged systems*

However, before we look at those examples, we need to understand the other extreme state of the relationship between departments. This is the more common problem where departments, which should be working closely together, seem to be largely disengaged from each other. On the basis that the problems are the systems, not the people, we need to understand what systems are encouraging this disengagement. To achieve this, we need to look at the concept of holding units.

## Holding units

So far, I have repeatedly compared service pathways to the analogy of a relay race. However, in organizations, relatively few connections pass directly between units. For example, a patient who needs X-rays after seeing a hospital consultant would probably have to wait in the radiology waiting room. When an item in a supermarket passes to the customer, it has often been waiting on the shelf for some time previously. Such pathway flows are not like the baton in a normal relay race. The flow is more like an adapted relay race. In this type of race, the runners do not directly pass their baton to the next runner. Instead:

**There are boxes at the points where the runners would normally pass batons.**

Under these circumstances, each runner takes a baton from the box at the beginning of their run. They then run, with the baton, to the box at the end of their run. They then drop their baton into the box and run back to their starting box to retrieve another baton. All the runners just keep cycling through these stages. So any individual runner only knows from which box they collect batons and to which box they deliver them.

In this scenario, batons placed into the first box will all progressively pass through the series of intermediate boxes until they finish up in the final output box. This means there is still a baton pathway. However, not a single runner may be aware of the route of that pathway. Now imagine someone wanted to move a set of batons, one at a time, from a box at the start to a box that was 400 metres away. We will assume the protocol of this game is that no single runner is allowed to run more than 100 metres at a time with any single baton. So, no single runner could take the baton from the start box to the finish box. A manager could solve this problem by splitting the 400-metre pathway into four controllable gaps. He or she could achieve this by placing three boxes 100 metres apart along the pathway, with additional boxes at each end. The manager could then assign the responsibility for each of the activities to four subordinates.

This may seem like a bizarre relay race. However, the point is that batons would flow along the pathway, with no one directly controlling the coordination of the individual flows.

Odd as it may seem, this is a far better analogy to the way inputs flow through organizations to become outputs. In this analogy, each runner is acting as the control system, coordinating their local actions of running with the baton. In fact, the situation in organizations is even more complex, because there is not just a single relay race, with a single baton and a single sequence of boxes. The analogy is more like a situation where there were many different relay races, with different shape and colour batons going into different sequences of boxes.

To complicate matters further, each runner is running in various different relay races, which are all taking place simultaneously! Changing our analogy, from direct baton passes to boxes, is far more fundamental than it might appear. In effect, we have now created the conditions that are almost certain to create silo mentality. Each runner is disengaged from all the other runners.

So now, the first half of the relay service pathway looks more like the picture below.

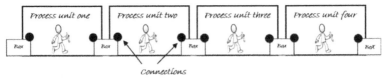

Connections

Under these conditions, no one has to coordinate their actions with other runners to "pass the baton". They just have to drop or collect batons from the boxes. There are still connections. These are the dropping into the box and taking the baton out from the box. However, the boxes have become "holding" units. These make a third type of unit, after process and connection units. In this scenario, no one is trying to minimise the overall time taken for batons to move from the start to the finish holding unit. That overall performance coordinating system is now missing. This is more like the legal situation before the Leadership Game. Under these circumstances, there are many reasons why the batons could take too long to make their journey. For example, the boxes could all be in the wrong positions. In principle, the runners could improve pathway performance by changing the position of the boxes until they minimised the time taken for batons to flow through the pathway. However, in the current scenario, the runners are not part of a performance system that would do this. The runners are just in the process units that carry out the separate activities in the service pathway. They are behaving correctly to the protocols of their individual systems.

In other words, we can now see that service pathways consist of a set of process, connection and holding units. However, the connection units are just used to put batons in and take batons out of the boxes, rather than passing the batons directly to the next runner. In this scenario, the units involved in the service pathway do not have any inherent way of changing or improving the pathway.

In the same way, while the relay runners remain solely in their own units, we can assume that they are not able to change behaviour or performance. They will only change their behaviour if they metaphorically exit the service pathway, and then enter a different system, with a different protocol.

### The inherent problem of holding units

The point with holding units is that no one is carrying out any activity inside the holding units. So there is no activity changing the state of the entities waiting in holding units. However, those states will still change. For example, anything left for a length of time in a holding unit will age. Consider the entity is a product on a shelf in a supermarket. A shelf is a holding unit. If the product stays there for any time, it may become out-of-date. Therefore, unless someone is continually checking the sell-by dates, the products could become dropped batons, as assessed by the external assessor – the customer.

Nevertheless, holding units provide some major advantages. For example, in a supermarket, staff do not have to hand each item directly to the customer. They just load the shelves. Then different customers take the products they need from the shelves. However, we need to fully understand the issues related to holding units because they are critical to improving pathway performance. So we will investigate holding units in more detail in the next chapter.

## Summary

In this chapter, we have seen how the GAME loop is equally applicable to developing maps and using them. In effect, GAME loops split complex challenges into a set of smaller challenges, which can be addressed by specialised units. We have seen how maps enable continual, short-term goals to eventually achieve long-term goals. We have again seen why we should not rely solely on vertical management control. The two extreme scenarios are departments at war or disengaged departments. Neither is conducive to high-performing organizations. We have also seen that organizational pathways are more like adapted relay races, with boxes for the batons at the connections. We called these boxes holding units. Such holding units have advantages. However, they also have disadvantages. They help encourage the disengagement of the different groups involved in the pathways. So this is the issue that needs to be addressed by the Leadership Game.

# Chapter 5

## Mapping the pathway connections

### Review and overview

In the previous chapters, we have looked at a range of concepts related to horizontal pathways. In this chapter, we need to start reviewing those ideas in more detail. That will allow us to see how the separate principles fit together. That will then enable us to see how we can split a high-level, organizational challenge into its controllable components. We will also take a closer look at the problems caused by pathway holding units. We will see how benchmarks, at the holding connections, are spread across three different categories. We also look at a case study as an example of how to apply these principles. We use that case study to better understand the difference between the management and leadership roles mentioned in the first chapter.

### A general view of pathways

So far, we have looked at simple examples of service pathways. These have included pathways for products, services and patients, to name but a few. However, in more general terms, a pathway is simply the route that needs to be taken from a starting state to a desired future state. So we can also use the term pathway to describe the route needed to transform the whole organization. That pathway will include the series of stages taken to change the organization from its current state to the state we require. At least in principle, the desired future state could be defined in the organization's vision statement. However, we will be looking in more detail at the usefulness of vision and mission statements in the final chapter. For now, we will assume that somewhere there is a description of the desired final state of the organization. This could be as simple as a set of benchmarks that define that desired state.

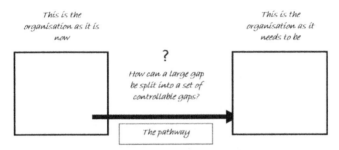

To start identifying the stages in that pathway, we need to split the complex problem into a set of controllable gaps. So the first question we need to answer is: where do we start when organizations are so complex? In organizations relying only on the vertical structure, that analysis is carried out vertically.

### The vertical structure

For example, we have already identified that we can consider the organization chart as a map of coordinated units. We can consider these as business units.

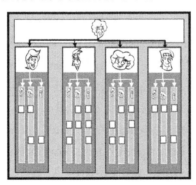

Thus, the organization is a unit which consists of several departmental units. At the top of the organizational unit, the chief executive acts as the coordinating system for those departmental units. The departmental managers act as the internal coordinating systems for the section units within departments. Even staff members, who do not have subordinates, still act as coordinating systems. They act as the internal coordinating systems for the various process units described as responsibilities in their job descriptions. So staff units include the process units coordinated by each staff role.

We have seen that, when a chief executive only uses the vertical structure to split down the problem, the process starts with their view of the future organization. As mentioned in previous chapters, the chief executive may then split that view down into performance targets for departmental managers. The same process is then repeated down the vertical hierarchy.

### The second critical responsibility

However, setting performance targets implicitly means that everyone has a second, critical responsibility. The first responsibility is to carry out the daily, operational duties. This is often referred to as "the day job". The second responsibility implicitly ensures that everyone is also responsible for helping to bring about changes to improve performance.

These changes should be the ones that help the organization achieve its goals. However using the vertical structure to cascade targets for the second responsibility creates numerous, disjointed performance targets. Those targets may have no clear relationship with the stages in the pathway required to transform the organization. Instead, the targets just increase people's focus on their own silos. That makes collaboration even harder. Nevertheless, it is worth repeating that:

*Any approach to cascading performance improvement means that everyone has a second, critical responsibility*

*That critical responsibility is to help bring about the changes needed to help the organization achieve its goals*

## The horizontal structure

However, as we have seen throughout the previous chapters, organizations have a second, complementary structure. That second structure of performance systems is based on the horizontal service pathways. Those pathways can be mapped across the vertical structure.

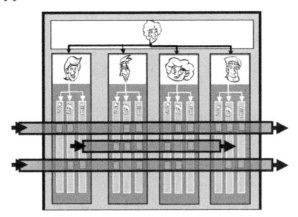

We have also seen these horizontal pathways consist of the individual processes, which are the responsibilities of individual staff members in the vertical structure. When we map those process units along the pathways, it automatically reveals the connections between those processes. For the moment, we will assume that all those connections involve holding units. In other words, we can consider all connections as holding connections. Those connections are shown below as crossed circles for clarity.

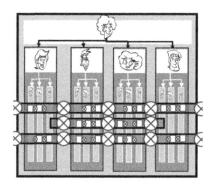

The larger internal circles represent the pathway connections between departments. We know the vertical structure defines who is responsible for which process units. So, in the vertical structure, who is responsible for the effectiveness of those connections?

As I briefly mentioned at the beginning of this book, when we only rely on the vertical structure for coordination, the departmental unit boundary is the boundary of control of department managers. Therefore, each departmental manager is typically only responsible for the coordination within his or her department unit. This means that, at least in theory, departmental managers are not responsible for anything outside their departmental boundaries.

Again, that technically means that departmental managers are not responsible for the effectiveness of the pathway connections between departments marked by the large crossed circles. They are the responsibility of the chief executive. Indeed, it is not even clear who is responsible for ensuring that products or services, delivered at the end of the pathways, consistently meet the standards needed by external parties such as customers or clients. So, for example, a manufacturing manager may justifiably blame a high level of returns on the purchasing department for providing low-quality components. Alternatively, he may blame the HR department for causing long delivery times. This could be because the HR department is not recruiting sufficient staff to fill vacant positions.

We know that successfully achieving any benchmark standard, along the pathway, is likely to involve coordinating the actions of several roles. However, as I briefly mentioned in the first chapter, it is difficult to directly delegate collective responsibility to any group for achieving a benchmark. This is because, as we have seen, they can all blame other members of the group.

The same problem even applies within a department. This is because each subordinate is technically only responsible for the processes within their direct control. So, in theory, the manager is always responsible for all the connections in the pathway flows between subordinates. However, we will see that most pathways are much more complex than the diagrams suggest. This means that, in real environments, the number of connections is far higher. The fact that most of those connections involve holding units complicates the problem even further.

### The holding unit scenario

To better understand the problems associated with pathway holding connections, consider a scenario where customers phone in orders for products. An operator enters the order details into the IT system and prints a hard copy. We will assume the name of that operator is Lynne. Les is another data entry operator. For the moment, we will assume that Lynne has to physically pass the hard copy of the order to Les. Les then looks at the hard copy of each order and checks the available stock. He then produces a delivery note so that the goods can be despatched.

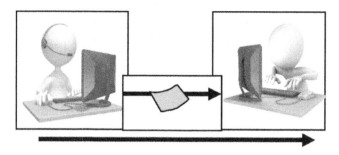

So when Lynne physically passes each printed order, it is equivalent to an ordinary passing-the-baton type of connection unit. Now, let us change the scenario to one where Les is too busy to collect the individual orders. So Lynne just places the printed orders on Les's table. The pile of orders on Les's table now becomes the holding unit.

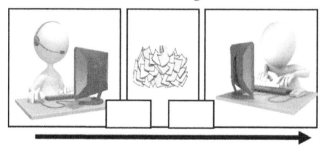

Both Lynne and Les may be working hard. However, if there is no collective coordination between the two, then the flow of orders could easily meet a bottleneck.

As we have seen, with silo mentality, neither Lynne nor Les feels they are responsible for the holding unit that makes the connection. The unprocessed orders could start building up in the holding connection on Les's table. Alternatively, if there were no orders in the holding connection, then Les would be waiting with nothing to do. Yet at the same time, potentially Lynne may not be coping with the influx of orders.

While the orders flowing along the pathway are physical documents, there is at least the advantage the pile of waiting orders would be visible. However, now let us assume the company upgrades the computer system. This upgrade means that Lynne enters the orders into a database, while Les uses the information in the database to create the delivery notes. Now, there is no reason to print the orders. The orders are just stored as data on a network disk drive. This means the ever-increasing backlog of orders is no longer visible. To make matters worse, the invisible bottleneck of orders, in the holding unit between the two internal processes, is causing another gap. The bottleneck is causing an ever-increasing delay in the overall time taken to dispatch the goods. This time delay is probably also invisible to other people inside the organization, including managers. It may well remain invisible until customers (the external assessors) start complaining.

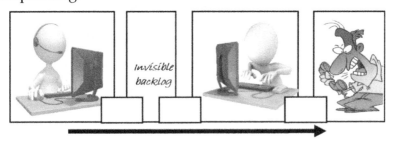

Even then, no one, who is carrying out the separate processes along the pathway, is likely to consider it as their responsibility to address the problem. In each operator's thought bubble, the boundary of their responsibility is the boundary of their own, system. So, from their individual perspectives, problems at the holding connections are the responsibility of their managers. Yet, if managers cannot physically see any problem, they are unlikely to take action to prevent a crisis.

As we have already identified, relay race teams would not be effective or successful if none of the runners felt responsible for helping to deliver effective baton passes. Yet this is what is happening in this scenario. Here, the waiting orders are equivalent to a pile of dropped batons. Yet, if the two operators were in different departments, then potentially, neither departmental manager would perceive an urgent need to ensure their departments engaged in collaborating more effectively. So the problems, created by the vertical system's inability to create a responsibility for the performance gaps, are more than just theoretical. They are real.

### *Responsibility for pathway effectiveness*

Nevertheless, these problems immediately vanish once people's second responsibility focuses on improving pathway performance, rather than just their own local performance. In other words, the problems vanish when people become accountable for the maps of the pathway gaps.

If the two operators were to assist each other in sharing the workload and coordinating their processes, it could potentially reduce the backlog very quickly. We have seen that they cannot be made directly responsible for minimising the backlog. However, we have also seen that they *can* be collectively responsible for *accounting* for the *documented evidence* of the gap at the holding connection.

In other words, they can be responsible for mapping the number of orders in the holding system. That can be achieved by each being responsible for recording the number of orders in the holding system on alternate days. They *can* also be responsible for presenting collective proposals to solve the problem. Then by definition, if they obtain their manager's buy-in to their own solutions, they are likely to be highly motivated to implement those solutions.

This may seem to be a roundabout way of engaging groups to *feel* responsible for removing the actual pathway gaps. However, as we have seen, it cannot be achieved directly through the vertical system. Moreover, although it may be complicated to understand, it is very simple to implement. It is also a fast way of achieving the desired result.

### Solving real-world complexity

The problem is that the real world is typically much more complex than the holding system example. Pathways are more complex, and there may be several benchmark standards required at each holding connection. However, the principle still applies. The simple solution is to ensure the people in control of the pathway are responsible for mapping all the pathway connections together with their related benchmarks and evidence of the gaps. To understand how we can achieve this, we first need to understand the various types of benchmarks.

## Quality, Availability and Cost benchmarks

Indeed, if we are going to map benchmark standards at this detailed level, we need to realise that such standards fall into three main categories. The three categories are Quality, Availability and Cost (or cost-effectiveness). So we can use these three benchmarks to assess the capability of a unit. This is achieved by recording the certainty of a unit delivering an output to the benchmark standards in all three criteria.

### Quality Standards

Quality standards define the standards needed to ensure the pathway output is fit for purpose. Thus, there would be quality gaps if the supermarket product was damaged or stale. Equally, in any organization, if a requested report contained wrong information, that would also be a gap between the quality standard provided and the quality standard needed.

### Availability standards

Even if an item is to the required quality standards, it may not be delivered to the right place at the right time. For example, in the supermarket, if the product you want is out of stock, then there is a performance gap in the availability standard. There would equally be an availability gap if you wanted four particular items, and only three were on the shelf. If the supermarket records how many items are out of stock each day, or the total out-of-stock days for all items, then those would be the performance gaps of availability.

### Cost-effectiveness

Cost-effectiveness is the third benchmark criteria that we need to control. As we will see in later chapters, there are different aspects of the cost criteria. One is the cost to the service provider in providing the service. Another is the cost or price of the service to the service customer. For simplicity, we will assume the two costs have a fixed relationship. So, if the product price at the supermarket was higher than another supermarket, then we would consider that to be a cost gap. In this way, the cost criteria of benchmark standards can be considered as a measure of efficiency in providing the required quality and availability. In other words, the cost criteria include any benchmarks that indicate the cost-effectiveness of the pathway.

### Improving service pathway performance

So, to improve the performance of a service pathway, we may need to improve the capability of the pathway unit to consistently meet one or more of the pathway benchmark standards. If the pathway was for patients through a hospital, that might mean achieving better health outcomes (Quality), in shorter times (Availability) at lower costs (higher efficiency).

### A performance system for each benchmark

We have seen that, if a benchmark is not being consistently met, it needs those people, who collectively control the standard, to take control of the performance system for that benchmark. In effect, when people are in the pathway performance system, they are playing a team video game for a specific benchmark. In that system, they progressively improve their ability to achieve that standard consistently. Then, that control system becomes the business-as-usual, feedback control system in the service pathway. The members of the team can then move onto their next challenge.

However, identifying such benchmarks and performance gaps, at all the connections, is rarely an important feature of traditional maps or measures used within organizations. In fact, traditional mapping often ignores connections. So it is first worth reviewing the common mapping methods and how we can adapt them to include connections and benchmarks.

## Traditional Maps

### Process maps

For example, one of the simplest and most commonly used types of map is the process map.

Process maps show the sequence of processes. However, they do not show what metaphorical batons pass between processes. Nor do they show the likelihood of dropped batons, or what set of benchmarks need to be met between processes. Also, when a specialist creates a map of the process flow, the only person owning the map is the person who developed it. It may well help groups to recognise where their individual task fits into the bigger picture, but, on its own, it does little to create a high-performance culture.

### The same problem with project maps or Gantt charts

When organizations have major projects, they often develop project plans. These are more sophisticated, one-off process maps. There are many different formats for these maps, but the best known is the Gantt chart.

**GANTT CHART**

| Job1 | SAM | | | | | | |
| Job2 | IAN | | | | | | |
| Job3 | JOE | | | | | | |
| Job4 | SAM | | | | | | |
| Job5 | IAN | | | | | | |
| Job6 | JOE | | | | | | |

The Gantt chart uses arrows to show a sequence of tasks. It may have proposed dates for starting each task. However, those dates are typically only guidance for the project manager. Once early deadlines slip, then it is likely that the rest of the dates start to become almost meaningless.

Unfortunately, this visual layout still does not help to engage the people who are in control of the tasks. Theoretically, people can see the tasks that involve them. But this does not help create 'ownership' of the map, the connections or the challenge. Again, the project manager may well be the only person owning the map. In such circumstances, we have separated the map keeper from the people in control of the processes.

## Swim lanes

More recently, there has been a trend to change the format of the information in Gantt charts towards a format that uses swim lanes.

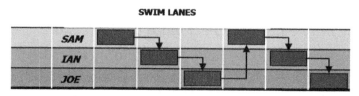

This format is analogous to the lanes marked out in a racing swimming pool. On the map, each lane represents a specialist role, group or department. In effect, it is a horizontal presentation of the various people units, showing their various processes.

In itself, this different format will not make a dramatic difference to ownership. However, it starts to highlight the individual responsibilities of various departments or people involved in the project. Nevertheless, in this format, the connections still appear less important than the actions. They are just arrows showing the sequence in which the processes need to take place. Yet it is connections that people need to coordinate collectively. So the map still does not show: what is passed at the connection; who is responsible for accounting for the benchmark standards; who is accountable for identifying potential gaps or their solutions. This means there is little chance that the people carrying out the separate processes will collectively own the connections.

## Maps based on a simplistic concept

Essentially, these are the maps we might use if we were the only person carrying out all the necessary actions. Such maps rarely tell us much about the nature of the standards required the connections. Nor do they tell us who is collectively accountable for any performance gaps in meeting those benchmarks. Indeed, when involving groups of people, these maps can be counterproductive. I once saw a project plan that involved getting agreement from the trade unions. The process was documented "meeting with unions". The relevant manager agreed that he was the person to meet with the unions. The day after the meeting he informed the project manager that the item on the plan was now completed. He had had the meeting with the unions. He had indeed completed the task. However, the following day, the project manager learnt that the union officials were so incensed at being "told" what was happening, they were holding a strike ballot!

Although this may seem an absurd example, it highlights the basic weakness of maps based on processes or activities. Such maps fail to define what success or failure look like for each activity or process. Even when they apparently have time standards at the connections, those benchmarks are for the completion of the activity, not the achievement of the quality benchmark of the outcome. So, before we can use these forms of maps as a basis for Leadership Games, we need to adapt them to contain the important information. That information includes the critical benchmark standards at the connections.

### Connections between swim lanes

For example, earlier, we saw that traditional swim lane maps show processes and the people or departments that are responsible for these processes. The connections are just arrows showing the process sequence. However, in the Leadership Game, we have seen the connections are as important as the tasks or processes. So, the connection units need to define all the benchmarks.

**SWIM LANES**

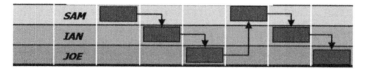

Those are the standards necessary to successfully achieve the desired outcome. It is worth reiterating the connections show WHAT is passed, as well as the relevant benchmark standards of quality, availability and cost.

## The UK Bank case study

To better understand how we can apply this mapping approach to organizations, we are going to look at a case study. This study involved the accounting department of a leading UK bank. At the end of every month, the department collected all the financial and management information from all the bank's national and international branches and departments. It then collated them into a sophisticated set of management accounts. Ben was the department manager. Within the department, there were five separate accounting sections. Each section consisted of between seven and fifteen qualified accountants, with one manager for each section.

The month-end pressure was considerable because head office needed to produce financial and performance reports as soon as possible after the end of a month. The department sent specific blocks of data to the head office on agreed days throughout the following month. Accounting rules were continually changing, as were the various IT systems. The problems and delays each month were getting progressively worse. Head office was continually complaining about the quality and timeliness of the information provided.

To show their frustration with his department's services, the head office sent Ben a copy email of every query raised with any of his sections. In the previous month, he had received over forty emails of queries and complaints. Ben had relayed head office's frustration to his section managers. However, the consensus was that the problems were not their fault. They felt the problems were caused by a lack of resources and external departments not providing information on time.

Ben agreed that some issues did originate with external departments. However, he felt there were also significant internal problems with how his sections coordinated the overall process with each other. These monthly issues became more critical each quarter when substantially more financial data needed collating. The year-end procedures were even more demanding.

Ben asked me to help in mid-December, just before the start of the approaching year-end. He wanted me to help the managers to try to bring order and rigour to the way they coordinated the end-of-period processes. A few managers were unhappy at taking time out during such a critical period. Nevertheless, they reluctantly agreed to have a two-hour session to try to identify any internal issues.

### Mapping the connections

Before the session, I had brief one-to-ones with the section managers. I then had a discussion with Ben. I explained that one problem was that section managers focused on their section's processes, rather than on the benchmark standards of the services they were providing. They all considered their purpose was to "load data sets" into the database. I discussed this with Ben and explained that this view needed to change. This was because the section managers currently considered the limits of their responsibilities as carrying out their processes. They were not assessing their services from the perspective of the external assessor. In this case, those assessors were head office and other sections using the data. In other words, everyone in the accounts department needed to change their perception of their role. They needed to see that the purpose of what they were doing was to enable the head office to produce and use accurate and timely financial performance reports. I explained to Ben how he could address this in the early part of the session with section managers. We agreed that he would give the introduction to the session. This part of the session was designed to group the relevant information that managers needed to develop the necessary, high-level frame of reference. Ben would then leave the managers to map the connections.

Ben started the session by thanking the managers for making time for the session during such a demanding period. He made clear that he was aware of the pressures they faced. He briefly outlined the fact that they all knew there was intense pressure to reduce costs. He continued by emphasising there was also an urgent need for head office to have timely and accurate monthly performance information for the directors. Ben also mentioned that they were all aware that the latest set of changes to the accounting rules would make life even harder for the department. There was little chance of the department increasing its headcount to address the new complexities. So they needed to find more effective ways of providing the head office with timely and accurate information.

At this point, Ben paused. He asked if everyone agreed that this was a reasonable description of the current state. Immediately, one manager responded the problem was getting timely information from all the bank's other departments. Ben agreed that this was a problem, but said that it was no longer acceptable to just blame other departments. First, they needed a structured way of checking their internal transfers between sections. They needed to address any internal issues before looking at external problems. He explained the purpose of the session was to introduce a simple way to keep track of such issues. This needed the cooperation of all the managers.

Ben explained that the aim was to dramatically reduce the number of complaints from head office. He asked how the head office could raise so many queries about the quality of the data supplied, almost as soon as they received it. After a short, but awkward silence, one manager responded that the managers in the head office could see problems as soon as they printed off their reports. So Ben asked the managers whether, if they were members of head office, they would be able to spot the problems so quickly. They all agreed that they would because they were all qualified accountants. So Ben asked why they did not spot them in their own department. The managers replied that their job was to simply load the data into the database, not to look at reports.

At this point, one of the section managers had a light bulb moment. He said that he thought it would only take a few minutes to run the same reports as the head office. That way, they could check the quality of the datasets that they loaded. Ben responded by saying that this was exactly the type of simple change they needed to improve their service. They also needed to take the same approach with the internal connections between sections. In effect, the database was the holding system. The datasets were the components that were passed between sections, via the database holding system. Datasets were sets of tables similar to spreadsheets of data.

Whenever a dataset was passed, the managers needed to agree on how the section providing the data could quickly assess the quality before passing it to the next section. Every time a section provided data to either another section or head office, they should always check the report from the perspective of the user (the external assessor).

Ben then explained that for the November monthly accounts, he received forty complaint emails from head office. He said that they all knew the workload in January would be much greater, because it involved producing accounts for the full financial year, with new and complex accounting rules. So he then asked everyone to predict the number of complaint emails the department would receive for the year-end, if they did not alter the way they worked. He then asked them to write the number on a sticky note.

The estimates from the managers varied from eighty to one hundred and fifty complaints. At this point, the mood of the managers changed. They all became more serious. They had started to assess the performance gap! Ben then said he was going to leave the session and return in about an hour. He explained that I would show the managers how to set up a simple map that would allow them to identify how to improve their current methods. This introductory part of the session took less than fifteen minutes. But it grouped all the relevant information to provide the context and an initial assessment of the gap for the next stage in the GAME cycle.

I then started my part of the session. I outlined the principle of creating a map of the benchmark standards at the connections. I explained that most project maps consisted of processes or actions. These were like the 'running with the baton' processes in relay races. I showed them an example of their own process maps. I then explained that, as they already had these maps, we needed to look at mapping the connections.

I explained the connections were similar to 'passing the batons' in relay races. Each connection would pass information between different sections or departments, including the head office. I also explained that every baton pass had a set of benchmark standards. These defined whether the baton pass was successful or whether it was 'dropped'. If the passed baton did not meet the benchmark standards, it was a 'dropped baton'.

I explained that for any service to be of value to the user, it had to meet standards that broadly fell into three categories of quality, availability and cost. I explained that it was the certainty of achieving the relevant benchmark standards that was important. Therefore, it was essential the supplying and receiving sections should agree on the benchmark standards needed at the connections. In this case, the group needed to agree on the benchmark standards for quality and availability (the day and time needed). I explained that they needed to create a map of the baton passes. They were going to use sticky notes, with which the managers could briefly document the standards. For example, a note, representing information passed on a particular day, needed to have the time of day that it was required. Any late transfer would be a dropped baton. Similarly, they should make a note of any quality checks on the note. For example, there might be a simple report they could use to check the quality of the information before they transferred it. If this were the case, they could document the report name on the note, with the aspects of the report that they needed to check.

I had earlier used Blu Tack® to cover all the four walls of the room with a row of flip-chart sheets. Each sheet represented a day and had horizontal lines, as shown in the diagram below. These lines defined the swim lanes for various sections and departments. In the following diagram, the teams are labelled as A to E, with head office (HO) and external departments (Ext). The first day of the month was day 1.

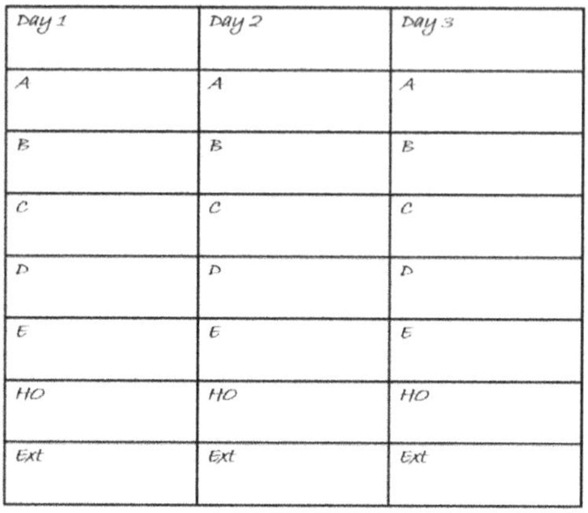

| Day 1 | Day 2 | Day 3 |
|-------|-------|-------|
| A | A | A |
| B | B | B |
| C | C | C |
| D | D | D |
| E | E | E |
| HO | HO | HO |
| Ext | Ext | Ext |

Each section manager had two packs of sticky notes: one square and one arrow-shaped. I explained the arrow-shaped notes represented the information they sent from one section to another. The square notes represented information received by one section from another. The aim was to show what information needed passing, on which day, at what time and to which section.

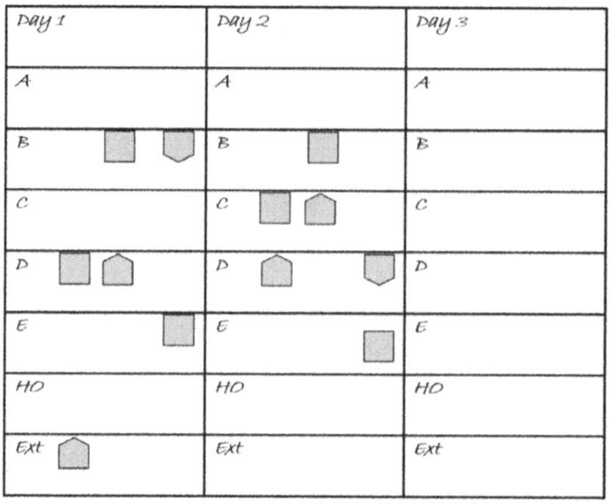

The group then collectively looked at each day until they reached the end of the month, agreeing on the transfers and critical standards.

Jim, one of the managers, kept complaining, "We know all this already. This is just a waste of time." Yet, during the exercise, Jim repeatedly disagreed with his colleagues on the timing of the information transfers. Each time Jim would tell his colleagues that they were wrong. Then his colleagues would say something like, "No, don't you remember, we agreed last month that my section needed this information by 3 p.m. at the latest." Each time, Jim had to reluctantly agree.

The overall number of transfers was so large that the flip charts on three sides of the room were filled with sticky notes. Nevertheless, the group completed the task a few minutes after Ben returned. They then took turns to talk Ben through the various transfers. In other words, they all accounted for all the connections, to Ben and their colleagues. There were areas where Ben asked for further clarification. There were also a few transfers to head office that Ben identified were wrong because of various recent changes. Also, some of the reports used to check the quality had to be amended. Nevertheless, at this stage of the session, there was clearly the beginning of collective accountability for each connection.

## Defining the protocol for using the map

I had earlier explained to Ben that this session was to proactively develop the map of benchmark standards at all the connections for the whole month. It needed to be followed by high-frequency reviews. This meant there needed to be daily reviews of progress. So before the first session ended, Ben explained to his managers how he wanted the daily reviews to work. He said that his new manager had asked Ben to give him a daily briefing at 10 a.m. each morning. So Ben explained that he wanted team representatives to carry out that daily briefing. This should ensure they were both fully updated on progress and were confident that outstanding issues were being addressed. Ben's manager could schedule just 20 minutes each day. So to make this meeting brief, the presentation was to involve just one section manager in rotation every day. That section manager should present the progress of all teams, not just their own team.

Ben also explained that this meant section managers would need to have their own short meeting late in the afternoon of the previous day. This meeting was to ensure every section manager was aware of the overall progress and could identify any problems that needed addressing urgently. In this way, the manager presenting the following day would be fully briefed. Again, there was some resistance to this protocol, especially from Jim. He felt that they were under far too much pressure to have meetings. I had briefed Ben that this might happen. So he remained firm and confirmed that this was the new way of working. In other words, he defined the protocol, or rules of the game, for both the review sessions between managers, as well as the presentation reviews to him and his manager.

### The daily reviews

Over the three weeks following the first session, the managers followed the new protocols. The managers met late each afternoon to discuss issues that might affect baton passes the following day. Because of this, they were accountable to each other for fulfilling their commitments for the next day. Section managers made commitments in front of all their colleagues, near to the deadlines. These meetings reduced opportunities to dispute who said what and when. Similarly, because each section manager took turns to present progress to the senior managers, each section manager had to account for the progress of the whole system. They all had to have the 'big picture' or leadership view of the pathway progress.

So each day, one section manager, in turn, presented to Ben and his manager. The room used for presentations was the room with the map of the connections. The duty section manager often referred to this map in any discussions. There was also a graph of the total number of email queries received from head office.

Near the end of January, managers reviewed the success of the new approach. The first obvious sign of success was the number of complaint emails from head office had decreased to less than ten, even though the prediction had been much higher. This was impressive, given the extra complexity of year-end accounting.

Three of the section managers said they were amazed at the difference. The three managers had sat next to each for over two years. Two of the section managers had to supply information to the third manager, who then processed it and sent the results to the head office. The managers explained to me that, before this exercise, parts of each month had become nightmares. The manager, who was receiving the data, continually complained about the information he received from the other two. Even though the three managers socialised well together on a personal level, they had continued having work-related problems throughout the previous two years. Yet after the simple mapping exercise, there were almost no problems throughout the month end.

Talking to Ben at the end of the first month, he confided in me that, at the beginning of the month, he felt uncomfortable with the new approach. Even though he was consistently aware of almost everything that was happening, he initially felt out of control. This was because he had been so used to being continually involved in fire-fighting. Nevertheless, he soon saw the team were now dealing with most of the issues themselves.

The section managers were so impressed that they asked me to run a similar exercise for their teams but at a more detailed level for individual staff members. Because of the larger number of people involved, I ran a slightly adapted version of the mapping exercise in late January. All members of staff attended a three-hour session in a room where they sat at tables in their team groups. Each team used small sticky notes on five A3 sheets. Each team used one A3 sheet to map the internal transfers within their own section. They then used separate A3 sheets to map the transfers to each of the other sections.

Once the teams had completed their own sheets, one member of each team paired with a member of another team to check the information on the A3 sheets, showing the transfers between the two teams. In other words, each A3 sheet showed the connections and benchmark standards between each set of two teams. They then returned to their own teams to confirm the updates on their own team maps. At the end of the session, they were all asked to return for another short, one-hour session the following week. They were asked to use the time between sessions to identify any issues and to agree – with both their own team and other team members – on the proposals to streamline the overall process.

The teams did this with great enthusiasm. They presented all of their proposals to Ben and the section managers the following week. Without exception, the managers considered all the proposals to be significant improvements and quickly approved them. A similar review format was used throughout the following months, during which time the head office emails reduced to negligible levels.

### A useful technique or something more?

Again, it would be easy to consider the mapping used in this case study as just another useful sticky note exercise. But that would miss the point. Developing and using the map changed the way that people collaborated without making any effort to directly change behaviours. It was a classic case of a group in control of the horizontal pathway, using the Leadership Game to improve performance.

### The reason for the success

The reason for this success is the same reason as in all the case studies that we consider. It was a rules-based challenge, focused on finding and removing the benchmark gaps in the service pathways. Each group was collectively accountable for the evidence of their success. It may have looked different from other case studies. However, it went through the same stages that we identified in earlier chapters. This brought together individual control of the processes with peer accountability for the mapped benchmark standards at the connections. This combination focuses everyone on addressing the gaps that would stop them from achieving a common purpose. It ensures that everyone is viewing the capability of their service unit from the perspective of the external assessor.

### The sticky note map of benchmarks

When groups use a map in this way, everyone involved is aware of what everyone else is doing. For Ben and his teams, the original mapping exercise created a common frame of reference for the benchmark standards needed at the connections.

*So one of the key aims, of the first mapping exercise, was to identify those benchmark standards that were needed at the connections*

*It also identified who was accountable for those connections.*

This stage of the Leadership Game started to transform the group's perception of their roles. It changed their perception from carrying out the processes of loading datasets to providing services to the benchmark standards needed by the head office. Yet, if the map they had proactively developed was never actively used, this mapping would have been a waste of time. However, the group who developed the map of the connections had to keep referring to that map. That created the same peer accountability towards team-members as taking on a collective challenge in ordinary team sports.

## Management and Leadership

In the first chapter, I related management to the vertical structure of ensuring resources were available for a pathway. I also related leadership to the horizontal performance systems. By making these definitions, I was not trying to identify the "right" definitions of management and leadership. I am only defining how I use these two terms in this book. However, these definitions allow us to identify the different roles that Ben played in the case study.

Before my first session with the managers, Ben had been taking the management role. Every time one of his section managers had a problem, which they could not immediately solve on their own, they passed it onto Ben. So Ben was forever crisis managing. However, just before the first session, Ben started to take the leadership role. He understood the protocol that would create a high-performance team. That protocol was that the group first had to develop the map of the required benchmarks and the connections. That map was part of the performance board of the Leadership Game. Once they had developed that map, there had to be a high frequency of the group using the performance board to coordinate their actions. There also had to be a high frequency of each of the group members being accountable for the performance board. The rules or protocol of the game were not negotiable. So when Ben met resistance to "playing the mapping game", he stood firm and did not yield. So then he was taking the leadership role.

Often, this is the hardest part for managers who believe in "empowering" their direct reports. They feel uncomfortable in standing firm in the face of resistance to mapping. Yet, from this definition of leadership, it is everyone's critical responsibility to account for the map of the pathway gaps. People will only collaborate if the rules of the game ensure collaboration. If they are not accountable for the map of the gaps, the outcome will not be the one required. So accounting for the map is the fail-safe control system.

## Splitting the organization horizontally

We can also learn another lesson from this case study. The initial session focused on the pathway at the level of the managers. The second session with the teams was focused on the same horizontal pathway but at a more detailed or lower level. In other words, the high-level service pathway of the accounts department was to provide the head office with accurate and timely performance information each month. That high-level service was progressively split into more and more detailed service pathways.

We can now consider this as a general approach to transforming organizations. For example, at the beginning of this chapter, we viewed the organization as a vertically structured unit. In that unit, everyone had two responsibilities. We then saw that the second responsibility was more effective when it was focused on accounting for the map of the gaps in the horizontal pathway performance. So it makes sense to view the top level of the organization as a single, high-level service pathway. Then we can progressively slice the pathway into thinner and thinner, horizontal slices.

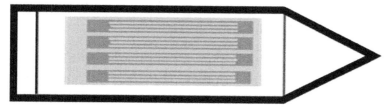

For example, consider the scenario of a clothing retail chain, which commissions its own designs and manufacture of clothing items. It could sell thousands of different product lines. However, at the top level, the service pathway would be a single pathway. That pathway would start at outlining the concept of a new product line. It might end at the customer purchasing the item, or after any after-sales service, such as returns or exchange. Yet that single pathway could, in principle, be immediately split into thousands of component pathways, one for each product line.

The advantage of this horizontal split is that focusing on the performance of a single product line is far more manageable than looking at the whole organization. Furthermore, we could apply a rule that any proposed changes to the pathway of a single product must be applicable and scalable to apply to every other similar product pathway. However, by looking at a single product line, it is much easier to test any early changes to improve performance.

We could also use a similar approach if, like car manufacturers, the organization only had a few basic models, but thousands of different parts. The highest level view would be a single manufacturing pathway for all cars, from concept, design, tooling, manufacture, after sales service, all the way through to the part being obsolete and no longer supplied or supported. That could be immediately split down into the pathway for a single part. That pathway might start at the design of the component for a concept car. It could cover the whole lifecycle of the part, through its manufacture, assembly, after sales service and replacement. Similarly, a restaurant chain, with hundreds of outlets, could split the complex organizations down into various pathways. It could obviously look at pathways in a single restaurant. It could look at each item on the menu as a single pathway. It could look at a single customer.

So at the most detailed level, we could be looking at the experience of a single customer, ordering a single menu item at a single restaurant, on a single occasion. However, even having split down the complex organization into simple pathways, we can still go further. We can then split that simple pathway into its component process and connection units. Each connection could show how all those baton-passes needed to join the individual stages.

However, even when we have split a single pathway down to this level, we can still analyse issues at an even more detailed level. We can look at each individual benchmark standard needed at any pathway connection. As explained in previous chapters, when the pathway system is not consistently meeting the benchmark standard, it is a signal of an ineffective control system. To correct that state, we need a performance system for that benchmark. Most such control systems are in the control of more that one person. The group may be from different departments or functions. So although we may have split a complex problem into small areas of focus, each benchmark provides a potential scenario for a team Leadership Game.

## Reducing complexity to repeating simplicity

Of course, we would only go into this level of detail if we needed to. However, the point is that with this approach, we can easily zoom into the smallest level of detail. We can also zoom out from any detail to see its contest in the highest level of the big picture. This is a far more effective way of finding solutions than progressively vertically splitting an organization into the individual people. However, even more importantly, it is much easier to understand the relationship between any Leadership Game and the high-level organizational pathway. For example, consider the scenario where the organizational challenge was to provide services of the highest quality and availability, at the lowest possible cost. That would mean that there would be a direct relationship between the organizational goal and all other finer pathway benchmarks of quality, availability and cost. In other words, anyone could easily account for the relationship between their current Leadership Game challenge and the organizational goal. So, over the following chapters, we will see how we can use such power to help transform whole organizations.

## Summary

In this chapter, we have seen how to split down the complexity of an organization into finer and finer horizontal pathways. We have seen how to further split the pathways to their benchmark standards at the connections, where each standard could potentially be the focus of a Leadership Game. We looked at traditional forms of mapping to see how they would need to be adapted to identify the benchmark standards. We also looked at the bank case study that used this approach. This helped identify practical examples of the differing roles of management and leadership.

# Chapter 6

## Mapping back from the future

### Review and overview

In the previous chapter, we saw how groups in the bank accounting department used the Leadership Game to transform complexity into the repeating simplicity. In that example, connections related to the transfer of data sets. However, most situations involve many different types of connections. This means they seem far more complex than the bank example. So in this and the following chapters, we are going to see how we can use the Leadership Game to help analyse more complex situations. We will see how it can help to identify which groups need to be accountable for which maps of what gaps. We will also see how those maps show the sequence of cause, effect and consequences of any issue.

### The systems people control

Throughout the previous chapters, I have repeatedly explained that case studies can often seem like the magician's illusion. Our own circumstances always seem so much more complicated. One of the key reasons, why our problems seem so complex and stubborn, is that we tend to view them from the perspective of vertical management. From this perspective, we often assume that our issues are caused by "people problems". So, when managers look at their own circumstances, they may seem unrelated to any case study. It also often seems the people involved in the case studies were more open to change than our own people. So we need to keep reminding ourselves that it is the systems, not the people that are the root cause of organizational problems. Although people vary, we will see that:

**Organizational behaviour is ultimately a result of the systems people control**

We have seen this in all the previous examples. Once the relevant Leadership Game performance board was designed, and the relevant group brought together to play by the game rules, the problems almost solved themselves. Clearly, few managers have the same problem as the case studies. Yet it is important to remind ourselves that the case studies in this book are not meant to be solutions for managers to copy. Each case study has been chosen to show particular aspects of the psychology and principles of how the Leadership Game generates fast change. In other words, the examples all show that people's behaviour automatically changes when their system changes their protocol-in-use.

Nevertheless, there often seems to be so many different issues that it is difficult for managers to see how to engage their staff to solve multiple problems simultaneously. If managers are going to use Leadership Games, they need to start by developing their own performance view. So they need to start by analysing the relevant organizational pathways. Only when we can carry out this analysis can we design Leadership Games that address our own specific issues.

### Designing new Leadership Games

In other words, if we want to replicate the success of the case studies, we need to be able to design a Leadership Game that exactly fits our own requirements, rather than just trying to copy a case study. To achieve this, we need to always remember that all Leadership Games are based on developing optimum pathway performance. In chapter four, we looked at the principles of mapping pathways from a set of connected units, using the example of driving to Durham. The problem with that simple example is that the driver, who was planning the pathway, was the same person directly controlling all the sub-systems. This is because the driver was driving the car along the whole pathway. However, the issues with organizational pathways are that the component pathway stages are all controlled by different people or groups. However, we need to understand how to create joined-up pathways, which consist of units controlled by different groups.

### *Flying to Durham*

So, we are now going to put the problem of travelling to Durham into a real context. This will help us understand how to analyse pathways and identify critical benchmarks at the connections, even when different groups control the various units. For example, imagine the scenario where one of my clients was based in Durham. So, let us assume that I agreed to run an in-house programme to help a group of managers use the Leadership Game. In this scenario, I would have agreed on the date, location and start time for the first session. So now I have to ensure I will be at the Durham venue, ready to start the session, on the correct date, at the agreed time. I may have looked at the solution of driving from my home in South London. However, we will now assume that I have now rejected that solution, and decided to look for a better way of making the journey. We are now going to assume that I am investigating the solution of taking a scheduled flight.

Again, planning this sort or journey is the problem solving that we often carry out, almost without thinking. It seems so trivial that we never need to define each individual step in the overall planning process. However, if we are going to develop the performance view of more complex problems, we need to look in more detail at the steps we take intuitively in solving such everyday problems.

Again we will see, those stages are more complex than most of us would imagine. The reason, why we need to understand the psychological stages of problem-solving, is that we often need to structure the Leadership Game in the same way. That way, we can ensure groups progressively work through the stages in the correct sequence. This means that groups need to have the right information and be asked the right questions in the right sequence. We will see this is the protocol that changes groups into high-performance teams. So, defining how we solve simple journey planning will help us understand how to create the correct sequence of questions.

The main point to remember here is that to reduce a complex problem to a set of simple solutions, we always need to design the pathway. That pathway will take us from the starting point to the desired finishing state. The pathway will consist of a set of units, which are capable of completing their own specialised tasks within the overall pathway. As there may be many different ways to solve every problem, we usually start by selecting one type of unit that could potentially provide the main, or most critical, part of the pathway.

Originally, I had selected driving on the motorways as the primary unit for the journey pathway. However, I now need to look at the method I would use to develop and implement the full pathway, using the GAME loop for a scheduled flight.

Even in this scenario, we would start with the initial map we created in chapter four. That included a map of England, with the starting and finishing points added. We had assessed the gap as 250 miles. Previously, we had started to map the highest level by assuming that there needed to be a pathway that was capable of taking us from our starting point to our final destination.

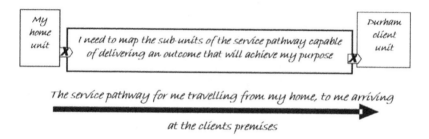

The difference with our current solution is that I have chosen the "scheduled flight" unit to be the main unit in my overall pathway. So this is the major or critical unit of the plan. The original group of information for this journey was a map of England, with the starting point and final destination. Before I can add the scheduled flight unit, I have to find the flight connection units nearest our starting and destination points. In other words, I need to add this to my group of information

### Group

In other words, the connections I need are the nearest airports to my home and my client in Durham. This is because we can view airports as holding connection units for scheduled flights.

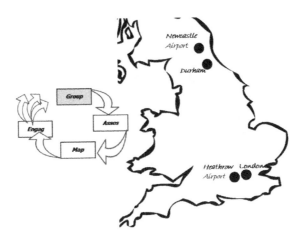

## Assess

This group of information creates a high-level map, where I can assess both the gap and the level of certainty of finding a solution capable of addressing the gap. Once I assess that it is worth progressing with the problem solving, I can move to the next stage that maps the various stages, or smaller "controllable gaps" of that solution.

## Map the controllable gaps

So, most of the gap, between London and Durham can be addressed by taking a scheduled flight from London (Heathrow) Airport to Newcastle Airport. I can map that "flight" as the middle pathway system, which is one of the controllable gaps. I can also map the airport holding units.

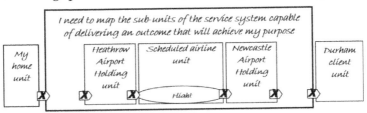

While I am in airports, I am not moving towards my destination. Of course, we could map the detail inside these holding systems to see the pathway sequence from arriving at the airport to the flight departure. However, that is a level of detail we may not need at this stage of planning.

I now have to map the controllable gaps on either side of the airports. These are the gaps that need process units to connect my home and the client's premises with the airports. So, I decide I will get a taxi from my home to Heathrow Airport. For the final part of my journey, I will use a hire a car to allow me to get from Newcastle Airport to my meeting place in Durham. The reason I am hiring a car is that I will be in the area for several days. So, the hire car company is the unit that takes me from Newcastle to Durham. The taxi company is the unit that will take me to Heathrow.

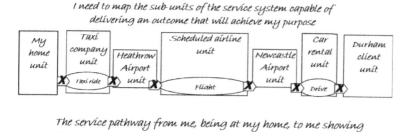

*I need to map the sub-units of the service system capable of delivering an outcome that will achieve my purpose*

*The service pathway from me, being at my home, to me showing managers, at the clients premises, how to implement the Leadership Game*

So, at this stage, I have completed the first part of the mapping process. That is to map the set of process and connection units that provide the full, joined-up pathway for my challenge. However, the plan still does not have sufficient information for me to start using it. So I now need to move to the next stage in mapping the gaps.

## Mapping benchmarks back from the purpose

In order to achieve success on this challenge, I will need to meet a number of final benchmark standards. For example, one critical benchmark is that I arrive at my destination before 10 a.m. on the relevant day. This is an availability measure. So I need to add that to the group of information already on my map. There is an important fact we need to remember here. To map all the benchmarks needed to succeed, I now have to *plan back* or upstream along the service pathway, from the desired result to the starting state. That means I can start planning backwards from the benchmark of the required, latest arrival time.

For example, the drive from Newcastle Airport to Durham is roughly half an hour. That means I need to be driving my hire car out of the airport before 9 a.m. That means that I need a flight that arrives by 8.20 a.m. at the latest. As it is a seventy-minute flight, I need to book a flight that leaves Heathrow before 7.10a.m. If I can identify the most likely flight, I can plan back from the take-off time, to assess the latest time I need to be at the check-in desk at Heathrow. From there, I can plan further back to calculate when I need the taxi to be at my home. So I may estimate to leave at 5.30 a.m. I can then plan back even further, to decide when I will have to set my wake-up call or alarm.

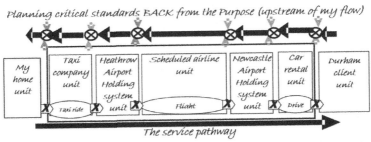

*Planning critical standards BACK from the Purpose (upstream of my flow)*

*The service pathway*

This may seem obvious. We are doing this all the time. However, many people do not realise that they can use the same approach on service pathways. In other words:

*We can identify all the benchmarks, needed to achieve a purpose, by progressively planning back from that purpose, upstream of the service pathway*

Indeed, the latest check-in time at the airport is clearly a critical benchmark in this pathway. So, all the previous control systems need to be designed to make this a fail-safe standard.

## Mapping systems to meet critical benchmarks

However, arriving at the right location and time are only two of the benchmarks that are critical to achieving my purpose. Another benchmark is that I arrive with the correct dress code (a quality standard). As I am working with senior executives, we can assume that a suit is the correct outfit. Even this standard can be traced back, upstream of the flow, to the process of getting dressed before I leave home. So that is a benchmark that I have to meet before getting into my taxi to leave for Heathrow.

Similarly, I can trace the critical quality benchmark, of arriving with my laptop, back to having the laptop in my possession before leaving home. However, ensuring the laptop has the correct information may need to be traced even further back along the service pathway. I may have to undertake the process of loading that information onto the laptop the previous day. In effect, I could have a mental list of the critical benchmarks I need to achieve before leaving home. I would use this mental list in the same way a pilot checks the fail-safe list before takeoff.

Of course, we regularly do this form of planning without this type of conscious effort. Yet even in this simple example, we can see how we have to plan all the different benchmarks, needed at the end of the project, back from the eventual purpose, upstream along the service pathways.

### Engage – by making psychological contracts

However, even having completed these stages of planning, I still cannot actively start using the plan to proceed to my destination. The big difference between this solution and driving my car is that, other than my home, none of these units is under my direct control. So, before I can use them, I need to ensure that there is a commitment from each of the supply units to carry out their part of the plan at the appropriate times. In other words, I need to create contracts with the three supply units.

When we talk about contracts, we often assume that it means a legal contract. However, a legal contract is just a formal and documented form of agreement, which helps ensure there are consequences for failing to meet the obligations of the agreement. However, I may phone a taxi company to book the cab I need for my journey. That can hardly be called a legally binding contract. So, in the Leadership Game, the term "contract" means a psychological contract or agreement. However, the certainty that a plan will deliver the outcome to the necessary standards is dependent on the strength of the psychological contracts made with the parties involved in the plan. So the strength of the contracts, or the level of "buy-in", is yet another factor we need to take into account when developing our plans or maps.

Therefore, the equivalent in an organization, to me driving to Durham, would be a manager planning a solution that he or she was going to use themselves. The organizational equivalent, of me developing the plan to fly to Durham, would be a functional or project manager mapping a solution or project, which relied on various other parties to complete. In the latter case, the project manager may need to create psychological contracts or get buy-in, from others to carry out the necessary processes.

So, returning to my trip to Durham, I would now need to book the flight, the taxi and the rental car. I will start by looking at the most critical system. This is the scheduled flight. Once I have booked that, I will reserve a hire car. To do that, I will check they have a suitable model (quality benchmark) available for when I arrive (availability benchmark) at an acceptable price (cost benchmark). For example, I am unlikely to book a Ferrari or a Rolls Royce. This is not because those cars are unsuitable quality. It is because the cost would be unacceptable for this purpose.

### Actively using the plan

Having created contracts with the various external systems, I can now start to actively use my map of the solution, whenever I am ready. In this case, that will mean setting my alarm the night before my journey or loading my laptop the previous day. Before I leave home, I will have to ensure that I am wearing a suit and have my laptop with me, loaded with the correct information. Of course, I may arrive at the airport slightly later than expected. In that scenario, I may quickly check my mental map of benchmarks at the connections. I may then decide to run to the check-in desk to ensure that I arrive before my flight closes. Although this started as solving an everyday problem, we can apply exactly these mapping steps to all the service pathways in organizations.

### Cause and effect pathways

However, as briefly mentioned at the beginning of this book, we can view service pathways as the pathways of cause, effect and consequences. For example, if I am likely to be late arriving at the check-in desk, I can follow the downstream flow on the map and predict the consequences. I will miss the flight and not arrive at my destination on-time. If I arrive without my laptop, I could in principle, use my map to check upstream until I could see the problem was that I did not have the laptop when I left home.

Normally, these causes are so obvious that we do not need a map to trace causes and consequences. However, in more complex organizational scenarios, which involve different people, we will find that allowing them to analyse the upstream and downstream cause and effects, is an incredibly powerful technique. It is a simple way of engaging the people inside the pathway to develop the external performance view of their pathways. In other words, it is a simple way to engage the horizontal performance structure of an organization. To understand exactly how powerful this approach is, we are going to look at another case study.

## A case study – plastics factory

The case study in question involves a plastics factory in the North of England. David was the general manager of the factory. When I asked him what issues he would like me to help with, he looked embarrassed. He explained that he did not know where to start because there were so many problems. However, he said that as far as he was concerned, the underlying problem was there was a blame culture rather than a "can do" culture. Even senior managers seemed to feel that all the problems were someone else's fault and outside their own control. This meant that no one was solving any of the recurring problems. David considered that he needed help to change the culture quickly, as there were too many problems for him to sort out on his own.

I started by asking David to give me some background to the history of the plant. He explained the plant was on a large site that was originally owned by a British chemical manufacturer. In its heyday, the company had been very successful. However, over the years it had failed to keep up with the foreign competition. David explained that historically, the workforce had been mainly male, but that was slowly changing. He continued explaining that the factory manufactured coloured plastic pellets for injection moulding machines. It employed about 500 people who worked in shifts, 24 hours a day.

Many of the company's immediate customers were using the moulding machines for producing plastic mouldings for cars interiors. These were then supplied to the car manufacturers. However, different moulding companies were often supplying parts for the same car manufacturer. Each car manufacturer had a small number of approved suppliers of the coloured plastic pellets. This meant that, in effect, the main customers were the car manufacturers.

At this point, I briefly explained the approach we were going to use. The principle of the approach was to engage people, within each service pathway, to work on the capability of their pathway to consistently meet the necessary benchmarks. Where a benchmark was not consistently met, it would be the basis of a Leadership Game. So any performance gaps would, in effect, have their own performance board. I explained the Leadership Game engages the relevant groups to work with maps of the performance gaps in the service pathways. This was analogous to people in a maze having the advantage of using a map of the maze to plan the fastest exit route.

So I asked David to map the pathways through the units or organizations, which he had just described. I also asked him to identify the "baton passes" or pathway links between them. I explained that, as he continued explaining the issues, he needed to annotate the map. In that way, we could group all the relevant information together in one place.

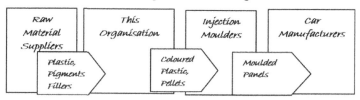

So he drew a basic map showing the different units involved in the pathway from the suppliers of the raw materials to the car manufacturers. He then noted the connections showing what flowed between the units. He then continued with his description, adding notes to the picture as he went along

David explained that one of the great challenges faced by the car manufacturers was to assemble a car with many different moulded parts, so they all had the same matching colour. Different parts of the interior fascia of cars were from different compounds to give suitable strength characteristics. Making sure that they all appeared to be the same colour was far more challenging than most people realised. This meant colour matching was a critical quality requirement for the factory. So David updated the map with the words "Colour matching of panels is critical" with an arrow pointing to the car manufacturers. He then explained this meant it was essential the pellets made by the factory met tight colour standards. So he annotated the map with that information. At this stage, I briefly interrupted. I explained that this was a good example of working upstream of a pathway to see the relationship between upstream standards and downstream consequences.

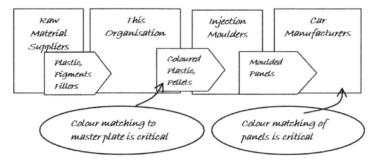

David then continued by describing how the previous owners had recently sold off a number of its factories. One of those factories was the one that David managed. The new German owners were previously one of its competitors. Now those new owners expected substantial improvements in the overall performance. However, they used a different set of Key Performance Indicators for their factories.

By these indicators, David's factory had far worse performance than comparative factories abroad. So he needed a way of quickly transforming culture and performance. Again David wrote on the map "new indicators – lower performance than all other factories in the group." I also asked him to draw some squares on the map to represent the graphs showing the comparative performance of different factories for each KPI.

I explained to David that we needed to break down each pathway into its component pathways. Then, at each connection, there are a set of critical benchmarks that needed to be met to achieve overall success. We would compare the difference between the current service pathway and the pathway as it will be when we have transformed culture and performance. I explained there were typically three main categories of benchmarks: Quality, Availability and Cost. So I asked him to map the main issues that most urgently needed addressing, in each of those categories. He marked the map with the following comments: "Quality - colour & tags", "Availability – always supply as promised – shorter predicted lead times", "Cost – reduced by at least 10%".

On the quality issues, David first explained the problems with colour matching. He repeated that even the very slightest variation in the colour of different parts of a car's interior looked terrible. So, if the colour match of each batch was not right the first time, it could cause considerable downtime. The downtime was to allow for the adjustment of the pigments in the mix to ensure that every batch matched the master colour plates. David also explained the equipment at the factory was old. When it was slicing the plastic rods into small pellets, the cut was not always clean. So sporadically, there were often tags or burrs on the pellets. These tags caused problems in the customer's injection moulding machines.

On availability, he said that batches were usually made to order; although the volumes manufactured were increased to ensure they could keep some excess production for stock. However, there was a monthly cycle of colours. They started the month with the lightest colours and ended the month with the darkest. This was because between each colour batch they had to clean the machines, to ensure that old traces of pigments could not affect the colour produced. They used the light-to-dark sequence was because if they had just completed a black batch, and about to run a white batch, it would take a longer time to clean the machine. In turn, this was because even the slightest trace of black could ruin the run of white plastic. However, if the change was just from one shade of cream to a slightly darker shade, then the clean could be completed much quicker.

David then explained they scheduled the cleaning downtime in the monthly plan for each machine. However, there was so much unscheduled downtime that the factory rarely supplied the orders as promised. Unfortunately, the sales manager often made the problem worse. If a customer was complaining about a late delivery, the sales manager would insist the factory run a particular batch outside the scheduled sequence. That obviously delayed further all the other scheduled orders. However, it also increased the unscheduled cleaning time if a dark colour had to be run in the middle of a light sequence. David explained the downtime also increased costs because it made the factory inefficient.

Once he had written these issues on the sheet, he said that those issues were only part of the story. He said there were many other cultural problems. These included: no interest in improving performance; senior managers continually arguing and blaming each other for the problems, rather than working together to solve them. So David then added those items on the sheet.

I then explained to David that this was our high-level map. We now needed to create a lower level map looking at the service delivery pathway inside the organization. I explained that we were cycling around the GAME loop. On our high-level map, we had grouped all the relevant information. We were now going to look at one gap at a time and create a pathway map for each gap. We would then break down the gaps and map the contributory, controllable gaps. To achieve this, we needed more information about the pathway inside the factory system on our map. We needed to understand the pathway from the starting point of the factory inputs from the suppliers to the finished outputs to the customer. To explain the approach, I used an analogy of mapping the pathway from my home to my client in Durham, which I as described earlier in this chapter

After describing this approach to David, I asked him to map the main section units carrying out the key processes, with the main pathway connections. So, he drew a rough pathway map. First, suppliers delivered different pigments, fillers and plastics to the factory stores. These were then transferred to the weighing bay as needed. This was the beginning of the production line. The first stage was similar to weighing the ingredients for a cake. Each batch of plastics had its own specific recipe of plastics pigments and fillers. The factory staff then weighed the various ingredients in the weighing room. The staff then put the mixture into a hopper and mechanically mixed it thoroughly. They then transferred the mixture into one of the four main extrusion machines.

They then heated each batch and further mixed it in the machine, so it was a consistent soft plastic. It was then forced through dies to make thin plastic rods. At the end of each machine, as the rods cooled, they were cut into pellets by rotating blades. These machines were like giant meat mincing machines. The difference was the output was coloured plastic pellets. The pellets flowed into bags. Samples were inspected, and the bags of pellets moved to the warehouse for later shipment to the customers.

So David drew the internal pathway of processes and connections. I explained that, for him to understand the Leadership Game approach, we were first going to look at just one issue. Once he understood the approach to address one issue, mapping the others would be much easier. I explained that we were going to use copies of this lower level, more detailed pathway map, to look at the individual problems documented on the high-level map.

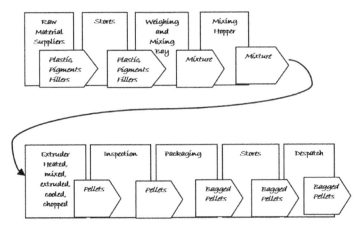

So, we agreed to start with one of the simpler issues. That was the problem of tags. So David made some photocopies of the map of the factory pathway map. Then, on one of them, he wrote "Tags" at the top of the map.

### Tags

I explained that this was going to be part of a performance board focused on the issues related to tags. The aim was not to solve the issue directly. It was to ensure the people, who were most able to directly control the issue, were accountable for the performance map. That map would be a performance view of the pathway, including how they were addressing the problem. So I used a large sheet of paper to start sketching out what the performance board might look like. I wrote the title TAGS at the top. The problem of tags was a quality issue of the plastic pellets.

So I asked David what the downstream consequences were of having tags on the pellets. He said there were several. As soon as the quality inspectors noticed tags coming through the production line, they should tell the shift manager to stop the line until they could resolve the problem. However, if they did not stop line in time, some of the sacks with faulty pellets could have already been moved to stores. This meant that they would probably get delivered to the customer. The customer would then often complain and return the material. If the customer returned the product, it had to be reworked. In other words, the pellets would have to go through the machines again, to be melted, extruded into rods and cut into pellets again. So tags caused downtime, customer complaints, and rework. That increased costs and delayed other deliveries.

So I enquired what information was readily available on the downtime, rework and customer complaints about tags. The reason I asked was that this was the information that needed to be grouped on the performance board for tags. It was part of the performance view. David said that historically, the organization measured almost everything. One of his staff was good at creating graphs. So he was confident that it would be easy to have graphs of downtime, rework and complaints associated with tags.

He agreed that, if they suddenly addressed the tag problem, that change would be clearly reflected in all the graphs. So we started to make a separate mock-up of the control panel for tags. It included the service flow and the relevant graphs.

### Looking at the causes of tags

I then asked David to work upstream, from the end of the service pathway, and identify the first process or connection (going backwards) that was critical to whether tags were produced or not. He immediately put an arrow to the "cutting" process. He explained this was the process that determined whether there are tags. Then, working downstream from the cutting process, I asked him to mark any places in the pathway flow where tags would be identified. He put in an arrow pointing to the final inspection process.

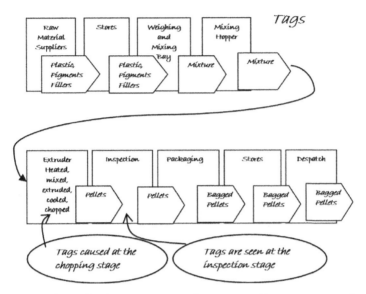

Having identified cutting as the immediate cause of tags, I explained that is was not our job to solve the problem. I explained that if we tried to solve the problem, we would have to "sell" our solution to the people who would need to change. Our job was to identify the people who could potentially collaborate to solve the problem and ensure they were accountable for developing and implementing a successful map of the solution.

So I asked David to list the various groups who had any knowledge about tags or carried out any actions related to the cutting process. He wrote on the performance board mock-up: Quality Inspection, Operators and Fitters. He explained the Quality Inspectors would see the tags when carrying out batch inspections. The fitters changed the cutting blades when necessary. The operators might adjust the blades when cleaning between colour batches.

I explained the way to quickly solve the problem was to

engage a group from those roles to account for the performance board. However, finding and carrying out any solution was a three-stage approach. We were going to:

**Prove small; prove a small rollout; prove the full rollout**

In other words, we would start by engaging one small group to start to solve the problem on one shift on one production line. Once that was successful, we would then test the rollout across the other shifts on the one line. Finally, we would prove the solution could be rolled out across all shifts on all lines.

Within a few days, David had discussed the requirements with the relevant section and shift managers. Between them, they helped David arrange a session that included two operators, two fitters and one inspector, who were all from the same shift. He had also arranged for a wallboard to be put up to act as the Tag performance board. Further, he had arranged for a simple way to print out the relevant graphs. These included: maintenance (Tag) downtime, kilos of (Tag) rework and number of customer complaints about tags. The graphs could be based on data filtered by machine and shift.

David ran the first group session, with me facilitating. He started the session with a description of the big picture, including how customers were complaining that tags on the plastic pellets were stopping their injection moulding machines working. He explained he was well aware the machinery in the factory was old. However, the tags were an intermittent problem, so there must be specific causes that needed to be addressed. This part of the session was so all the individuals involved could *group* the relevant information as the first stage in the GAME loop. He then asked them all to think about the scenario where tags were just starting to be produced by one machine. In effect, he was asking them to *assess* a situation where tags started to appear.

He then asked them to think about any information that they were aware of, which could be relevant to causing the tag problem. He then engaged them in the sticky note GAME, similar to the one used for the departments at war described earlier. This was the *map-the-gaps* stage. He asked them all to write each idea on a single sticky note. Once they had all finished, he asked each person, in turn, to put up one note on the flip chart and explain what the information was. He then asked that any similar notes be put in the same circle. He then asked the next person for their idea and repeated the process. There were only a few groups of notes. These included:

"Re-sharpened blades". This highlighted that some time previously, managers had started sending blades away locally for re-sharpening. This was because re-sharpening was much cheaper than replacement blades from the manufacturer. However, the re-sharpened blades did not last as long. Yet the maintenance schedules for replacing the blades were based on the manufacturer's blades.

- "Torque". This referred to the fact that, when the operators finished cleaning the machines between batches, they did not always tighten the blades correctly. If the blades were loose, tags appeared.

- "Delays in replacing the blades". This referred to the fact that if the inspectors noticed tags and the shift manager stopped the machine, it could be some time before the fitters came and sorted out the problems. This could lead to considerable unscheduled downtime.

- "Letting tags through". This related to the fact that,

if tags occurred near the end of a run, shift manager may let the batch finish, in the hope the customer would not notice or complain. Managers were motivated to do this because they knew there was often a long delay in getting the fitters to look at changing the blades.

- "Predictable". There was only one note for this item, and that was put up by the quality inspector. Yet it was the item that caused the most surprise among the rest of the group. The inspector explained that it was easy to predict some time in advance when tags would start appearing. That was because, when she inspected the pellets under the microscope, the cut face of the pellets started showing grove lines well before tags appeared. These grooves suggested the cuts were not clean and that tags would soon start appearing. No one else in the group had realised this, because neither the fitters nor the operators carried out inspections.

However, as they discussed the possibility of prediction, one of the fitters identified another opportunity. He said that anyone could predict that tags would appear shortly if they inspected the state of the blades before each batch. To the fitter's knowledge, this inspection was only carried out if it was part of the planned maintenance schedule. So David asked for another note to be put on the flipchart, saying "Condition of blades".

David realised that this was an appropriate point to intervene. He asked the group "So who is responsible for checking, before the start of each colour run, that the blades are in a fit state to complete the run without tags?" There was an embarrassed silence. After a short while, David said "OK, well that is the type of question that I would like you to consider. If necessary, define a new set of rules or protocols that will ensure tags do not appear.

Before the meeting, I explained to David the aim of the session was to ensure the group felt accountable for developing, carrying out and proving the protocols for avoiding tags. I explained that the solution should provide the highest possible level of fail-safe control. In other words, we needed to try and make it almost impossible to supply customers with tags on the pellets. To achieve this, protocols needed to be developed to cover three aspects. These were: Prevention, Contingency and Failure.

### Prevention, contingency and last resort

Prevention protocols were the protocols for preventing a pathway from failing to deliver the desired result. Inspecting the state and torque of the blades before each colour run would be an example of a prevention protocol. However, the group also needed to develop the other two protocols. The contingency protocol would be the protocol that they could carry out if it looked as though tags would appear before the end of the run. The last resort protocol would be the protocol used if tags appeared. In other words, although the service pathway would have failed, the fail-safe system would ensure that no faulty pellets were sent to the customers. I explained that the purpose of the contingency and prevention protocols is to try and prevent the last resort protocol ever being triggered. Thus, when identifying the contingency protocol, it is important to define the standard that we are trying to prevent.

So, David explained to the group that he would like them to go away and first think about the problem. He said they should then have a meeting among themselves to develop the details of how they needed to coordinate their actions, which would best address the issue of tags. He explained that their proposals should cover three areas

1. Prevention Plan - How to prevent tags

2. Contingency plan - if warning signs appeared

3. Last resort plan – if tags did appear, how could they be spotted immediately to ensure no faulty pellets got through to the customer.

He also explained that any proposed solution had to ensure the minimum of downtime. He explained that he would like them to present their proposals at a meeting in three days. As long as they could get his and the shift manager's buy-in to the new way of working, he would like them to immediately start the new regime on at least one of the machines. He showed them how to use the reporting programme to print the graphs of downtime and rework. He explained that he would like them to take turns updating the challenge charts every day. He would also like them to have a brief meeting as a group every day to agree who needed to do what to ensure that tags were no longer a problem.

At the following session, the group presented their proposals for a new way of working. This included the blades should be "certified" by a fitter every time the operators cleaned the machine between each batch. This would mean the fitter had assessed the state of the blades and the tightness of the blades as being fit to complete the next batch without producing tags. Once they had proved the principle, the fitters would train the operators so operators could certify the blades

The plans also included how the inspector should contact

the fitter if they could see the early warning signs that tags would appear before the end of the batch run. However, it also included random pellet inspections carried out by fitters, operators and inspectors to check for any warning signs that tags were imminent.

David and the shift manager were very happy with the group's proposals. Within a week, the group had performance boards for all the machines, not just one. The problem of tags vanished almost immediately for the shift concerned. However, without any formal rollout of the new protocols, the other shifts started carrying out the new procedures. Within two weeks, they had completely addressed the problem of tags across all the machines and all the shifts.

I think they have been a bit over-enthusiatic with the sticky notes

Of course, this was only one of the issues that David faced. So, in the next chapter, we will see how David used the same approach on several other issues simultaneously. However, before we do that, we need to understand what David did to change a group of individuals into a high-performance team, capable of transforming the performance of the pathway. Indeed, we need to start identifying the separate stages of the Leadership Game and the roles within those stages.

## The four stages of the Leadership Game

If we reviewed all the previous case studies, we would see that most had the same, four-step sequence of stages. We can consider each stage as a system, based on a GAME cycle. Each stage prepares the information necessary to engage the next level system. Each of the four systems has its own rules and roles.

The four stages of the Leadership Game are:

- Analyse and plan the game
- Team engagement session
- Team problem-solving sessions
- External review and accountability sessions

The first two stages are one-offs because they relate to developing the map. The last two stages have high-frequency cycles. This is because they relate to consistently using the map. So let us now look at each stage in more detail.

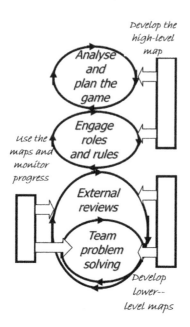

### Analyse and plan the game

In each example, the manager involved had first to carry out the analysis of what needed to be achieved, and who would be players in the Leadership Game. In many examples, I facilitated the manager to go through the GAME loop steps to map the various, high-level gaps and identify the groups that needed to be involved. So in this example, I facilitated David to map out the service pathway and document the issues on that high-level map. In effect, this stage designs the template for the performance board that groups will use in the Leadership Game. In this stage, the format of the next stage needs to be carefully defined, together with the rules of the resulting stages. However, simply because a manager has developed the performance view of the pathway, does not necessarily mean this is the actual map used by the team. Often, it is better for the team to start from scratch to develop their own version of the map.

## *Team engagement session*

Once we have identified the challenge, and the group who can potentially collaborate to achieve the challenge, we need to engage that group in playing the relevant Leadership Game. As we have seen in the previous examples, the groups were initially engaged by progressively taking them through the four stages of the GAME loop. They became accountable for solving the various issues because they identified for themselves, who was accountable for each issue. Further, they learnt the rules of the game. They learnt they would have to present their solutions to the manager and the other members of the team at an agreed date and time in the near future. That presentation is in the review session system, which creates upward team accountability.

## *Team problem-solving sessions*

Before the teams presented their solutions, they needed to get together to develop their solutions. This is called the team problem-solving system. In such sessions, the teams may well be developing lower level maps for their next presentations.

## *Presentation & review-creating upward team accountability*

This is the system that creates external accountability. That accountability can be split into two parts. The first is accountability for the planned solutions. This is where a team has to get the buy-in for their plan, from their manager. The second is accountability for progress. This may simply be the accountability created by a publicly displayed graph. It is important to remember that the reviews sessions and graphs act as important parts of the fail-safe system. We have seen that making apparently small changes to these systems can have disproportionate consequences. So, we will look in more detail at the manager's role in the review sessions at the end of the next chapter.

### *Ownership of the performance board*

Collectively, these four stages ensure the relevant teams develop ownership of the performance board. They achieve this by ensuring the people involved are continually accountable for the gaps in the maps of the service pathways shown on the performance board.

## Summary

In this chapter, we have again seen how the mapping technique used in the Leadership Game can progressively reduce complexity to repeating simplicity. That technique identifies the number of component gaps that need to be addressed to remove high-level gaps. We achieve this by planning back, or upstream, of the purpose to identify the required benchmark standards. So the pathways give us the connections between cause, effect and consequences.

We have also seen that the way to implement changes is to prove small, prove a small rollout and then prove the full rollout. This chapter also described that strategies should also include systems for prevention, contingency and fails. Finally, we clarified that the Leadership Game could be viewed as four sub-systems. Understanding the roles in these systems will provide us with a clearer view of leadership. These are the roles that we will investigate in more detail over the following chapters.

# Chapter 7

## Leadership to transform a manufacturing company

### Review and overview

In the last chapter, we saw how the Leadership Game addressed one quality issue of the many issues in a manufacturing factory. In this chapter, we will look at a more structured approach that could have been used in more complex situations. Then we will then see how David used the Leadership Game to engage the organization to simultaneously address the many other issues that he faced. In the next chapter, we will see an example of the Leadership Game, transforming an organization in the service sector.

### The power of mapping

The Leadership Game, when correctly designed and implemented, will always give a rapid transformation and performance improvement. However, as we have seen in previous chapters, just doing "something like that" will often fail. Indeed, it is easy to again imagine slight variations in the previous case study that would have stopped it from being successful. For example, let us assume David had only included operators in the Tag Leadership Game described in the previous chapter. That group may not have been able to solve the problem. The same would have applied if the group had only consisted of fitters or inspectors. Indeed even having the correct mix of skills does not always guarantee the group will be able to "brainstorm" complex causes of problems. For example, in the tag session, David used a form of brainstorming to identify the possible causes of tags. This is a simple and powerful way of identifying possible component gaps. It also helps develop the collective ownership of the overall performance gap. That ownership means that, even if the group did not identify all the critical causes at first, their motivation would be to continue finding and addressing any extra causes. However, in complex or critical scenarios, we may need a more formal analysis technique. To achieve this, we need a better understanding of how units transform a set of input states to output states.

### Unit maps of the organization

We have seen that we can represent a system or unit by a boundary. So we will assume that our first map is just a boundary with a descriptive name. We can now "lift the bonnet" of the unit and look inside. Inside the boundary, the unit has a protocol defining the internal roles, structure, and actions. So a football system has a set of rules, roles and definition of allowable and disallowable actions. However, nothing can happen in a unit until people and other resources enter as inputs to take up the internal roles. As I mentioned at the beginning of this book, this is like actors taking roles in a play. However, slight variations in the inputs can have a disproportionate effect on the standards of the outputs. To understand how this can occur, I am going to use the analogy of making a meringue.

### The meringue

A meringue is an item of sweet food made from a mixture of egg whites and sugar, which is baked until crisp. In principle, it is simple to make. You first crack an egg and separate the egg white from the egg yolk. Then you whisk the egg white with some fine sugar into a fluffy mixture. You can then put the fluffy mixture into the oven to bake until it becomes crisp.

So, to start with, let us consider just the whisking process of the overall meringue making system. For simplicity, I will assume the cook uses a hand whisk to whisk the egg whites and sugar in a bowl. The cook's aim is to whisk until the output becomes a light and fluffy mixture. In other words, "light and fluffy" is a quality benchmark for the output of the whisking unit.

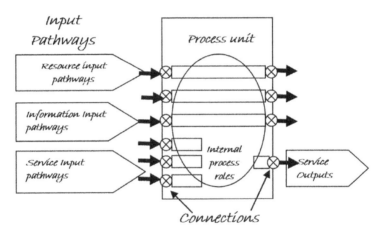

Although meringues should be simple to make, there is a potential issue. If there is the slightest amount of grease in the mixing bowl, then no matter how much you whisk the egg white, it will not become a light, fluffy mixture. The bowl may look clean. However, the cook may have hand washed it in washing-up water that had previously been used to wash greasy bowls. Under those conditions, there could be a thin, invisible layer of grease around the bowl. This invisible layer is enough to stop the whisking from creating the needed fluffy state. So, to achieve the critical output benchmark of "light and fluffy", the process needs a critical input benchmark of the quality, or cleanliness of the bowl. That success benchmark is the bowl is "grease free".

### Initial conditions

In fact, in our meringue example, various other input standards can stop the mixture from becoming light and fluffy. For example, the cook may not have separated the eggs properly. This could mean there is a small piece of yolk in the mixture. This is fatty enough to make the whisking fail to create the light, fluffy mixture. A greasy whisk would have a similar effect. A bad egg would also cause a problem. Indeed, if we consider environmental conditions as inputs, these could also affect the output benchmarks. If the kitchen is too hot or humid, this could stop the mixture from becoming light and fluffy. So we can say that:

**The initial input conditions of a process unit have a critical effect on the output standards**

This means that:

**We can trace the cause of output issues to one or more input gaps**

This gives us a generic approach to analysing the cause of any issue. We can start by identifying all system inputs, with their related quality, availability and cost benchmarks. We can then identify which of those input benchmarks are likely to be causing the failure to meet the necessary output benchmarks. For example, consider the scenario where we were often failing to achieve a light, fluffy mixture. In those circumstances, we would look at the supply systems to see if they were consistently supplying meeting the necessary benchmarks.

We could have applied this approach to the tag example in the previous chapter. The cutting blades were one of the critical inputs to the chopping system. So rather than just brainstorming possible causes, we could have first identified all the inputs to the cutting system. Then for each one, we could have identified the benchmark standards necessary for each input, needed to ensure the output consistently met the benchmark of being tag free. So when defining the input quality benchmarks of the blades, we would have found that these included "being sharp; damage free; tightened to the correct torque". This is just a more formal and fine-grained approach to problem-solving, working upstream to find those conditions that are critical to success. This can be a powerful technique for solving complex issues. We can also see how this approach was used to solve one of the other important problems in David's factory.

## Finding upstream causes
### Colour matching

You may remember from the previous chapter that colour matching was critical in the manufacture of coloured pellets. Failure, to ensure the colour of each batch met the benchmark, could cause several problems. These included an increase in machine downtime, rework, returns and costs. So I discussed this with David, using a copy of the original service pathway diagram that he had created. We put the heading of "colour matching" on the sheet. I asked David where the colour match was assessed in the pathway, and by whom. He marked the inspection process as including colour match test. He also marked that the quality control section carried out the colour test. He then explained what happened when the batch did not meet the colour standards. In that case, the quality department would use the colour testing machine to calculate how much of each different pigment had to be added to the mixture to bring it to specification. They would then advise the mixing bay and supervise adding the pigments and remixing. The process was then restarted. Once the new mixture had worked through the extruder, the colour match was tested again.

So I asked David to mark on the sheet the consequence of not getting the right colour benchmark first time. Again, he wrote on the diagram "colour matching downtime" and "Colour matching rework" and "increased costs".

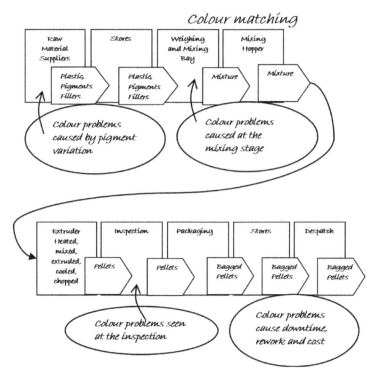

I then asked him to again work from right to left, upstream of the pathway in the diagram to identify possible areas that could cause a mismatch. He marked the "machine not cleaned properly between batches". He marked the mixing bay as "not enough care in weighing pigments and ingredients" and "not mixed thoroughly". At the beginning, he marked the pigment inputs as "variation in batches of pigments from suppliers."

I explained the issues with weighing, mixing and cleaning, were clear examples of the colour inspection separated from the systems that could affect the colour match. In other words, the colour control systems were inherently ineffective.

I then asked what control system they used to ensure each pigment met the benchmark standards. He said he was not sure. He thought the quality control department should check it. However, he was not sure that they did check. They often complained they were too busy getting the batch colours correct to spend time checking the pigments. They felt that it was not their responsibility, because the suppliers should be checking that. In other words, there was no internal control system to check the colour quality benchmark of the pigment pellets.

So, the next day, I visited the mixing bay. It was clear the operators doing the mixing were all fairly young. They were just carrying out the work of measuring the ingredients without any real idea of the consequence of even small variations could have. They explained that several "old timers" had retired in the last 12 months, and now all the operators in the mixing bay were relatively new. They saw their job as loading the mixer with the batch ingredients, rather than ensuring the pellets were the right colour first time. When I asked them why they thought there were so many problems ensuring the batched matched the benchmark colour plates they said that is was because the different batches of pigments varied.

I also visited the quality control department, where they inspected colour matches. The manager explained the operators in the mixing bay did not realise the importance of measuring all the compounds accurately. She had complained so often that she had now given up complaining. When each batch came through, a colour-testing machine identified what extra pigments were required to create a colour match. So, she went up and supervised adding the extra pigment, and that usually solved the problem for that batch. I asked her about the problem about the master pigments being inconsistent between batches. She said she thought that was a myth. She explained that they had a small test extruder in the quality control department. These were like small "toy" versions of the factory extruders. She explained that when there were new pigment batches, she used to make test colour plates using the new pigments in the testing machine. She never found a problem with the pigments. However, she admitted that she did not continue to test every new pigment batch because the machine took so long to clean after each test.

I discussed this with David. I confirmed my previous view that this was a case where inspecting the colour match was separated from the activities that controlled the colour match. However, at the moment, the operators in the mixing bay did not have the necessary skills to either inspect the colour match or understand how their actions were affecting the colour match. I explained that we needed to use the same progressive approach to solve the problem: prove small, prove a small rollout, and finally prove the full roll out.

So, we agreed the Quality Control Manager should start by giving one of the groups from the mixing bay, a colour matching training session. This was going to use the small test extruding machine in the quality control room. The three operators in the first group were shown how to measure out the test mixture of pigments and plastic fillers on the small set of scales in the room. The manager showed the group how to load the mixture into the test extruder. The extruder then heated and mixed the mixture and extruded it into a small square testing plate. The manager then allowed the plate to cool and took it to the colour tester to test it against the master colour plate for that product. She then asked the group of operators to individually carry out the same process and check their plates for a colour match against the master. So each operator carried out the process, which they considered as a trivial task.

However, they were all genuinely shocked when all of the test plates they had made failed the colour match test. They started to see a gap in the way they carried out their duties. Before the quality manager asked them to repeat the exercise, she gave the group a short presentation that I had given her. This was about the critical nature of initial conditions. It used the example of making a meringue.

She explained that getting an output of the right colour was similar to making a meringue. The slightest variation of the weights of different ingredients could mean the output would need to be reworked. She explained that if there was slightly too much of one pigment, the effect would be exaggerated if there was slightly too little of another pigment. She also explained that if the machine was not clean, that could also ruin the colour match. She then asked the operators to repeat the process of mixing the ingredients and producing a new test plate. At the second attempt, all three operators produced plates that passed the test.

The manager then showed them how to clean the machine and test a new batch of pigment. This was just a matter of taking the one pigment, mixing it with plastic filler and making a test plate to check in the colour tester against the master plate for that pigment. Each operator did this for one of the pigments. This time all three plates passed the test.

The operators, in the mixing bay, agreed to a new protocol where they tested new batches of pigment in the quality room and cleaned the test machine. The quality manager oversaw the process. It never showed any problem with the pigment. However, the operators from the mixing bay also updated their control board for colour matching.

Previously, when a new batch was put through one of the main production machines, the quality inspector was the only person who tested the batch against the master colour. Now they changed the protocol so the operators, who did the mixing, had to come and test the colour of the first pellets off the machine. They had to leave the test plate with the colour machine test printout and a signed certificate showing who had verified the colour match was to the necessary benchmark. This brought together the colour assessment and control of measuring the ingredients. In other words, the people in the system were assessing the output as external assessors.

The other change was the performance board in the mixing bay now showed the colour testing downtime and the colour rework tonnage. In this scenario, the mixing bay operators were now accountable for the successful colour matching of productions batches. This made them much more careful in weighing the different ingredients. Soon all the mixing bay operators took the colour matching course. However, word had spread about the meringue story and what happened in the first training session. So, usually, the operators were careful to make sure their first attempt was a successful colour match. In a short time, nearly all the batches were "right first time". Soon, it was the exception rather than the rule the first colour match did not meet the necessary benchmark. In fact, the mixing bay operators became distraught if the colour match was not right the first time.

At the beginning of the project, the graphs on the colour control board showed substantial amounts of colour matching downtime and rework. Soon the graphs went down to negligible levels, and the mixers took great pride in showing visitors their control boards.

This colour mixing example may look like a different problem to all the previous examples. However, it is not. The original problem was caused by a lack of a capable colour control system in the service pathway. By training the operators to assess the colour quality that resulted from their processes, it massively improved the ability of the control system. Soon, the new control system became the normal control system in the service pathway.

## Changing the culture

### The visit

Although tags and colour matching were two of the most critical problems that David faced, there were many others. Shortly before the start of the colour matching training, David asked for another meeting with me. He explained the new owners had insisted that he send a delegation of staff and managers to see how the German factory was run. That was the most efficient of all their factories. David had been trying to put off such a visit. He explained to me the original British owners had often tried to do this. However, the culture of the factory was one of what he called the "male ego", where the men always felt they had to brag about how much better their own factory was. So, when staff went on such visits, they often saw it as an opportunity to point out what the other factory was doing wrong, rather than identifying what lessons they could learn. Often, after such visits, he would get complaints from the manager of the factory visited. Those complaints would be about the behaviour and rudeness of the staff from his factory. Even where the visits passed without incident, rarely did staff or managers carry out any significant changes on their return.

Nevertheless, the new owners had now insisted on the visit taking place. So he had reluctantly asked for volunteers to go on the visit. However, he had now seen the list of volunteers. He considered all the volunteers were ones who had volunteered for previous visits, and all had the "male ego" problem. They had all caused problems on their previous visits. David was worried that this visit would also be a disaster. He said that he had scheduled some time to meet the group in the next few days before they left. He was concerned that no matter how he impressed on the group the importance of being well behaved, they would still try to prove that they were better than the other factory.

I explained that people automatically change their behaviour, as soon as they enter a system where they perceive they have a different purpose, roles and responsibilities. The way to ensure that people understood their different roles and responsibilities is to create a system where they are accountable, to their peers, for the outcome and effectiveness of the system. I explained that often, when people are sent on visits, they feel it is a criticism of them personally. They form their own "in-group", with those working in the other factory as the "out-group". Therefore, in their minds, the way they succeed is to highlight any of the failings of the out-group in the workplace they are visiting. One way to overcome that issue is to start by engaging the group in identifying problems in their own factory. This allows the group to focus on trying to spot ways of overcoming those issues. However, even in this scenario, it is essential to ensure the group are aware that they will be accountable to their peers for presenting ideas that would transform their own factories, performance.

I explained that we could use the GAME loop to help understand the way to address the problem. It would show the sequence in which the information needed to be presented at the meeting, to change the perception of those making the visit. So the first stage, of the session with the visiting staff, was to *Group* all the relevant information onto a single map. This meant that we needed to assemble all the information that would allow the group to assess the gap for themselves. Once they assessed there was a gap within their control, they would see the need to map some of the controllable gaps.

So David and I started to assemble an overall control board which listed the new KPIs used by the new owners. It also showed the last three month's performance of both the British and German factories. This showed a large gap on every graph. We also included a large sheet showing the main sequence of the processes used in the factory. That was the picture described in the previous chapter.

David said he was not comfortable with the graphs. He said his management training had always taught that managers should focus on highlighting the positives and encouraging people to repeat their successes, rather than criticise the poor performance. He continued that he considered it was a manager's job to motivate people with positive feedback, rather than de-motivate them with negative feedback.

I explained that it was important to distinguish between the two different approaches to change. The first was the vertical, top-down, face-to-face communication between managers and subordinates. People rarely like being criticised. So, continual criticism can break down the relationship between managers and their staff. However, there was a second way to bring about change. This was to ensure the people, whose actions can affect performance gaps, are collectively responsible for accounting for the performance gaps in the horizontal service pathways. In other words, no one is blaming them for performance gaps. They are collectively being asked to check the gaps and identify ways they could alter the coordination between them, to address the system performance gap.

I explained that it is important to understand the difference between the two approaches. For example, presenting a graph, which shows the difference in performance between the two factories, allows the audience to assess the difference for themselves. There is no need for the manager to explain that their factory's performance is lower. However, the manager needs to display the information in a way that allows the audience to assess the gap, rather than the manager explaining his or her assessment. However, he should be ready for some of the audience to try to discount the information as fake news. Typically they may say that factors outside their control or responsibility are causing the gap. In such scenarios, it is essential that, although their concern needs to be acknowledged as at least partially valid, they cannot discount the entire gap as outside their control. This is because we need to focus the group's attention on those aspects of the gap that are within their control.

I explained that one way to do that was to move the group straight onto the mapping the controllable gaps phase of the GAME loop. I reminded David of the sticky note exercise, used to solve the tag problem. One way to use that approach would be to ask the group to imagine "the week from hell" and to write out notes for anything that would go wrong.

They could then classify their ideas. By definition, they would have identified a series of performance gaps. He could then explain that these were the types of issues the party needed to focus on during their visit. They needed to identify whether the German factory had methods that avoided these problems. Also, they needed to see whether the German factory was doing anything differently, which could account for the difference in performance.

So, together, David and I developed the presentation. It started with an explanation of the new KPIs the new parent company used. It introduced the note exercise with the question "What types of ideas should we be looking for?" and "Imagine the week from hell." At the end of the exercise, the presentation stressed the group should look for any other ideas as well as the ideas for the problems listed.

The presentation ended with a slide explaining the visiting group needed to develop their own presentation of all the ideas they had identified. These were the changes that would allow the British factory to close the performance gap with the German factory. David explained the presentation that the group developed would be given to the rest of the factory staff in several training sessions. He would also explain that, where possible, a member of the visiting group would be available at each of the training sessions to answer any questions from their peers. This made it clear that the visiting group would be accountable to their peers in the rest of the factory for the success of their visit.

Although I was confident this presentation would have the desired effect, David was still not convinced that it would be enough to overcome the male-ego problem. He still felt this particular group could focus on areas where the British factory was working more effectively. So I explained the presentation needed to be clear about its purpose, as well as the protocol or rules of the game. The presentation needed to define that David was not interested in hearing about a single area where the British factory was superior. So David developed his own simple, unusual way to address the competitiveness of this group. At the end of the presentation, David would stress the role of every person visiting the German factory was to "steal" as many ideas as possible. This last statement is not one that I would usually recommend in this scenario. However, it made David feel more comfortable that it would help him focus the attention of this particular group. He considered that it would give the group a focus and make them feel as though they were on an "undercover" mission.

David made his presentation to the group a few days later. However, he was now prepared for any of the objections he was likely to face. For example, there was an immediate response to the slide, which showed the graph of the lower performance of the British factory. One person shouted out the extruding machines in the British factory were older and more unreliable the German factory. David agreed that their equipment was indeed older. However, he then explained how one group was already making progress on some of the main problem areas, such as tags and colour matching. Further, there was always something to be learnt by understanding how other factories worked. Anyway, he emphasised the fact that the British equipment was older, simply meant that they had to be even cleverer than their German colleagues in getting the most out of the machinery. He then continued to run the "week from hell" exercise. At the end of it, he stated that he was sure that if they could find solutions to some of these problems, he had no doubt the gap would become smaller. Although the session went exactly as planned, David was still not convinced the visit would be a success. However, the group left for their visit two days later, leaving David to wait and see what the outcome would be.

Indeed, even before the group returned from the visit, David received an email from his counterpart in the German factory. The German manager congratulated David on sending such an eager and attentive group on the visit. The manager explained the group were continually asking probing questions and making detailed notes of the answers that they received. The manager further said that it was a pleasure having the group and that they were, without doubt, one of the most interested groups he had ever shown around the factory.

On their return, the group collectively presented their findings to David and three other senior managers. All the managers were impressed. In fact, the group had already started to use some of the ideas. David thanked the group for their hard work. He also repeated the training manager would use the group's presentation in training sessions across the factory. He repeated that ideally there would be at least one member of the visiting group at each of those presentations to answer any questions. The training sessions would be a combination of the original sticky-note exercises and the group's presentation of their findings.

However, even before the formal launch of the training programme, some other groups were already using the new methods. Once the training manager had completed all the training sessions, the shift managers produced a single list of improvement projects. Anyone could add new projects to the list. Everyone had to put their names against at least one improvement project. The Shift managers worked together to help ensure there was no duplication of projects across shifts. Each project had its own project control map. However, in practice, many of the staff had already started collaborating, across boundaries and shifts, to improve performance. Each project team also regularly presented their progress to their managers. In a short time, all the Key Performance Indicators were showing big improvements.

Within a few weeks, most staff were engaged in various change projects. Almost every aspect of performance was clearly improving. However, because of the backlog of orders, the factory still was not running as smoothly as David wanted. When I discussed this with David, he accepted there were improvements across the factory. However, he said that he still had a major problem.

### Senior managers

He explained that his three senior managers were continually arguing with each other and complaining to him about each other. These were the sales manager, operations manager and purchasing manager. David said that essentially, the sales manager was always complaining the operations manager was inept because he was not delivering orders according to the plan. The operation manager complained the sales manager was always insisting the production schedule was continually altered to supply any customer who shouted the loudest. Also, as the schedule was continually changing, the purchasing manager could not always ensure the right materials were delivered on time. Every time the factory was short of the right material, they had to change the production schedule again. Such changes put the factory further behind. I explained to David that it was the same problem. Each manager only focused on their part of the big picture. What he needed was for the three senior managers to all commit to the same big picture. Put another way, they needed to all own the same control board.

I explained that, for the senior managers to act as a team, they needed to be accountable for the success benchmarks that they could jointly control. They needed to be accountable for the control board showing the extra predicted delays and costs caused by rescheduling. So, after various discussions, David found a simple way to calculate the increase in the total number of days late that the orders would be, every time the schedule changed.

I explained there needed to be a clear and accepted protocol for regular meetings of the three managers. This would be a new system, with its own rules or protocol. The first rule would be there could be no change to the production plan without agreement on the consequences, from all three managers. Further, even when the three managers agreed, they had to get David's buy-in to the change. A second rule could be the three managers had to meet once a week to agree and commit to the following week's production schedule. A final rule could be that the extra delays, created by any change, should be identified and documented at the meeting. For example, if the sales manager wanted an urgent order put to the front of the queue, he had to agree to the fact the list of subsequent orders would all be later than predicted.

David asked me who should come up with the rules. Should he ask the three managers to set the rules? I explained although that might seem a good approach, in the real world, it is not usually possible. I explained that David needed to give the three managers the initial rules. He could say that once they could convince him they could get it to work, then they would no longer have to get his buy-in.

So David had a meeting with the three managers. He explained that he expected them to collectively account for the production schedule control board. They were to agree on the schedule at the end of each week for the following week and update the board for him to view at any time. The board would also show the trend of the total days behind schedule of all orders. He would expect the adherence to the production schedule to improve over the following weeks, so changes to the plan became the exception rather than the rule. He said that he would also expect to see an improvement in the graph on the board.

Within a few weeks of introducing the new protocol, almost all the conflict between the senior managers ceased. They were now all accountable to each other for developing and using the production schedule each week. Within three months of starting the various changes described, the performance and culture of the factory transformed beyond recognition.

## Leadership Game review protocol

### The external reviews

In this case study, I only briefly mentioned the review sessions that the project teams had with their managers. Yet this is an important part of the Leadership Game. In the previous chapter, we identified the external review was the last of four Leadership Game systems. This system consisted of two parts. The first was the review of the team's plans. The second was the review of the progress, which may be created simply by a public graph. The review of the plans is where the teams have to present their proposals to their peers and their manager to get their buy-in to the teams' proposals. This stage helps create the fail-safe system, which connects the vertical and horizontal structures. So we need to look in more detail about how to run these sessions effectively.

### The review session dilemmas

In most cases, the Leadership Game automatically reduces complex requirements into smaller component issues. Typically, each such issue has a fairly simple solution. So getting buy-in to those solutions is usually straight forward. However, in more complex scenarios, if the reviewing manager does not use the correct protocol, he or she can unwittingly affect the group's ability to develop into a high-performance team. This can happen when managers feel they need to tell the group what they need to do. It can also happen when managers believe they are just "empowering" subordinates to find solutions to problems. Under these conditions, managers often face seemingly insoluble dilemmas when team present their solutions. This is because, managers can find themselves presented with plans they consider will not achieve the desired outcome, or will have unacceptable consequences.

Here, the problem is the group presenting the plan are already committed to their solution. After all, they have emotional ownership of that solution, because they developed it. If the manager tells them why he or she thinks it will not work, it can easily destroy that motivation and ownership. On the other hand, the manager could allow the group to continue with their plan, and learn by their own mistakes. However, the manager's superiors could then view the manager as inept for allowing staff to work on an obviously unworkable solution. When such problems arise in the review sessions, the issues are usually caused by a lack of a common view of the rules or protocol of the reviews. So, ideally, all parties would have the same mental model of the performance view before they start developing any solutions.

To understand how this can be achieved, let us look at the format and different roles that need to be taken in a review session.

## *Review format*

Such reviews should always be in the format of the team standing at the front of a room, formally presenting the documented evidence on their performance board. As previously mentioned, reviews should never take the format of groups sitting around a table with their manager. This format just creates a talking show, where no one is accountable for anything. Initially, for Leadership Game reviews of simple challenges, the formal presentation format will be sufficient to create the relevant psychological conditions. It is only when the issues become more challenging that the format needs to become more structured.

We will be investigating much more complex Leadership Games in the final chapter. There we will be looking at the transformation of large organizations. However, here, I will briefly outline the next level of rules, which can be introduced if the review sessions clearly need a more structured approach to be effective. This might be the case, for example, if these arguments were occurring in the review sessions.

Such scenarios could be avoided by using the sticky note GAME protocol that we first saw in the departments at war case study, and which I have mentioned several times since. So, the rule would be that any questions about the presentation should be written on a sticky note. Then at the end of the presentation, the questions can be categorised on the flip chart. Once that has happened, the presenting team can make sure that at least one member is accountable for each issue. That could mean providing additional evidence at the next presentation. However, this level of formality would only be used where necessary.

### The Socratic Method in the review systems

The most effective protocol available to managers in a review session is to use what is called the Socratic Method. This is a method attributed to Socrates, who was a philosopher in ancient Greece. He is best known for his approach for engaging his students to solve problems by asking them probing questions. By asking such questions, he ensured that the students had to work out the solutions for themselves, rather than just learning solutions from someone else. Carried out correctly, this can be one of the most powerful ways of engaging people in learning. However, part of the skill is in knowing which questions to ask. The other part is to know which questions not to ask.

We have seen, in the Leadership Game, groups are never asked to provide instant solutions. The protocol used is quite simple. First, they are asked to assess a high-level gap and to split it into the lower level controllable gaps. Then they are asked to self-select which groups are to be accountable for those gaps. Next, they are given a date by which they need to jointly present their proposals to gain the buy-in from their audience. So by definition, before they present, they need to collaborate to agree their proposal.

This means that questioning in the review sessions is always to try and get the group to identify the gaps that need addressing. We have seen that this can be an iterative process. This is where further gaps are identified in the proposals. Then, in principle, the proposals are only accepted once all the gaps have been addressed.

So the questions that a manager needs to ask are the ones

that engage the group in identifying the gaps for themselves. However, this is very different to the role many managers are used to. In a traditional, top-down management role, managers often act as the coordination systems. In other words, the manager assesses an initial gap and mentally maps the controllable gaps. The manager then delegates the separate solutions to the relevant subordinates. Often, when such managers do try to engage groups, they ask the groups for solutions. Yet, as we have repeatedly seen, these are exactly the questions that should not be asked in the Leadership Game. In the final chapter, we will look at the whole range of questions, which can be asked when dealing with plans to transform whole organizations. However, for the moment, we will look at just a small set of questions that managers can ask to start developing their Socratic skills.

For example, one critical benchmark of any plan is that it has the maximum certainty of achieving the desired outcome. So a manager may ask "How certain are you 0-100% that your solution will achieve the necessary benchmark standards?" The typical answer may be something like "we are 95% certain". Many managers would be happy to agree to a project with that degree of certainty. However, in the Leadership Game, the leader's role is to ensure that teams always address avoidable uncertainty. The Leadership Game is all about mapping the gaps. So, the five per cent uncertainty is a gap. The team needs to map the controllable gaps that are causing that uncertainty. Therefore, the next question should be "So what reasons are causing the uncertainty?" Often, groups will want to talk about those items without documenting them. It is essential that they document each item on the flip chart or on a sticky note placed on the flip chart. In this way, they are starting to develop a map of the gaps.

I often ask delegates at my master classes what they think the next question should be. Often, they will say something like "So what are the solutions?" Most delegates are surprised when I emphasise that the protocol for the Leadership Game is to try to avoid instant solutions. Often, if we allow general discussions about instant solutions, the meeting ends with no one being accountable for addressing the issues. Therefore, I remind delegates that the aim of the review sessions is to develop accountability. In effect, we need the team to map the controllable gaps, with the names of the people who are accountable for addressing each of those gaps. The people who are collectively accountable will then need time to develop high-quality solutions, which are more likely to gain other people's buy-in.

This means that, at the point where the issues are on the flip chart, the next question is "so who is going to be accountable for each of those issues?" In effect, you need to know who will be accountable for developing a solution and getting the necessary buy-in from all concerned. So this is exactly the same process that we have repeatedly seen before. Then, one or more people have to put their name against each issue. Once that has happened, the manager taking the role of the external assessor can re-enforce the point. He or she can comment that they look forward to seeing the group's presentations on the solutions the following week. If faster solutions are required, the review session could be sooner.

Of course, you could face a scenario where the team consider they are 100% certain of success, even though they can see problems. So, if there is an issue, which you consider the team have not identified, then you can again ask a suitable question that will ensure they add it to their map of the gaps. For example, you may think the team have not considered the effect of their plan on a particular department. In that scenario, you can ask whether the team has the buy-in from that department. If it does not, you can again ask the team to put that gap on the flip chart. Then you could ask who will be accountable for gaining the buy-in from that department. Of course, there are many other questions, which could be asked in more complex challenges. We will be looking at those in more detail in the last chapter of this book.

## Summary

In this chapter, we have seen how small gaps in the benchmarks, of the initial conditions of a system, can have a disproportionate effect on the success benchmarks of the system output. We saw how we could use this knowledge to track down seemingly minor issues that are having major performance consequences. We have also seen that many cultural and performance problems can often be caused by relatively few upstream issues. We saw how transforming the performance and culture of a manufacturing factory was far faster and simpler than traditional literature would suggest. Finally, we looked in more detail at the review stage of the Leadership Game.

# Chapter 8

## The invisible leader of a service organization

**Review and overview**

In the two previous chapters, we looked at the transformation of a manufacturing organization. In this chapter, we will look at the transformation of a service organization. We will see the same principles apply. However, in this chapter, we are also going to use this case study to help understand how it is possible for successful leadership to be almost invisible. We will also see how someone with no direct executive authority was instrumental in transforming an organization.

**Universal principles**

*Manufacturing vs Service*

As we will see in the following chapters, we can view most organizations as hybrid organizations, rather than either service or manufacturing. After all, most people would consider a restaurant or fast food chain to be a service organization. Yet the pathway of actions to produce hamburgers or meals is, in principle, the same pathway type needed to produce any manufactured product. For example, consider the sequence of interactions, which make up the overall service provided by a restaurant. They are not that different from the sequence of interactions provided by sales, support and servicing of manufactured products such as cars. So, the principles of the Leadership Game are the same for either type of organization.

### *Engaging the pathway lead roles*

In the previous chapters, we have assumed the manager, who planned the game, would take on the visible lead role of the Leadership Game. However, in some situations, a manager does not have the direct authority over all the potential team members to take on the visible lead role. In that scenario, the first stage has to include planning how to engage some of the lead roles. The second stage includes the engagement of those lead roles. So, to understand how lead roles are engaged, we are going to look at another case study.

## The housing case study

This case study involved a housing association in the UK. Housing associations aim to provide high quality, low-cost housing for those who cannot afford private rents. At the time of this case study, a government body called the Audit Commission regularly assessed housing associations. The Commission graded associations on a 0 to 3-star scale. Just before my involvement, the Audit Commission had assessed the housing association in question as failing, with a zero star rating. This meant that it was one of the lowest performing associations of the four thousand similar organizations in the UK. The report gave a list of immediate improvements the association needed to rapidly complete, to ensure it at least moved to one star. The non-executive board insisted the managing director complete the changes immediately. This he did by using the traditional top-down management approach.

Each of the non-executive directors had specific areas of oversight. Simon, one of the newest non-executive directors, was responsible for overseeing the performance of the organization. I had previously worked with Simon on several challenges, in his role as operations manager in various organizations. He arranged a meeting with me to explain how shocked the non-executive board of directors were at the assessment. However, from his previous experience with the Leadership Game, he knew how to apply it when in a management role. However, he was unclear how he could apply the principles when he was not in an executive role. He felt the Leadership Game could be used to transform this organization. However, as a non-executive director, he had no authority to implement it.

Simon considered the association should be more than just aiming to be a one-star organization. He wanted to see it aiming to be a three-star organization. However, the managing director showed little interest in achieving that standard. Indeed, the managing director did not even believe it was possible. I explained that to understand how to use the Leadership Game in such circumstances, Simon needed to understand how to engage the lead roles. For us to understand the issues Simon faced, we first need to understand the nature of the Audit Commission inspection.

The Audit Commission split its overall assessment into six hundred Key Lines of Enquiry (KLoEs). These six hundred were grouped into six categories, each with roughly one hundred KLoEs. In broad terms, each line of enquiry related to an external or internal service. Against each criterion, there were two descriptive statements. The first would be a description of how an excellent (3-star) organization would deliver the service. The second would describe how a fair (1-star) organization would deliver it.

For example, consider the KLoE related to debt advice. It asked, "Does the organization ensure that service users receive effective welfare benefit and debt advice to maximise income and manage debt?" Against this criterion, it provided the following two statements:

An organization delivering an excellent service: "Proactively signposts service users to other agencies that can maximise their income, whether in arrears or not."

An organization delivering a fair service: "Has protocols with some agencies that can maximise tenants' and leaseholders' income, but these are not managed in an effective way to the benefit of tenants".

These assessments define the same type of hell and utopia frame of reference that we saw in the factory housekeeping example in chapter two. When I had a brief look at the assessment manual, I asked Simon how long he would expect the organization to achieve a three-star assessment, if everyone collaborated to achieve that goal. His answer shocked me. He explained that, so much needed changing, it could take up to three years to bring about the changes. This was mainly because there were only forty staff. They needed to carry out the changes while carrying on business as usual. I explained that it would be prudent to put an initial "peg in the sand" of two and a half years to allow for any slippage and implementation.

Simon discussed with me how he could successfully use the Leadership Game under these circumstances. I explained that because this was a change involving the whole organization, some of the lead roles needed to be taken by those at the top of the organization. The managing director was not going to provide visible leadership because he did not consider that goal was possible. So initially, all the non-executive board would need to provide that leadership. This meant that Simon would first need to get buy-in from each of the other board members before he could progress this any further.

So Simon arranged informal one-to-one "chats" with each of the other non-executive directors. The purpose of these discussions was to see whether the other directors would each agree the organization should aim for a three-star ranking, rather than stay at one star. Simon explained to each director that he had successfully used the Leadership Game elsewhere. He explained that he considered that it should work at the association. However, it could only work if there was a commitment at the top to achieve that standard. Simon also explained that Pat, the managing director, was not enthusiastic.

Simon found that, individually, all the non-executive directors were enthusiastic about achieving three-star status. So, he asked the chairman to formally bring up the subject at the next board meeting. At the meeting, there was unanimous agreement the association should aim to achieve three-star status. I then worked with Simon to help him design a way of controlling the six hundred Leadership Game performance boards.

He set up six Excel workbooks, one for each category of KLoE. Each workbook had a front master sheet and about one hundred other sheets, one for each KLoE in that category. Each sheet showed the description and number of the KLoE, together with the two descriptions of fair and excellent service.

Then, in groups, all the members of staff of each department were asked to identify which KLoEs they thought related to their own department. Then they were asked to assess on a zero to three-star scale of each Key Line of Enquiry, which was within their department's area of responsibility.

Potentially, the total number of stars possible was three stars for each of the six hundred KLoEs. In other words, the maximum score was eighteen hundred stars. However, the staff collectively gave an average of less than one star per KLoE. The total number of stars awarded for the six hundred KLoEs was five hundred stars. In other words, the staff agreed that they were not yet even at a one-star status, which would have needed six hundred stars.

Simon entered all the first assessments into each of the six hundred worksheets. The front master sheet in each workbook showed the total score of all the KLoE worksheets in that workbook. He also combined the information on the front sheets of each of the six workbooks on a master workbook. This, in effect, showed a bar chart of the gaps, in comparison to the eighteen hundred stars needed for a three-star organization.

The first total gap was thirteen hundred stars (1800 maximum less 500 assessed). This meant the organization had to gain ten stars each week for a hundred and thirty weeks (roughly two and a half years) if they were to achieve three-star status within three years. This assessment made progress easy to check whether the housing association was on track to achieving three stars within the allotted time.

From his previous experiences with me, Simon knew the implementation approach was to start by proving the Leadership Game on a small-scale. Once he achieved success at that scale, it would be easy to roll out. Therefore, Simon decided to start with just one group within the organization. This was the Asset Management Team. They were responsible for fifty-five KLoEs. The total they had awarded for their fifty-five KLoEs was fifty stars. This meant there was a gap of one hundred and fifteen stars, which they would need to address, for their department to achieve three stars overall. That meant the department needed to aim for almost a one-star improvement each week, over two and a half years.

Simon then had a short session with the five members of staff in the asset management team. Simon arranged for the Sue, the manager, to explain to the staff members that they could select whichever services or KLoEs they would look at each week. However, the aim was to try to gain one star each week. The group selected one of the KLoEs, which they felt they could quickly improve. Simon explained they had to return each week and present their progress to Sue, each time they thought they had increased the standard of one KLoE by one star. The aim of the presentation was to get the approval from the Sue that it was at the standard needed.

At the first presentation, after the first week, the group was embarrassed. They hadn't managed to achieve a one-star improvement. However, they explained that it was just taking a little longer than they anticipated. So, they would still like to take one or two other KLoEs in the meantime. That way, they could be working on those simultaneously. Sue agreed to this approach, and by the second presentation, the group had indeed achieved one-star improvement in one KLoE. They were also well on their way to achieving a second.

After each presentation each week, they updated all the worksheets to show the current standard, even if there had been no change in those particular KLoEs. The asset management team decided to place their graph in the boardroom. This was the room used for meetings. Very quickly, the other groups wanted to know how the asset management team were managing to reduce their star gaps.

Also, the board of directors gave the managing director the objective of achieving three-star status by ensuring that all staff were consistently checking their progress towards three-star status. However, this needed relatively little effort because the approach spread virally to the other departments. Those groups then all started weekly selections of the next star to be address and weekly presentations. The board also asked that the teams made some of their presentations to the board.

Soon, the whole organization was involved. Over the following months, the association progressed to the first milestone of a two-star organization. They confirmed this by using an outside consultant to make an independent assessment. Once the consultant confirmed the two-star status, the staff baked a "Two Star" cake and arranged a "Two Star" party in the boardroom, as can be seen in the photo.

An external facilitator then asked the staff what they had achieved during the process. Again, as can be seen from the photo, they came up with some surprising answers.

These included: "Be the best at what we do", "Better communication between departments" and "New way of thinking". It is important to remember there was no initiative promoting these ideas. These were just a natural result of the Leadership Game.

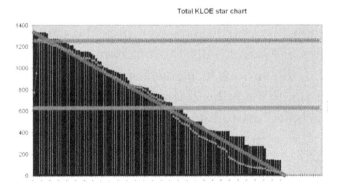

Total KLOE star chart

Within three years, the housing association had indeed moved from being one of the worst of four thousand organizations to one of the best (at least, as judged by the Audit Commission's criteria). This all happened without any major effort on the part of managers. The transformation occurred purely by applying the Leadership Game.

Also, it happened without anyone in the organization having any detailed knowledge of the psychology behind the Game. However, Simon knew the principles. This is how he could engage both the lead and the team roles of the Leadership Game.

## Badges of excellence are no guarantee of future success

Badges of excellence, such as the one just described, are useful in defining some of the benchmarks of excellence. However, particularly in the commercial world, they are no guarantee of future success. Indeed, they are not even a guarantee of future survival. There are many examples of organizations, achieving prestigious awards, such as the Baldrige Quality Award, before going bust. This is because such approaches often only focus on achieving quality standards. Yet, quality alone is not enough for success. However, we can learn several points from this case study.

The first is that introducing the Leadership Game needs someone to engage the necessary lead roles. Of course, in most scenarios, the same person may well plan the game and take the lead roles. However, later in this chapter, we will look in more detail at the various lead roles, and how to engage them. The second point made by this case study is the association needed to achieve many hundreds of success standards. The Leadership Game made it simple to engage everyone in the organization in progressively achieving the large range of standards. The case study also showed how the Leadership Game spread virally, once the first game was demonstrably showing success. Equally importantly, the case study showed that:

*It is very simple to ensure that everyone is the organization can account for the way they are assisting the organization in achieving its goal*

Anyone in that organization could have shown a visitor the various pages that showed the collaborative improvement projects in which they were working. Those pages were their version of performance boards. They could also show the direct link between their projects and the organizational goal to become a three-star organization. This last point is going to be particularly important when, in the last chapter, we look at the general way of transforming whole organizations. We will see that one of the very early milestone benchmarks is to reach the stage where everyone is working form their performance boards. That is the stage where everyone in the organization can account for their part in collaborating to help the organization achieve its goals.

I don't think they have really got
the idea of performance board games

However, there was also another part of the case study, at which we have not yet looked. That is the improvement of a specific Key Performance Indicator.

### Using the Leadership Game to improve a KPI

After Simon's first session with the asset management

group, most KLoEs progressed without any further
intervention by Simon. However, one KLoE stated excellent
organizations consistently identified benchmark standards
and improved their Key Performance Indicators (KPIs) against
the other best-performing housing associations. One of the
KPIs, which had ceased to improve, was that of rent arrears.
The staff had completed the KLoEs that could affect arrears,
such as the debt advice KLoE mentioned earlier. That had first
reduced arrears slightly, but then the amount of arrears did
not continue to decline.

Traditionally, each manager was responsible for one or
more KPIs. The KPI for arrears had been allocated to Fred, the
finance manager. So, Simon went to see Fred to understand
why the KPI was not improving. Fred explained that three of
his staff spent a great amount of their time, on the phone,
chasing rent arrears. However, as far as Fred was concerned, it
was the housing department that caused the problem, not the
finance department. The housing department consisted of
several housing officers and a housing manager. The nature of
housing associations is that they provide housing for the more
"vulnerable" members of society. These included the poor or
those with drug addictions. Fred considered that, if the
housing department selected tenants predisposed not to pay
their rent, then it was not his fault that arrears levels were so
high.

So, Simon went to discuss the matter with Jane, who was
the housing manager. Simon asked Jane if she felt there was
any way the housing officers could help with reducing the
rent arrears. Jane replied that she had had various
conversations with her housing officers. However, they
considered that their job was to help and assist vulnerable
tenants. They considered the tenants were their clients. They

were reluctant to become debt collectors as well. They felt that this would break down the relationship they had with their tenants.

Simon came to discuss the problem with me. He explained the control of whether the tenant paid their rent on time was in the control of the tenant. So he could not see how the Leadership Game could apply to arrears. After all, you could not get the tenants to play the Leadership Game. I agreed that delivering payment was in the control of the tenants. However, there were three other systems related to the pathway of rent payments to the organization. These systems were the ones I described in the factory case study in the previous chapters. They are the prevention, contingency and last resort systems. In this case, the prevention system was the system that helped ensure the rent payment system did not fail in the first place. The contingency system was the system that kicked in as soon as there was a failure to pay rent on time to correct that problem. The last resort system was the system that triggers at the point where it was clear the debt would not be paid.

All three of these systems were in the control of the organization. However, the most important one was prevention. The prevention system should focus on helping tenants keep out of debt. There should also be a focus on a contingency system that helped people get out of debt with a formal payback programme. The contingency system aimed to ensure that a tenant's debt never reached the clearly defined level that would trigger the last resort system of debt collection.

I explained the tenants' behaviour would depend on their view of the protocol, or rules of the game, about paying rent. Therefore, these systems should concentrate on ensuring that tenants' mental protocol focused on taking the necessary action to ensure they kept out of debt and kept their tenancy.

After further discussions with me, Simon arranged with Fred and Jane to have a session with a group that consisted cf both finance and housing officers. I agreed on the format of the session with Simon, so it followed the sequence of the GAME loop. Simon started the session by presenting a slide of the housing association's vision and mission. He then reiterated the purpose of everyone in the organization was to help the organization support, vulnerable tenants.

Simon continued that they all knew that one issue with such tenants was that they were not good at controlling their finances and easily got into debt. Of course, none of this information was new to any of those attending. However, this was the *Group* stage of the GAME loop. Simon was grouping all the relevant information to provide a context or mental model. That was the context from which the staff present could assess for themselves that there was a need to develop a more effective way of working.

Simon then continued explaining that the organization needed to find better ways of helping tenants keep out of debt, rather than just trying to collect the outstanding debt. In effect, the best way the association could help tenants keep their homes was to help them keep out of debt. Simon explained the principle of the thought bubble and that people behave fittingly to their mental protocol in their thought bubble.

He had a slide showing a person with a thought bubble saying – "I need to make sure I pay my rent and other bills to prevent getting into debt." Simon then explained that every rule should have a contingency plan. Thus, he showed another slide with a different thought bubble. This bubble said, "If I know I will not be able to pay my rent on time, I need to contact my housing officer". This was where some people would be unable to pay the rent for no fault of their own. This was most likely to occur if, for example, they had not received a benefit payment on time. It was the policy of the association that, as soon as a tenant was aware that they would not be able to pay the rent, they should immediately contact a housing officer. This was to agree exactly when they would be able to pay the debt. It was also a policy that, if a tenant went into arrears, they had to agree on a schedule to repay the debt over a reasonable period.

So in the meeting with accounts staff and housing officers, Simon explained that every interaction between tenants and staff should take the opportunity to re-enforce the "rules of tenancy" in their thought bubbles. He also showed a slide with the total amount of rent arrears owed by tenants. It also split down the total debt into the amount under an agreement to repay, as well as the amount outstanding with no agreement.

Simon explained that debt without an agreement was a sign of how many people were not using the proper rule in their thought bubble. He then showed a graph showing the average levels of rent arrears per hundred tenants of three-star, two-star, one-star and zero-star housing associations. He then asked the group if they had any idea where their organization's level of debt was. Rather sheepishly, they predicted it would be at the zero or one-star level. Simon proved their prediction correct by showing that their organization was near the bottom of the zero star organizations.

At this point, one of the accounts officers said that it was not a fair comparison, because the other housing associations were in more affluent areas. This meant they had fewer problem tenants. So they would obviously have lower arrears levels. Simon agreed that a simple comparison was not fair. However, it was still useful to keep the graph updated to see if their organization was getting better or worse than similar organizations.

Simon then asked the group to identify all the ways for tenants to pay their rent. The group then listed all the possible ways including, direct debit, paying at council offices, post offices and banks. He then asked them which way was most effective at keeping people out of debt. They unanimously agreed that Direct Debit was the most effective. However, one of the housing officers pointed out that some tenants did not have bank accounts.

Simon then displayed a slide showing the current ways that tenants paid and in what percentage. It showed that only 30% of tenants paid by direct debit. It did not even list payment via post offices, because the association did not yet have arrangements with the post office to accept payments on their behalf. Simon then asked the officers why such a small percentage of tenants paid by direct debit. After some general discussion, it became clear there were several reasons. One of the main reasons was historical. Where tenants had been given choices in the past, about how they wanted to pay, they often chose not to use direct debit. Simon then asked, "If we could increase the percentage of tenants paying by direct debit, what effect would it have on arrears?" There was general agreement that it would have a dramatic effect.

Now the housing and accounts officers had been able to Group the relevant information about debts. From that information, they could assess there was a gap, which was potentially within the control of the organization. For example, they could aim to increase the number of tenants paying by direct debit. Simon now needed to get the officers to map the controllable gaps. He now asked them to complete a sticky-note exercise. This was to identify all the possible opportunities they had to engage the tenants in signing a direct debit authorisation for paying their rent and keeping out of debt. The exercise identified many opportunities. These included on tenancy sign-up, immediately the tenant missed a payment; on agreeing on a payback plan with the housing officers, as well as several other opportunities. The officers agreed that these would be good places to start in their drive to keep tenants out of debt. They agreed that they would have weekly review meetings and would use graphs of the percentage of tenants still not on direct debit and the level of arrears.

Sure enough, even after a few weeks, both graphs started showing big improvements. Similarly, the comparison graphs with similar organizations showed improvements. However, after several weeks, the rate of improvement in the graphs started to level off. At this point, Simon explained to Jane, the housing manager, that she needed to facilitate another mapping session after the officers had finished their next normal weekly review session. Having seen Simon run the first session, Jane was happy to run the sessions needed to refine the plans even further.

As we have seen, the purpose of all mapping sessions is to split down a complex problem into its controllable component gaps. We have seen the standard way to achieve this in the Leadership Game is the sticky note GAME. So this was the approach that Jane used to facilitate the group in progressing further. Once they had completed their normal weekly session, they could all assess there was still a gap, because the improvements had almost stopped. This was the point at which they could potentially map a more detailed set of controllable gaps. Therefore, Jane asked the officers to carry out another sticky-note exercise. She asked them to identify how to split those people still in arrears into different groups that needed different approaches to help keep out of debt. One of the splits identified was to divide tenants with arrears into "can't pay", "won't pay" and "forget to pay". Another was "those with bank accounts" and "those without bank accounts". Jane then asked everyone to put their name on a note and make sure at least two people were looking at each scenario. She asked the teams to get together and work out the best solutions for each group. She stressed that every presentation had to get the buy-in from everyone else.

The following week, the groups presented their ideas. Then the whole group agreed their plan of action for the following weeks. This cycle of progressively splitting issues down, into more manageable problems, repeated several times over the following few months. It continued until the level of arrears had become so low the performance exceeded that of three-star housing associations.

### Who was the leader?

Now we have seen how the transformation occurred, we need to return to understanding the lead roles that brought about the transformation. Transforming this housing association involved everyone being committed to the common goal of becoming a three-star organization. However, what is not so obvious is the answer to the question "Who was the leader who aligned the organization?" Much of Simon's involvement was largely invisible to most people in the organization. His informal discussions with the non-executive directors would not normally be considered as leadership. His development of the Excel spreadsheets simply needed some advanced knowledge of Excel. The two or three sessions with small groups of staff seemed to be little more than coaching or facilitation. The non-executive board members simply went with the idea of being a three-star organization. The managing director's main contribution was not to hinder the progress of the transformation. So who was the leader of this transformation?

In one sense, we could say the non-executive board took the role of visible leadership. This is because they were the ones who insisted the organization should aim for three-star status. They were the ones who created continued accountability. They did this by asking for regular presentations from the various groups bringing about the changes. Yet they were not the ones to set up the sequence of events that would finally lead to success. Nor were they the ones who developed and carried out the plan to engage everyone in collaborating to achieve that goal. In effect, the most important role was the role that Simon played: The role of the invisible leader. This was the role that ensured the correct people filled all the other lead roles in the Leadership Game. Of course, in many scenarios, the visible and invisible leaders are the same person. In other scenarios, a visible leader's success may depend on their ability to select the right person for the role of the invisible leader. So, to understand how this later scenario can take place, we are going to look at another case study.

## The Police case study

This is the story of Brian, who came to one of my master classes. In one of the breaks, he came to me to explain that he had previously been a police commander. In that role, he had been responsible for transforming one of the lowest performing divisions of the Metropolitan Police into one of the highest performing divisions. (The "Met", as it is known, was police force responsible for Greater London). In fact, he had received a promotion based on his success. Brian also explained that, although he had received the promotion and moved to various other challenges, he never managed to reproduce the same level of success achieved in that division. Until now, he had never been able to understand why. However, my description of how the invisible leader plays a key role in transformations had now enabled him to understand why he had been so successful in that particular transformation.

He explained that, when he took over the job as commander of the low performing division, he knew he would need some help. So, he had asked Roger, the civilian corporate services manager, for his views on how best to approach the transformation. Roger had been surprised the new commander was asking for his views. Roger had explained that he had tried to engage the previous two commanders of the division with his own ideas on improving performance. On both occasions, they had rebuffed his proposals. This was because the commanders did not believe a civilian could understand the complexity of police work.

Brian explained to me that, attending my master class, he could now see the approach Roger proposed was similar to the Leadership Game. Brian did not know where Roger had learned about the approach, but as the new commander, he had been open to any new ideas. So the two had worked together to set up the system whereby both police and civilian staff were all collectively working on specific performance measures within their local control. Sure enough, within nine months, the division had transformed from the lowest performer in all the Metropolitan Police to one of the highest performers. To explain what this meant in practice, Brian related two stories.

The first story was about a group of police sergeants from neighbouring division, who were visiting Brian's division and having lunch in the canteen. At a nearby table, there was a group of local police constables (the starting rank in the police force). They were discussing how they were going to improve a key performance indicator. The visiting sergeants on the adjoining table started talking loudly. They were mocking the "pathetic" constables for using their lunch break to discuss performance indicators. So one of the young constables got up from his table and walked over to the group of visiting sergeants. The constable then leant over and addressed one of the sergeants. "Yes, sergeant, you are right. We are using our lunchtime to discuss how to improve policing, to make this area a safer place. But that is how this division has become one of the best performers in the Metropolitan Police, while your division is one of the worst!" Needless to say, the visiting sergeants looked embarrassed. They quickly finished their lunch and left the canteen.

The second story Brian described to me was when one of the deputy commissioners (one of the highest ranks) decided to carry out an inspection. The commissioner was very impressed, but was suspicious as to whether he was only seeing the outward "veneer". He considered it could not be that good throughout the division. He told Brian that he was going to inspect the garages, which consisted of mainly civilian staff. The commissioner saw a civilian cleaning one of the police cars. He asked the staff member what his role was in the division. The member of staff asked the commissioner to come over to their control board. He explained that one of the key targets for the police was to arrive at over 90% of all incidents, graded "immediate", within 15 minutes. So, one of his roles, in helping that target, was to make sure that any vehicle faults were corrected as soon as possible. So before he left at the end of each shift, he ensured the next shift were aware of what needed urgent attention. That way, a failure to meet the callout target would never be caused by a lack of available vehicles. He showed the commissioner the graph that displayed how this division was succeeding in exceeding the target by over two per cent. The staff member also explained that it was important to ensure that members of the public could be proud of their police force. That was why all the staff in the garage ensured that all police cars in the division were spotlessly clean. The commissioner was impressed. His report stated that he had never before come across such a dedicated division.

Brian then explained to me how, after promotion, he had struggled to match that spectacular success. He was even trying to write a book on leadership, to help him identify what he did that made that transformation such a success. Brian explained that he had always worked closely with the top ranks when trying to transform an organization. He had assumed that his leadership style would naturally cascade down the hierarchy. However, learning about the role of the invisible leader had made him realise that much of that success was created by engaging Roger as his invisible leader. Roger was the one who ensured that managers changed to taking lead roles throughout all the ranks in the division. Brian now realised that he should have always tried to take Roger with him whenever he took up a new post. Between them, they had made a great leadership team. However, neither of them individually had been able to fill all the roles needed to transform the organization. In other words, Brian had the motivation and the authority to engage his immediate subordinates, in working together to improve performance. However, what both he and his subordinates lacked was the knowledge of how to engage the whole organization in a hierarchy of Leadership Games. The corporate services manager supplied that skill.

Brian's story is not unique. Most of us are aware of leaders who have been successful in one organization, only to fail when they moved to a different organization. In many of those cases, the successful leaders failed to recognise the critical role played by their invisible leaders. That is why, to consistently achieve success with the Leadership Game, we need to understand all the lead roles with the Game fully. However, before we do that, we first need to look at the critical requirement of overcoming resistance to mapping.

## Overcoming resistance to mapping

In several the previous case studies, we saw that engaging people in the mapping process was not always as straightforward as it should have been. Occasionally, there was resistance to carry out even the simplest mapping task. The first point to realise is that resistance to start mapping is usually far easier to overcome that resistance to operational change. As we have previously identified, overcoming resistance to change can be difficult. This is because we are trying to change other people's established mental protocols. However, in principle, overcoming resistance to mapping is relatively straightforward. After all, usually, the mapping in the first team engagement stage takes less than one hour. The mapping for the following, frequent reviews may take just a few minutes a person each week.

However, as I have mentioned before, where problems arise, it is usually because a manager believes that his or her role is to empower staff to only do whatever the staff choose to do. As I mentioned in chapter one, we should not consider empowerment as a strategy. It is a *consequence* of people playing by the rules of a game. For example, players, in any game or sport, are empowered to make choices within the rules. However, they are not empowered to choose not to play the game of helping the organization achieve its goals. Nor are they empowered to change the rules to suit their own preferences.

The Leadership Game rules are designed to create the motivation, which ensures groups collaborate and improve overall performance. So, these rules of the game cannot be negotiable. We have seen, for example, the Leadership Game is unlikely to have the desired effect if only one person acts as map-keeper. We have seen the motivation to identify a solution (map the gaps) only occurs when people assess a gap for themselves. Of course, sometimes there may be a skill issue for particular people, in understanding how to carry out the duties of a map keeper. For example, I have had several cases where low-skilled, front-line staff, have not had any understanding of how to update a graph. Occasionally, we teamed those people up with a "buddy". This was the person who helped them update the graph. In other cases, we gave them a short training session in updating graphs.

In all those situations, the people involved took great pride in their graphs or maps. Yet the easy solution would have been to excuse them from that duty. However, the easy solution would have destroyed the motivation to collaborate as a team. So, it is nearly always worth the small amount of effort to train and engage people in the necessary basic mapping skills.

The one difficult area of mapping resistance occurs where people feel the information they are collecting could put their job at risk. This is the area that needs to be given the greatest consideration when developing Leadership Games. This is because Leadership Games should ensure that:

*People always win by playing the Leadership Game. They can only lose by not playing the Game*

In the final chapter, we will look at the specific conditions where the Leadership Game could potentially threatening people's livelihood. In such scenarios, there is a valid reason for resistance to mapping. Nevertheless, even this resistance needs to be addressed. However, there are more common situations that cause people to resist mapping. Indeed, there are situations where incapable people go to great lengths not to play the game, rather than be in a situation where they have to improve their competency. In those scenarios, we can adjust the rules of the game. That adjustment is to ensure that only those people, who are playing the game, can win. While people can only lose if they do not play the game. For example, we have already seen that, if a person failed to fill in the graph when it was their turn, that day's entry would show a zero reading. It would be clear to everyone who was not playing the game. This is a large deterrent to refusing to play by the rules.

In another example, I assisted a project, where area managers had a weekly review session. In that session, each manager took turns in presenting the information for the whole organization. However, there was one manager who always found an excuse not to attend the meeting whenever it was his turn to present. So the rest of the managers agreed to add an extra rule to the game. That rule was that if a manager did not present when it was their turn, then that manager had to make the next two presentations. In other words, anyone not playing by the rules, lost by paying a "forfeit". So, if necessary, we can adjust the rules to ensure we get the correct behaviour.

## Leadership Game roles

We have already identified that every pathway performance system involves a set of leadership roles and a set of team roles. We have also identified four stages of the Leadership Game. So we now need to look at those four stages more closely. We need to identify which roles are needed for each of the stages. The four component systems were: Analyse and plan the game; Engage the roles and rules; External team reviews/accountability; Internal team reviews and problem-solving.

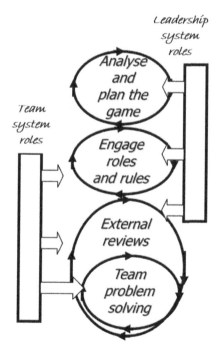

## 1. Analyse and plan the game

This is the work that needs to be carried out before team engagement can start. This stage aims to prepare the presentation and systems needed to ensure the success of the team engagement stage. In this system, there are five roles: Pathway analysis; Engage the figurehead leader; Design and activate the challenge information system; Design the engagement session, Design and implement the fail-safe system.

### a. Analyse the Pathway

This is the type of analysis that I carried out with David, the factory manager. It can happen at every level, from the highest organizational level to the smallest, most trivial pathway. However, whether you are going to engage the senior management team or a group of operators, you need to understand the pathway involved before you start to engage the team. Over the following chapters, we will be looking at this in more detail.

### b. Engage the figurehead leader

Any change requires a figurehead or nominal leader. That is the person or group who has the perceived authority, power or influence to be the apparent leader of the change. In some case studies, such as the legal example, it was the immediate manager who took the figurehead and all the other leadership roles. In others, such as the safety and housekeeping example, the training manager ran the engagement sessions.

However, the perceived figurehead or authority requiring the change would have been the factory manager. In the case of the housing association, Simon engaged the non-executive board to be the figurehead leader.

### c. Design and activate the challenge information system

Clearly, the Leadership Game is based on a performance board. That board contains performance information. In the first case study we looked at, the manager had to create a report to draw the necessary information out of the IT system. In the housing association example, Simon had to design the set of workbooks and spreadsheets. So the board needs designing, and the related information systems have to be implemented.

### d. Design the engagement session

To engage teams, a presentation or approach needs to be developed beforehand. The team-engagement is the stage that triggers the sequence of following stages. So, it is worth putting in some effort to ensure the session follows the GAME loop sequence. If the team engagement stage is designed correctly, all the other stages should naturally occur.

### e. Design and implement the fail-safe system

Although I have made this the last role in the planning system, it is the most critical. Previously, I have explained that accountability for the performance board is the fail-safe system. This acts as the lynchpin that connects the vertical and horizontal control systems.

So, by definition, if the fail-safe system is designed and implemented correctly, the Leadership Game cannot fail to achieve success. It is the external reviews that create accountability for the performance boards. So, this is the system that should be carefully thought through to ensure it is truly a fail-safe system. This includes ensuring the board has a schedule of team leads, roles and rules if necessary.

## 2. Engage the team roles and set the rules

The second system aims to ensure the relevant groups become accountable for presenting their proposals at the external review sessions. If the person running the session is not the figurehead leader, the group needs to feel that person is the representative of the figurehead leader. In other words, that role needs to be filled by someone who has the necessary direct or indirect authority or influence with the group.

So, consider the factory safety and housekeeping example. There, the training manager ran the session where the groups learnt to assess the state of the factory on the hell to utopia scale. The training manager also stated the new rule that everyone had to take turns in assessing as the external assessor. Technically, a training manager does not have that authority. However, in effect, he was explaining the new rule set by the factory manager. So, the person taking the lead on the team engagement role needs sufficient influence to ensure that the team members cannot ignore the fact that they have to take their own roles according to the rules in the challenge. Those rules may be that each team member has to present at the next external review sessions or act as regular map keepers. The team engagement lead role will also present the relevant information. This is the information that the team needs to group the relevant facts and enable them to assess the gap, which requires their action. The perceived authority of this role is critical. It is worth repeating that the Leadership Game can only be effective if the manager performs this leadership role of ensuring there is an effective psychological contract with the group. That contract needs to ensure the group plays the game by the rules and the agreed timings. This contract should ensure the group understand they have two roles in the organization. Their role, of carrying out their service delivery responsibilities, may be the most time-consuming. However, their role in assisting the organization in achieving its aims is the most critical.

### 3. External team reviews/accountability

This is the system that we looked at the end of the previous chapter. It is the stage where the teams present their proposals to an external assessor. So the external assessor is one of the leadership roles. We have seen that this role is typically a dual role. When a manager is asking probing questions, as an external assessor, he or she is also acting as a coach, using the Socratic Method. One aim of this system is to ensure that the teams have the method, motive and opportunity to run their own problem-solving sessions successfully. The other aim is to ensure their plans and progress are being assessed by an external assessor.

### 4. Internal team reviews and problem-solving

This is the system that only includes the roles of members of the team or sub-team. Here the group collectively map the solution, which they will present in the external review stage.

### The Leadership Game initiator

However, even though we have identified the various lead roles in the four stages, there is still a stage missing. Someone has to ensure those leadership roles are filled. In other words, in addition to the four stages identified, there is system zero. System zero has a lead role that fills all the lead roles in the other systems. All the lead roles could be taken by either the same person or different people. However, even with system zero, we have the same problem. Something has to motivate that person to take on the lead role of system zero. Often, that "something" is a crisis. So, many of the case studies occurred because a manager faced a crisis. That is when managers are most likely to take the leadership role of system zero. In the housing case study, Simon took the lead role in system zero. He engaged the non-executive board to take on the role of the figurehead of the challenge to become a three-star organization.

So, the lead role in system zero is the Leadership Game initiator. It is an invisible role, although it is the most critical of all roles. If no one takes the initiator role in system zero, then there is nothing to start the cascade of Leadership Games. So, the person taking the initiator role in system zero is the true leader. This is the person who has a clear understanding of the long term goal, and the ability to engage the relevant roles in the first stage of the Leadership Game. As we have seen, the manager or executive who takes on this role will often fill some of the other roles. However, in later chapters, we will look at an alternative when cascading the Leadership Game throughout a large organization. There, several of the leadership roles may be carried out by a small and dedicated "catalyst" team.

## Summary

In this chapter, we looked at the housing case study. This showed how someone, who did not have the necessary direct authority, launched and facilitated the early engagement of a whole organization. The case study also showed how easy it was to align a whole organization on achieving a badge of excellence. In addition, it showed how teams could use the Leadership Game to progressive solve the finer details of complex problems. We also saw how the invisible roles of the Leadership Game are just as important as the visible ones. This was shown in the example of a leader who was successful in one situation, but less so in others. It showed how the lack of later success was caused by a failure to understand the important role played by the invisible leader. Finally, we looked in more detail at the leadership roles of the four stages of the leadership game. We also saw that there was an additional stage, called stage zero.

# Chapter 9

## The control of variation

### Review and overview

In this chapter, we start to look at ways in which the Leadership Game can integrate other sophisticated problem-solving tools, to solve more complex problems. In particular, we will look at the different types of complexity created by variation. We will see how easy it is for different people to look at the same problem, and all come to different, and mistaken conclusions about the causes. We will then look at case studies to show how these issues can all be easily identified and addressed.

### Variation and performance

In many organizations, even when the same issues occur repeatedly, they often seem unavoidable. This is because they appear to happen at random. So managers spend much of their time crisis managing the effects of those seemingly unpredictable issues. Yet the apparent unpredictability is often just another illusion. This illusion is caused by a lack of understanding of variation, its causes and the protocols for minimising it. So we need to understand variation, as well as some of the powerful approaches that control it. In doing so, we will see how easy it is to integrate any problem-solving approach into the Leadership Game.

### *Solving more complex problems*

Many performance techniques use a simple problem-solving principle. That principle is that we can remove one performance gap by finding and addressing those upstream component gaps causing the downstream gap. We have repeatedly seen groups form high-performance teams when they use this principle to achieve a common purpose. However, this approach only works if the relevant group can identify the relationship between the upstream actions they control and the downstream performance gap they want to remove. The problem is that variation often creates a metaphorical fog, which can stop them from identifying the upstream causes of gaps.

### *Controlling variation*

We have already seen some obvious examples of variation control in the previous case studies. For example, variation was the fundamental cause of colour problems in the factory case study. Variations in the ratio of pigments, which were added at the beginning of the pathway, caused problems with the quality of the colour downstream of the pathway. In other words, a small extra amount of one pigment, combined with a smaller amount than required of another pigment, could cause a significant variance of the final colour produced. In turn, that error caused excess downtime and rework. That affected the on-time delivery and the cost performance. Similarly, in the same case study, variation was the cause of tags on the plastic pellets. In that case, it was variation in the torque and the state of the cutting blades. In turn, that variation also increased downtime and costs. So the consequences of not controlling variation can be enormous. It is also true that the potential benefits of controlling variation can be out of all proportion to the relatively little effort needed.

We have also looked at case studies where the control of

variation was less obvious. In the performance accounts department of the bank, the section leaders considered their job was to load data sets to the IT databases. The quality of those datasets was variable and caused problems in head office. These problems rapidly decreased when the people, who were responsible for loading the datasets, started checking the quality before loading. They did this by running the relevant reports and checking those reports. So controlling variation is relevant to all types of organization. In all these examples, the downstream pathway variation in standards was greatly reduced by the collective coordination of the people in the upstream processes.

In effect, the solution has always been the same. It was to first identify a benchmark standard that was not being met consistently. The next stage was to identify the group who controlled the relevant pathway processes. Once that had been achieved, the aim was to engage that group in collectively creating a performance feedback control loop. However, not all variation can be cured quite so simply. So to solve more complex challenges, we now need to understand the principles behind the control of variation.

### The basics of variation

Variation is an integral part of almost everything in our world. If they are measured with enough accuracy, no two items are identical. For example, if you use an electric hand drill to drill ten holes in a piece of metal, no two holes will be precisely the same diameter. If we measure the diameter of those holes accurately enough, we will find that each hole varies slightly from the diameter we were expecting. This variance is caused by the variation in the process of drilling. We may have applied slightly different pressure to the drill each time. Similarly, the angle of the drill will have varied a little each time. The drill bit will have worn slightly each time we used it. The temperature of the drill bit will increase when it is used. This is both because of normal friction and, as the drill bit becomes worn, it produces more heat.

Typically, if we measure each hole and plot the results on graph paper, this variation creates a bell shape curve. Most dimensions will be close to the average size. A smaller percentage will be slightly further from the average. Fewer still are a long way from the average.

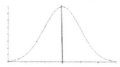

### Quality and reliability

This variation may not seem important. However, imagine the scenario where the drilled holes are for the unit to support a rotating spindle or axle. Imagine the spindles also suffer from variation. Some spindles will be oversize and some undersize. If we put a spindle, with an oversize diameter, into a hole with an undersized diameter, the fit is going to be tight. The friction created, when the spindle continually rotates, is likely to be high. This will increase the temperature and wear. So the unit is likely to break down prematurely. A problem also occurs if we pair an undersize spindle with an oversize hole. The spindle is likely to flop around in the hole as it rotates. Again, this could cause excessive wear and premature failure. This means the assemblies will have unpredictable reliability, with many premature failures. So it is not just the variability of single items that causes problems. It is the combined variability of related components that affect the final output.

Now imagine an assembly with hundreds or thousands of

parts that need to fit together in this type of way. Any failure of a single part could mean the failure of the whole assembly. In this scenario, it is easy to see how the failure to control variation leads to poor quality products and correspondingly poor reliability and reputation.

However, variation can similarly affect the other critical criteria of cost and availability. For example, variation in demand or variation in available resources can adversely affect the level of service an organization provides. So we need to understand how variation affects our ability to consistently meet the whole range of critical benchmarks. To achieve that, we need to first briefly consider the theoretical principles of variation that have been used to transform the quality of manufactured items. However, it is important to stress the reason for the investigation is so we can use the principles in a range of scenarios in any type of organization.

### *Ways of dealing with variation*

Therefore, let us return to our example of the hole and the spindle. Let us assume that it is possible to identify the precise gap between the hole and the spindle, which gives the maximum working life under normal working conditions. We can assume that a long, fault-free working life is one way to assess quality. So the more we reduce the variability of the gap, the higher the quality of the assembly.

There are potentially two ways to approach this challenge. The first would be to match all the oversize spindles with the oversize holes. In the same way, we could match undersize spindles with undersize holes, and correct size spindles with correct size holes. This approach is clearly impractical when manufacturing thousands of components. However, it is important to remember that this is a potential solution for other types of problems. We will call this approach "adapting to variation". For example, it is the approach that we may use to match the resources used in a pathway to meet variable demand. We will look at this method later in the chapter.

However, for the moment, let us stay with reducing the variation of manufactured components. For example, minimising the size variation of spindles and holes will help minimise the variation of the gap between the spindle and the hole. In turn, that is likely to reduce failures and improve the life and perceived quality of the assembly.

### *Statistical Process Control*

To control variation, manufacturers often use techniques based on a theory called Statistical Process Control (SPC). In simplified terms, SPC has two ways to reduce variation from the desired standard. The first is to reduce the variation around the mean value. The thinner the bell shape, the less variation there is. The more spread the bell shape curve, the higher the variation around the mean.

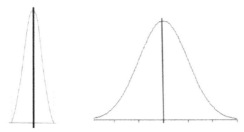

However, even with a thin curve of variation around the mean size, there could still be a problem. This would occur if the mean dimension was different from the required value. So SPC also aims to minimise the difference between the mean and specified dimension.

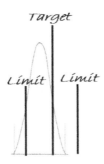

In effect, SPC helps control both these issues by regularly plotting the measures of samples during the production run. The variation among the samples will reflect the variation in the full batch produced. By looking at different patterns of the plotted graphs, it is possible to progressively identify and address the issues causing variation. However, most managers would not see how this is relevant to their own, everyday problems or achieving rapid change. Yet, it is very relevant. To understand why, let us briefly return to our example of drilled holes.

Image the scenario where one person is drilling holes, and another person is inspecting the components. The second person measures the diameter of the drilled holes. If the measurement is within a defined tolerance, the component passes the inspection. If the measurement is outside tolerance, the item is rejected and scrapped. In this scenario, all the outputs of the pathway are being measured. Now assume the inspector plots the measurements on a graph. To all appearances, the only difference is that we have added an extra, bureaucratic process of graph plotting. Yet, if we start to analyse the information on the graph, there has potentially been a radical change. For example:

*When a graph displays the trend of the mean over time, it is showing the change in CAPABILITY of the pathway system to meet the benchmark standard*

Even if we only plot the measure of one component in every ten, the graph is still displaying the change in the capability of the pathway system.

### *The trend could be a useful factor in predicting the future capability of the system*

So, for example, if the mean started to change, it is predictable that more errors would occur. However, the simple trend of the mean measure is not the only graph pattern that helps define the pathway capability. SPC provides a range of different ways of analysing the pattern of graphs to help identify and remove the causes of variation. So, it is worth taking a brief look at some of the SPC protocols, because they will be useful to many other types of pathways.

### *Different graph patterns*

For example, one pattern is when six or more measurements are one side of the previous mean trend. This suggests that something has caused the mean to shift and needs investigating. Similarly, if the last five measurements are consistently increasing or decreasing, something has caused a new trend away from the previous mean. Clearly, either situation could rapidly increase the variance of the components from the desired benchmark. Similarly, plotting the trend of the variation (rather than the trend of the mean) can provide essential information on the capability of the system. Likewise, outlying points on the graph are likely to suggest that some special cause has created a rogue outcome. So any changes in graph patterns would need immediate investigation. In other words, the graph pattern is not only an indication of future capability. It can also be an aid in tracking down the causes of variability.

### Seeing through the fog of variation

This may not seem applicable outside the mass manufacture of components. However, it is relevant to all sorts of different scenarios. This is because it helps "see through the fog" created by variation. For example, imagine a team in a retail outlet trying to assess whether different layouts of the products affected the number of items sold. Normal daily variation in sales could be more than any difference caused by changing the visual layout of the display. So just looking at a daily spreadsheet of sales each day would not help understand the effects of a change.

However, when plotting the sales on a daily chart, it might show the mean of sales during the days since the change was different from the previous mean. That would strongly suggest the change in the display had caused a change in sales. In other words, the analysis of the graph pattern would suggest that future sales would be improved by using the new display layout. Although this seems a trivial example, the point is that principles behind SPC can be used in many different situations. However, to gain an even better understanding of SPC principles, we need to apply these principles to our scenario of drilling holes.

## Prevention rather than cure

In our previous example, we had one person drilling holes, and one person inspecting the final components. The inspector was also plotting measures on a graph. We will assume that only one in ten measures is plotted. However, even in this scenario, the graph can predict the probability of future problems. In other words:

*By graphically controlling the system capability, you can avoid producing faulty products or services before they occur*

This has implications for delivering services to any set of benchmark standards. It also sharply contrasts with viewing a single set of measures, at a single point in time. That view is like driving a car, looking through the rear view screen. This is because we are looking at events that have happened in the past and that we cannot change. Besides, it gives us little information on what to do to create a better future. So, to better understand the implications of these facts, let us return to our simple scenario of drilling holes.

### Changing the pathway control protocols

We will assume the variation, in the diameter of the hole, can be controlled by the person drilling the holes. That person can take more care when drilling. They can also change the drill piece when it starts to wear. At first, we will assume two separate people take the drill operator and the inspection roles. The inspector plots the graph but does not have the skill or responsibility to analyse the graphical information. Only the manager has that skill and responsibility. In this scenario, would you predict the two people concerned would naturally work together to try to reduce the number of rejects?

Now let us try to predict if each of the following minor changes to the protocol would change the way the two people worked.

- The inspector is given the responsibility and training to understand the meaning of the patterns on the graph

- As above, with both people permanently remaining in their different roles, but the drill operator was also given training to analyse the graphs

- As above but the two people consistently changing roles

- As above, but they also have a graph of the trend of rejects

- As above but both have to regularly give a presentation to their manager on the ways they are using to reduce the number of rejects

By now, it should be clear the final scenario creates the same conditions as the Leadership Game. Each individual step may slightly improve the chances the two people will collaborate. However, it is the final protocol that creates the conditions of a fail-safe system that helps ensure the group work as a high-performance team. In other words, it creates the conditions most likely to motivate the team to collaborate in reducing rejects. This is because it creates the conditions where the team are collectively accountable for the maps of the performance gaps. Furthermore, they can see the evidence of their success. Indeed, once this approach is consistently applied, variation is likely to reduce to the level where 100% inspection is no longer necessary. This is because the use of SPC alone will predict if faulty components are likely to be produced.

### Where has variation control been successful?

So, we have seen that SPC is a powerful technique, which can be used in conjunction with the Leadership Game to solve more complex problems. However, to better understand how to use it successfully, it is worth briefly looking at where it has been used successfully, and where it has failed to live up to its promise.

SPC was originally developed in the 1920s. W. Edwards Deming was one of the best-known proponents. He made it a practical technique used in the US during World War 11. After the Second World War, General MacArthur, Allied Supreme

Commander of post-war Japan, asked a small number of US quality Gurus, including Deming, to help transform the quality of manufacture in Japan. MacArthur used his authority to ensure that many of the chief executives of Japan's major manufacturing companies became experts in Deming's SPC approach. However, in Japan, they did not just use statistical techniques. They also ensured that it was the frontline staff that used the technique to control variation in their production lines. This was the most effective way to use the techniques. After all, the more often the measures were taken, and the faster a potential problem identified, the lower the probability of producing a defect.

So in effect, the Japanese approach to quality improvement was clear. It was to engage those people, in the manufacturing pathways, to continually identify and address the causes of variation. This ensured the manufacturing teams consistently focused on reducing the variation of the final components. In other words, the Japanese approach was using the same principles that form the basis of the Leadership Game.

Progressively, Japan transformed from having a reputation of being a source of cheap, but shoddy goods, to a world leader in quality, manufactured products. That reputation helped the country become one of the largest economies in the world. Gradually, that reputation has decreased. Now, with a few exceptions, products produced by Japanese companies have little extra quality kudos than any other products. One of the reasons for Japan's more recent decline in reputation is partly because automation typically reduces variation. So, as competitors automated, the quality advantage reduced. Nevertheless, at the peak of Japan's reputation, Western companies often tried to absorb similar principles of controlling variation to improve quality.

## Western versions

However, when Western companies tried to copy the techniques used in Japanese companies, they often did it from the vertical perspective. They rarely use the horizontal approach to engage frontline staff in using SPC directly. Typically, they used separate teams of specialists, not directly involved in the service pathways. Needless to say, many Western implementations failed to achieve the success of the Japanese. As I have said many times before, small differences can have disproportionate consequences.

In effect, Western companies were like the man looking for his lost keys under a lamp post. A passer-by tried to help. The passer-by asked what the man was doing. The man explained that he was looking for his keys. The passer-by asked the man if this is where he had dropped his keys. The man replied that is wasn't. However, he was looking there because that was where the light was.

In effect, when we only understand the vertical system, then that is where the light is. We try to understand everything that happens in an organization from that perspective. From that perspective, it is always the managers' responsibility to motivate subordinates. From that perspective, if subordinates are not motivated to collaborate, it is the fault of the people, not the system. Yet, once we understand the horizontal systems, we have a torch to shed light on the real places where we can find the causes of the magician's illusions.

In effect, the performance board is where the light is. So we need to make sure the light is shining on both the problems and the solutions, which are in the collective control of the group accounting for the board. We have seen the performance board is more than just driving a car looking through the front screen. It is analogous to the view of the racing car video game. It is the visual focus of the challenging game that engages people in consistently improving the capability of their pathway systems. So the information on the board, and the way it is accounted for, are both critical to the success of the Leadership Game.

"I know we are trying to reduce variation, but I think this is ridiculous"

### *The performance board requirements*

So, we can start defining the requirements for the performance board. We can already see that the performance board should:

- Remove the fog of variation

- Show a leadership view of the pathway

- Provide evidence showing the past, current and predicted future capability gaps of the pathway system to consistently achieve one or more benchmarks of excellence.

- Contain information about the pathway contributory gaps and their accountabilities

- Be consistently updated in rotation by the people who can assess the meaning of the information they are updating AND who can collectively control that gap

- Have a fail-safe system. This is created by the documented responsibility of the individuals in the group. That is the responsibility to account for their collective success in assisting the organization to achieve its goals

### The format of graphs

However, although we have said the board should show the capability of the pathway system, the format in which it is shown is critical. For example, let us consider the scenario of a parcel delivery company, which I briefly mentioned in the first chapter. The company delivers a million parcels each month. The company may have a motto of being "A delivery company customers can trust." Now imagine the chief executive presenting monthly performance graphs to her section managers. Imagine the graph shows performance varying from 94% to 98% on-time delivery.

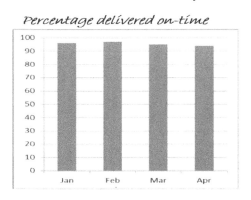

Percentage delivered on-time

Imagine you were one of the section managers at the presentation. Would you consider this showed there was an urgent need to collaborate with your peers to improve performance? Indeed would you even consider it even showed there was a crisis that needed addressing? Anyway, if it was the chief executive who was presenting the data, who would you consider owns the gap shown on the graph?

When I ask these questions in my master classes, most delegates agree the graph does not show any urgent need to fix a problem. Indeed that performance looks reasonable. I ask them to imagine they were the section managers and I was the chief executive presenting the information. I then ask them "in that scenario – who owns the gap?" They usually agree that I (acting as the chief executive) own the gap. When I ask "so who does not own the gap?" they agree that they (as section managers) would not own the gap. If they believe someone else owns the gap, there is no reason for them to collaborate to address the gap.

I then show them a graph with the same information presented differently. Consider the performance level of 94% on delivering one million parcels a month. That level of service would mean 60,000 upset customers each month. This is the issue I briefly mentioned in the first chapter.

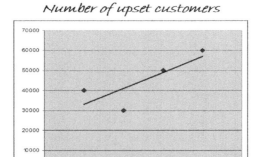

*Number of upset customers*

I then ask delegates whether they have ever waited in for an urgent parcel, only to find it was not delivered. They all agree they have. I ask them how they felt about the delivery company when that happened. They usually all laugh – as they would not like to put their feelings into words. I then ask them if 60,000 upset customers each month seems more of a crisis? Of course, it does.

However, even in this format, if I am presenting the graph, there is still a tendency for me to be the one who owns the gap. This is why, once the Leadership Game has started, the manager should not be the one presenting overall performance data to subordinates. Such presentations should be carried out by each member of the team in turn.

However, whenever we try and interpret the format of the graph, from a vertical perspective, it will result in the wrong solution. For example, I have seen some managers believe that all they have to do is to change the format of the monthly graphs being automatically circulated to managers. They often believe that culture change will automatically occur if they alter the monthly graph from a percentage performance to a graph showing the number of errors or returns. However, from a horizontal perspective, this is unlikely to have any great effect.

So, we need a clear protocol that will help us match up the correct format of the performance boards with the correct groups. Without such a protocol, the fog caused by variation can easily stop us from seeing the simple solution to the current problems. Our problem is that, if we view problems from a traditional vertical perspective, we are likely to identify the wrong potential solutions. Indeed, different people in different functions are all likely to be able to look at the same problem, but each identifies different solutions.

To help understand this problem, we are going to use a story about a fictitious bakery. Although this is not a real case study, it is based on the combination of real examples. It has been constructed to help understand several issues related to the fog caused by variation.

## The story of the bakery

This story is about an imaginary wholesale bakery, which has two main departments, each with 40 staff. However, as the bakery worked seven days a week, only 20 staff worked in each department on any one day. One department produced a range of different breads. The other department produced a range of different cakes. Combined, the two bakery departments produce about 250,000 loaves and cakes each week.

To ensure the freshness of its products, the organization has a strict policy on deliveries. Orders received from retail outlets by 3 p.m. one day, were dispatched by their fleet of vans by 4 a.m. the following morning. Any orders, or parts of orders not fulfilled by that time, were in effect cancelled.

The managers would like their organization to be the market leader in its area, but they are starting to lose business to competitors. This is because their competitors are more reliable in fulfilling the daily orders. When the senior managers gathered to develop their strategic plans, they made little progress. This was because each manager had different views on the most pressing issues, which needed addressing to enable the organization to become the market leader. So they agreed to adjourn the meeting for a week. This was to enable them to have time to collect factual data to identify which were the most important issues that needed to be resolved. To make the figures compatible, the accountant recommended the unit of sale as a "bakery unit", which represented either one loaf, or one cake. This was because, although the costs of the ingredients were different, the costs of production were similar.

At the following meeting, the accountant outlined the current performance and financial state from the information he collected during the previous week. He estimated that recent increases in costs were affecting profitability, and no matter what the longer term strategic plans were, it was essential that they improved profitability as soon as possible. He explained that they needed to make up the lost profitability by an increase in productivity of 10,000 units a week. He suggested the sales manager should have a short-term target to "improve sales by 10,000 units a week within three months". He also suggested the two bakery managers should each have targets to "increase productivity by 5,000 units per week within three months".

Following the accountant's presentation, the sales manager then explained that it was pointless asking him to increase sales. This was because they were already losing customers because of poor reliability in fulfilling orders each day. He then presented a graph of the performance for the previous seven days showing the number of lost bakery unit sales each day.

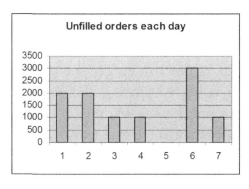

The sales manager showed that is was possible to increase sales by 10,000 units a week, simply by fulfilling the current orders. However, he agreed that it was essential the bakery performance improved, if they were to become a market leader. This was because the market would not take any increase in prices. Margins were already wafer thin, and simply increasing costs by increasing staffing levels would be counterproductive. So his solution was for the bakery managers to improve productivity to always fulfil current orders.

Then the manager of the bread department displayed the information he had collected during the previous week.

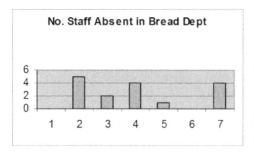
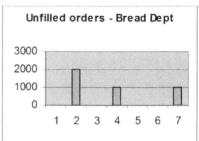

He explained the problem with unfilled orders was down to unreliable staff and casual absence. The graphs clearly showed the only days that bread orders went unfilled were those days (day 2, 4 and 7) where four or more staff were absent in the bread bakery. He believed the personnel manager should have a target of bringing in a system of penalties or dismissal for unreliable staff.

However, the personnel manager then stood up with the data that he had collected during the previous week. This showed that in the previous week, the bread division had lost 16 working days from short term absence.

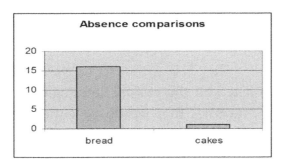

It also showed the cakes department had only lost one day. This clearly showed the problem was not with the staff personnel systems, but with the ability of the bread manager to motivate his staff. It was therefore important the bread manager went on a man-management course as soon as possible.

The manager of the cake department then stood up with the information that he had collected the previous week and explained that he felt the problem was due to the variation in demand. The bakery used to sell to many small retail outlets. The variation in demand for a large number of small outlets usually evened out to give a fairly predictable daily demand. Now they were selling to fewer, larger outlets and the daily demand varied dramatically, even though they had fixed staffing levels.

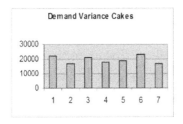

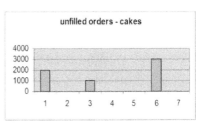

He used the graphs to show the days that cake orders went unfilled (day 1, 3 and 4), were the same days that cake demand exceeded 20,000 units. He considered there were two alternatives. Either there had to be a target for sales to get a higher proportion of business from smaller outlets, or the personnel manager had to recruit extra staff to cover the peaks in demand.

So they each listed all the possible strategies that they had identified, with the roles that would potentially have to use them.

- Increase sales by 10,000 units per week - sales manager

- Increase efficiency to produce 5,000 more units per week - both bakery managers

- Increase bakery efficiency to be able to cope with daily variation in demand and staffing levels - both bakery managers

- Increase the proportion of smaller customers - sales manager

- Create new personnel systems to reduce staff absence - personnel manager

- Reduce staff absence by attending a man-management course - bread bakery manager

They soon realised that, even if they made any of these alternatives part of an improvement plan, every strategy would have to be implemented by managers who believed they were the wrong solutions. Not a single manager was enthusiastic about using any of the strategies for which they would become responsible. Indeed, each manager had identified the cause of the problem as being in someone else's department. There was also another issue with some of the strategies, such as increasing the proportion of smaller customers or going on a man-management course. Even if they had been completed, there was no way of accurately predicting the effect they would have had on the problems of variation in demand and staff absences. Equally, for those strategies that had clear, predictable results, there was no way of finding what process would be most likely to achieve the necessary standards. This meant there was no real way of costing any of the strategies or calculating their relative cost and benefit ratios. As they would not need all the strategies, the managers continued to argue which strategies they should remove from the list.

So the Managing Director deferred any decision until he had been able to look at all the presented data and assemble it into a single spreadsheet. He considered there would probably always be a degree of variation, in both demand and staffing levels. So the MD decided to produce graphs of the variation, which the overall pathway would have had to cope with during the previous week. The graphs showed the pathway would have had to deal with a demand, which varied from a minimum of 34,000 units to a maximum of 40,000 units a day. It would also have had to deal with a staff variance of a minimum of 35 to a maximum of 40, as shown below:

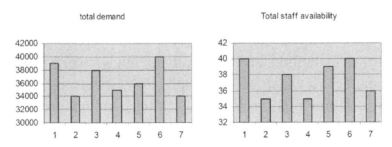

Also, to be able to achieve that performance, the next graph showed that on some days (days 3, 4 and 6) it would have needed a productivity rate of 1000 units per person:

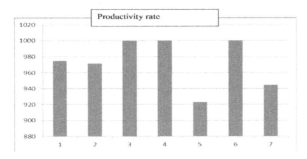

So, how far was the current system from being able to perform at that level? The Managing Director plotted the previous week's performance for both the Bread and Cake departments, as shown below:

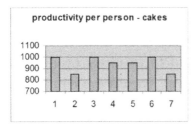 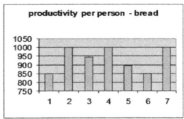

The graphs showed that both departments regularly hit this level of productivity. However, this was often on the very days that demand was greater than their ability to supply. The days, when they did not hit the productivity level, were when the supply potential was greater than the demand.

In other words, on some days, each department was slightly overstaffed, and on others, they were slightly understaffed. However, as the graph below shows, on no days during the previous week did the total demand exceed the potential overall supply capability.

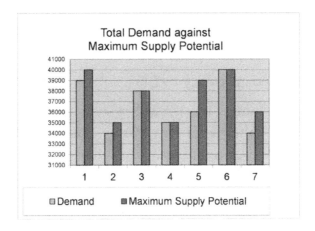

The graph below shows the under and over staffing levels for each department on each day:

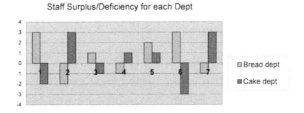

For example, on day one, the bread department had three too many staff, but the cake department had two too few to cope with the demand. On no days was there an under-availability of staff needed to meet all the total demand.

In other words, in this case, the solution does not lie inside either of the two service pathways. The solution needs a pathway between the bread and cake pathways, to share staff between them. In fact, they could solve all the problems if just three staff were flexible enough to move to where they were most needed each day. If such a pathway had existed in the previous week, it would have automatically achieved the following improvements:

- Increase sales by 10,000 units
- Removed under supplies
- Increased efficiency by 5%

Equally important is the overall system would have been running at a level that would encourage customers not to try the services of the competition. Thus, the potential benefits from such a simple change could be considerable. Further, the two bakery managers could jointly and easily assess the cost of using such a system. Additionally, the regular collection of the variation in supply and demand information would create data that was sufficiently statistically significant to enable accurate predictions of the potential future variations in demand and supply. This would enable the organization to quickly identify any changes that were occurring in either the demand or supply systems.

This story shows why we have to be careful when engaging groups in playing the Leadership Game. For example, consider an example where the managers had engaged groups in either of the cake or bread pathways in using the Game to improve on-time delivery. It is true that they may have been motivated to find ways of improving efficiency. However, if we assume that they were already working at peak levels, the solutions did not lie inside the separate pathways.

So, it is possible that neither group individually would have found a solution. In any case, the solution may not have been as simple as it first appeared. For example, let us assume the staff in the cake division needed completely different skills to those in the bread department. In those circumstances, just moving three staff from the bread section to the cake section would not work. They would not have the necessary skills.

In fact, engaging the relevant groups to share resources is such an important factor in improving performance that we are going to look at three case studies. Each case study will look at the different solutions needed in different scenarios. The first case study is in this chapter. The other two are in the next chapter. However, the case study that follows has been constructed from a combination of several real case studies.

## The Office – skills matrix

This is an example of an office of seven people. Previously, the group had an office supervisor. The supervisor had a command and control approach to management. Similarly, she tended to have just one appointed person for each job in the office. Recently, the supervisor had become ill and was now on long-term sick leave. The illness was such that she was unlikely to return. However, the post could not be filled while there was even a possibility that she would return.

Jack was the manager of the department. The administration office was just a small part of that department. He had hoped that, without the office supervisor, the group would automatically start breaking down barriers. He had tried to "empower" them to work across their current skill boundaries. However, that was not happening. The fact that each person had their own job invariably caused problems when someone was away sick, or on leave. This was because no one else either had the skills or felt responsible for covering someone else's area of work. As Jack had other responsibilities, he did not want to spend time directly managing and reorganizing the office. He considered he needed a way of engaging the group to organize themselves.

I had spent some time with Jack explaining the Leadership Game. I described the sticky note GAME used in the case study of the two departments at war. I explained that a similar exercise could be used to identify the skill gaps in the administration team. So Jack ran the first mapping stage of the Leadership Game with the administration staff. He started the session, grouping the relevant information, by explaining the conditions created by the supervisor being off sick. He asked the group whether anyone had any objections to carrying out an exercise for them to identify any training needs needed for the group to work together more effectively. Most of the group briefly shook their heads signalling no one had any objections. Jack then explained they needed first to set up a skills spreadsheet to identify who needed extra training or coaching in specific skills.

Next, Jack started the mapping-the-gaps stage. Everyone had a pack of square notes. Jack asked them all to individually write all the different jobs that they personally carried out. He explained that they should use one note per job. He also asked them to write their initials on the note, as well as a number on each note to show their current skill level for each job. "3" would show that they felt they were fully skilled at the job and never needed help. "2" would signal that they were fairly skilled, but occasionally had to ask for support. "1" would say that they were not confident about doing that job, even though they did it occasionally.

As the group started to write their notes, Jack put several flip chart sheets on the wall. Each sheet had a matrix of lines, so each space was the size of the sticky notes. When everyone finished writing their notes, Jack asked one member to put their first note in the top left-hand space in the first flip chart sheet. He then asked everyone else to put their note in the same column if they also carried out that job. He then asked the next person to put one of their next sticky notes in the second column. He again asked for all the other similar notes to be put in the same column. Within about 10 minutes, the flip chart sheets contained a complete skills assessment for all the jobs carried out in the office.

Jack then explained the columns on the flip chart sheets defined all the actions or processes the office team had to carry out. However, he also explained the only justification of spending any time carrying out actions, was to provide a service to another person or group. The office needed to provide services whether or not the person, who normally carried out the job, was in the office, on leave or off sick.

He then explained that each service needed a service champion. That person should try to ensure that several people had the skill to do the job. The champion would also ensure there was always someone in the office able to provide the service, even when there was sickness or holiday leave. Jack continued to explain that ideally, the service champion would be someone with a high level of skill for providing that service. That way, they could train anyone else in providing the service. In other words, the champion would ensure there was at least one service provider each day. However, he said there should be up to two service champions per service to help provide cover. Jack then made a quick assessment. He calculated that, for there to be two champions for all the services on the sheets, everyone would need to be a joint champion for three services. Jack then asked everyone to put their name on three sticky notes. He then asked them all to go the sheets and put their names on three different services for which they would be champions. However, there could be no more than two champions per service.

Jack also explained that he needed everyone in the office to be skilled in as many duties as possible. So he needed everyone to develop their own plan for working with other people in the office to gain the full range of skills. He said that everyone should aim to reach at least a skill level of 2 across all services over the next couple of months. If anyone felt they could not achieve that, they should come and discuss the problem with him.

I had previously described to Jack the case study of the legal team outlined in chapter one. I explained how the protocol was the group had a daily meeting to agree on how to assign the work. So Jack explained to the team there needed to be a short meeting, involving the whole group, at the beginning of every morning around the office flip chart. There was an agreed rota for everyone to take turns in being the "lead" for each meeting. It was the responsibility of the lead to ensure the meeting took place and that it was effective. Any service champion, who had an issue with providing the service that day, should put a note on the flip chart. After a brief discussion, anyone who was prepared to help on that issue should put their name next to the issue.

Jack also asked if any of the group used Excel. They all looked at Sarah, who was the one person who was considered as the expert in Excel. So Jack asked Sarah if she would mind putting the information on the charts into an excel spreadsheet. That spreadsheet should show the list of different duties, the champions and the current skill level of every member of the group. Sarah was happy to do this. Jack then explained that anyone who increased their skill level should enter the data on the spreadsheet. He also asked the person acting as meeting lead each day should check the date of the Excel file on the disc drive. If it had been changed, then to print the latest version and put in on the notice board. That way, Jack could see how the skills project was progressing.

Jack made a clear schedule of when he would be able to attend the morning meetings. This ensured the team would know when they would be able to ask for his help. However, in general, the team resolved most problems among themselves. These issues included arranging who would carry out which jobs, whenever someone in the team was on leave. They also agreed who would be helping who in developing their skills that day. It soon became clear the office ran effectively with little or no intervention from Jack.

In other words, this is another example of using the same mapping technique as the departments at war. However, this mapping exercise was aimed at the repeated mismatch of skilled resources for each of the service that they needed to provide. That mismatch was a repeating problem because of the variation in the availability of specific skill to cover all the services every day. This may seem a simple, small or even trivial example. However, there is no reason why a similar approach could not be used across a whole organization.

## When to use graphs

The previous case study did not use graphs. In effect, the public skills chart acted as the graph. However, it is easy to imagine a more complex scenario, which would need one or more graphs. For example, consider the star rating for skills identified the skill gap for each person for each service. The sum of all those skill gaps would give the total number of skill gaps for the office. If those gaps were going to take several months to address, the team could have used a graph. That would have shown the downward trend of the skill gaps over time. If that graph were on the wall, it would have ensured they were all accountable to Jack for their success in progressively removing the gap. It would have played the same role as the graph for the legal team in the case study in chapter one. That graph helped the group see their continued success in removing the backlog gap. It created accountability and the same type of motivation as a video game. So deciding on whether a graph is necessary will depend on the complexity and duration of the solutions. It will also depend on what is required to produce the fail-safe system. In this case, the fail-safe system was created by Jack being able to consistently view the performance board containing the training skills matrix.

## Summary

In this chapter, we have seen that variation is often the critical factor that needs to be controlled. Indeed, we saw that its control of variation was one of the most important factors in Japan's post-war transformation. We have also seen that variation can act as a fog, stopping us from seeing a trend toward a potential disaster. This is why trend graphs are an essential part of many Leadership Games.

# Chapter 10

## Controlling utilisation and costs

### Review and overview

In the previous chapter, we looked at some of the problems caused by variation. In particular, we saw that variation in demand and capacity could hinder the efficient use of resources. In this chapter, we are going to see that a failure to cope with the variation in demand is a common reason for the failure of previously successful organizations.

### The control of unutilised resources

In the factory case study described in previous chapters, we saw that quality problems of colour matching and tags in factory case study adversely affected the availability and cost of the products produced. In that example, we saw that improving the right-first-time quality, produced by the service pathway, improved both cost and availability performance of the service.

This is the underlying principle of many quality approaches. They focus on reducing waste caused by poor quality. So improving "right first-time" quality can simultaneously improve the quality, availability and cost factors of the service. However, there is another major cause of cost and availability problems. That cause is even more prevalent than problems caused by quality problems. That is a lack of control of unutilised resources.

### *Demand, capacity and backlog*

To understand this problem, let us first consider a scenario of a business unit that employs 100 members of staff to process applications from the public. We will assume that each member of staff can process 10 applications per day. This means the whole unit has the capability of processing 1000 applications each day. We will assume an initial state where the public is sending in exactly 1000 applications a day, and the unit processes every application the day it is received. So, everything is in perfect equilibrium. We will also assume the total daily cost of running the unit (including the cost of staff and buildings) is £100,000 each day. In other words, the total cost of processing each application is £100. We will assume the unit charges £100 for each application, so it is exactly covering its costs.

Now let us assume the demand increases by 100 applications a day to 1100 per day. As the unit is running at full capacity of 1000 per day, that is the maximum number of applications that the unit can process. Therefore, a backlog of applications starts to build up. That backlog will increase at the rate of 100 applications each day. In effect, those applications are waiting in a holding system at the beginning of the pathway. After ten days of the increased demand, there will be 1000 applications waiting in the holding system. This means that all applications are now taking two days to process, instead of the original one day.

After another 20 days, the backlog in the holding system is 3000, and the turnaround time has increased by another two days, to make four days turnaround for each application. Clearly, while demand is more than capacity, the backlog will continue to increase every day. However, the cost for each application remains constant at £100. Similarly, the organization continues running at a break-even level.

In other words, we can say that:

***When demand is greater than capacity, the backlog (in availability) will grow; the time to process (delivery time) will increase, but the cost per unit will remain the same***

Now let us assume that demand suddenly reduces to 800 per day. As there is a backlog, the business unit can continue to process 1000 applications per day. So the cost per application remains at £100, and the backlog reduces by 200 per day.

Now, we can see that:

***When there is a backlog, and demand is less than capacity, the backlog will decrease, but the unit cost will remain the same***

However, after 15 days, there is no backlog, but only 800 applications are coming in each day. So the business unit can now only process 800 applications. As the total costs remain at £100,000 per day, the cost of each application suddenly rises to £125. Yet the charge for each application remains at £100. So the total income is (800*£100) £80,000 per day. In other words, the unit starts losing £20,000 a day.

Now, we can see that:

***When demand is lower than capacity, and there is no backlog, then the overall unit cost will increase***

It is this scenario that is one of the most common causes why previously successful, commercial organizations progressively get into financial difficulties.

Typically, in the good years, demand increases and managers respond by increasing the capacity. They may take on more staff or expand their premises. However, when demand falls, even slightly, the unit cost (as calculated by all costs divided by total income or the number of units produced) increases. To add to this problem, often the expansion programme gains a life of its own. So expansion continues, and surplus capacity increases unabated. Quickly, the organization can start losing money.

Given the importance of balancing capacity with demand, it would be reasonable to assume that this would be one of the most important performance indicators for all organizations. In fact, relatively few organizations even check this indicator. Even fewer have protocols in place to constantly address the gap in the balance. However, the importance of the indicator means that it should be a critical benchmark in the Leadership Game. The gap in the balance has to be monitored and addressed, either by adjusting the work available (demand plus backlog) or by adjusting the resources used to provide the service. So in this chapter, we are going to look at various case studies that took different approaches to balance capacity with demand.

"I don't think you realise how long the backlog really is"

## The Registry case study

A UK government agency had twenty-three business units across the UK. Each unit was mainly responsible for applications from its local geographical area. I had previously helped Peter, the general manager of one of those units, to successfully address several internal issues using the Leadership Game. However, Peter was transferring to another unit. Peter's new unit was in the North of England and employed over three hundred people. Head office measured how all twenty-three units performed, using a spreadsheet of different Key Performance Indicators. These covered quality, turnaround time and efficiency. The main efficiency measure represented the cost for each application.

Peter's new unit was one of the top performing units for quality and turnaround times. However, it was the lowest performer on the efficiency measure. Over the five months following my involvement, it went from bottom to one of the top three business units for efficiency. However, before looking at this transformation, we need to understand how variation and trend masking helped to hide its poor performance.

When Peter asked me to help with his new business unit, he showed me the spreadsheet that head office circulated to managers each month. It showed the KPIs for the previous month for all twenty-three units. The current spreadsheet showed the performance KPI for Peter's unit was 4.6. The performance of the best unit was 6.2. Peter explained to me that, when he discussed this with the managers, they just said that it was the culture of the people in the North of England. The managers considered the staff were not interested in improving performance. Anyway, the managers would point to the fact that their business unit had some of the shortest turnaround times as well as the highest quality performance.

Peter explained to me the unit had been split into numerous small teams. This was to create a team spirit and ownership, to try and improve performance. It also allowed managers to identify the efficiency of all the different teams. That information showed that some teams were far higher performing than others. Peter felt the figures proved that this was a "people problem". He just needed to know how to motivate the "difficult" teams. He was thinking of setting up a reward system for the teams.

I explained that we first needed to look at the trends of performance, not performance figures for individual months. So, between us, we made a spreadsheet comparing the efficiency performance of Peter's business unit with the best performing unit over the previous six months. The spreadsheet showed there was a clear difference between the two units over that period. That difference varied from month to month. However, as soon as we made a graph of the trend over the previous six months, the picture was very different. It showed a clear trend of improvement for the best performing unit. It also showed a clear downward trend in the performance of Peter's new unit. Peter was quite shocked when I said that was good news. He could not see why a downward trend was good news. I explained that we had been grouping the information for people to be able to assess a crisis. At the moment, they were suffering from the boiled frog syndrome.

This name comes from a story about an experiment with a frog. Although the story is not true, it does create a useful analogy to one aspect of human behaviour. The fictitious story is about an experiment where a frog, which jumps into boiling water, will immediately leap out of the water unharmed.

However a frog, in a pan of water that is gradually heated until boiling, does not jump out. It does not sense any change, so it dies as the water gets too hot for the frog to survive. In other words, the change is so gradual that the frog does not sense any change. As with all control loops, if the frog does not assess a gap, it does not react. The gradual change in water temperature imperceptibly increases the frog's temperature. So when it is assessing the difference between its own temperature and the external temperature, there is no discernable gap.

The point of the story is to provide the analogy to the behaviour we see all around us. In effect, it was the behaviour in the early case study about safety and housekeeping in the factory. The problem is exasperated by variation. For example, managers may receive monthly spreadsheets of the performance of numerous performance measures. Each month there may be colour coding to indicate whether that month's performance was above or below target. From our knowledge of variation, we can assume that, even if the mean of all the measure was on target, every month the individual measure will vary between being above and below target. This alone means the spreadsheet is covered by the fog caused by variation. However, far more importantly, this type of variation in monthly spreadsheets masks gradual trends. So people do not sense a performance indicator is deteriorating. If they do not assess a gap, they see no need to act. However, rather than keep referring to boiled frogs, we will call this effect "trend masking". In other words, even though there is a definite trend in the performance that predicts a future crisis, no one realises because of variation in the normal monthly reports.

Once I explained this principle to Peter, I laid out the

monthly spreadsheets circulated to managers over the previous six months. I asked him to pick one at random. I then asked him to image he was a new manager and just received an email with the spreadsheet. How would that manager be able to assess which area of performance needed urgent attention? Rather embarrassed, Peter accepted that the spreadsheet, on its own, was of little use.

So I explained that, once they saw the graph of the trend in efficiency, and asked to predict the gap in six months, they would see the best performing unit would be twice as efficient. Then, they would immediately be able to assess there was a gap. That would be the assessment that would help engage everyone in bringing about the necessary change.

However, before continuing, I asked Peter to explain how the available work was split between the various business units. He explained that each unit was placed in a different area of the country. Each unit had its own catchment area where the applications came from. He also explained that each of the internal teams had their own catchment area.

So I asked, when there was no backlog of applications and if the unit suddenly improved its efficiency, where would the extra work come from? It took a few seconds for the question to sink in. Peter had never thought of that possibility. I explained that, to me, the problem was probably not down to the lack of work ethic in that area. The problem was the capacity of the whole unit was higher than the demand in the area the unit serviced. In fact, I suggested the difference in efficiency between teams might not be down to the fact that some teams had a higher work ethic. It may be the demand and capacity mismatch may be greater in the low-performance teams.

Peter took a few moments to think about the questions I was asking. Then he said, "yes, but in theory, if a team runs out of work, they can take work from the pool of overdue applications from other business units." So I asked if we knew whether there was enough work in that pool of overdue application to keep his unit running at the higher efficiency levels. He explained he did not know, but would have to look into it.

After some further analysis, we determined there was sufficient backlog to keep the higher performance level for some time. However, we also identified the informal protocol in the unit was that each team just had to service its own area. Few teams were currently accessing the pool of extra work. In effect, the culture was that both staff and managers did not see why they should have to do the work of other business units.

So I ran a session with the managers where I showed them the trend on unit performance in comparison to the benchmark performance of the highest performing unit. I asked them to predict what the gap would be within six months. They reluctantly identified the highest performing unit would soon be twice as efficient as their unit. That was enough for them to start sensing a gap.

I also explained the calculations behind balancing demand and capacity. Then I explained the local efficiency could only improve if they changed the protocol-in-use. It had to change so each team would need to regularly take on work from the pool each week, to make up its local efficiency performance.

The managers decided to use a planned away day for all the staff, to engage everyone in the unit. They showed the graph and explained how the efficiency of any team was affected by the variation in demand. They composed some exercises, for the groups on each of the tables. That allowed the groups to work out for themselves, how to calculate the work that they needed to take from the pool in different circumstances.

During the day, there were various other exercises where the teams identified ways of improving efficiency. Near the end of the day, the managers introduced the protocol that, from now on, it would not be the responsibility of managers to keep checking how the teams were performing. Each team would now have to monitor its own performance. Each team would decide how much work they could take from the backlog pool each day. Each team could do this by printing out the team report daily. That report would have two graphs. The first was the efficiency graph. The second was the amount of work taken from the backlog pool.

Within three months of the away day, the efficiency of the unit had improved by 40%, and they became one of the top three performing units of the twenty-three units across the country. In this example, teams controlled the gap between local demand and the capacity of the unit, by continually adjusting the extra work taken from the pool of backlogged applications. In other words, they balanced the variation in demand with fixed resources by taking work from the backlog.

However, the alternative is to balance resources to match the varying level of work required. So, we will shortly look at a different case study, where managers adjusted and shared resources to meet the variation in demand. However, before we do that, we need to look at the general way to map unused resources.

## The general solution

Previously, we created a map of the process for making a meringue, to understand the effects of initial conditions. In that diagram, we mapped all the external inputs with a direct connection to the process within the process unit. However, we now need to upgrade our mapping to reflect unused resources in a more realistic way. So we are going to assume that resources are only in the active process part of the unit, while the process is utilising them at its optimum performance level. This means that, when resources have been allocated to a process unit, but are not fully utilised, they remain in a special type of holding system, inside the process unit boundary. We call that holding system "unused process resources".

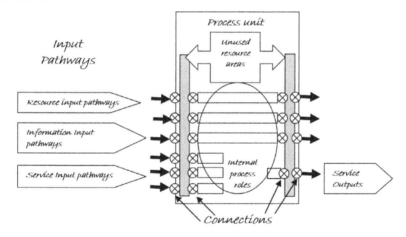

For example, imagine the scenario where a manager sends two skilled tradespeople to a site to build a wall. The manager has also arranged for the necessary materials to be delivered early that morning. However, when the tradesmen arrive, they cannot start work because the materials have not been delivered. In other words, the tradesmen's time has been allocated to the process unit, but that time is currently unused.

So that time resource needs to be mapped as being inside the process unit, but in the unused area rather than in the process itself.

Often, there is no physical movement between the unused area and the process area of a unit. For example, in the registry case study, the people in apparently underperforming teams probably did not move from their work areas, when they had less work to complete. However, the potential time in the unused area could easily be calculated using the benchmark standard set by the best performing unit. That would identify the time that would ideally be spent in the process area of the unit. The rest of the resource would be in the unused area. So the unused resource time is the gap that needs to be minimised.

Sometimes, having resources in the unused areas may help ensure the resources are consistently available when there is variable demand. However, resources held in this way are also increasing the total costs, without directly creating any value. So, in general, we will measure unused resources by their cost. This means that, from the horizontal perspective, the performance board needs to focus on minimising the cost of unused resource time. That cost is the gap that teams need to focus on removing. This contrasts with the vertical approach to the same problem. In the vertical approach, it is the manager's job to try and get his or her subordinates to work harder. So, to understand Leadership Game approach to minimising the cost of unused resources, we will look at another case study.

## The distribution hub

Some time ago, I was asked to help Sue, the centre manager of a site that was a major distribution hub for the transportation of letters and parcels. The centre consisted of a huge warehouse with twenty inbound lorry loading bays at one side of the building and twenty outbound bays at the other. The basic operation of this hub was simple. Lorries arrived at the inbound loading bays from all over the country. The hub staff then unloaded the cargo of sacks of parcels and letters, on to the inbound loading bays. Each sack had a label to show the final destination depot. So, staff then sorted the sacks on to various trolleys. A small power unit then pulled the trolleys around a circular track, which ran inside the warehouse. Staff then disconnected the trolleys at the relevant outgoing bays. Staff would then load the sacks on to the outgoing lorries, which then returned to their original depots. In effect, the sacks followed the pathway from their starting point to their destinations across the country.

The centre consisted of two, largely autonomous, units. One unit dealt with the high priority next day service. The other part of the centre dealt with low priority packages that had a delivery schedule of three or four days. The workload of the two departments varied greatly, from hour-to-hour and day-to-day. So the centre relied heavily on casual staff supplied daily by a local recruitment agency. Indeed, one of the largest individual costs of running the Hub was the cost of the temporary staff. Managers predicted the daily workload according to the day of the week and from information provided by the other hubs sending the cargo to the central hub.

The distribution hub was a 24-hour operation. The two departments had their own departmental managers, David and Jim, who were both directly responsible to Sue. Both departmental managers had several sections and shift managers responsible to them. David and Jim were each responsible for hiring the correct number of casual staff that they needed each day. The priority was to ensure that all sacks were loaded on to the relevant outgoing lorries before the last scheduled leave time. Any sacks, not at the outgoing loading bays on time, could be delayed in the depot for up to 24 hours until another lorry for that destination arrived.

There was one factor that was crucial in ensuring that sacks did not miss the scheduled outbound lorries. That was the hour by hour reallocation of temporary staff to the areas of the hub that needed them most urgently. Although the basic processes were simple, the problem was the variation in workloads during each day. The predictable variation became worse when there were even relatively small delays on the surrounding motorways.

The primary measure of hub performance was based on the number of sacks left in the hubs each day. All hubs had a 99.8% on-time delivery target. This was such an important measure of performance, the regional manager would have a video conference with all his hub managers most mornings at 7 a.m. each morning. Typically, the regional manager would berate any hub manager who had significant amounts of mail not transported out of their hub. It was not a pleasant experience for any of the unfortunate centre managers, who were the target of the regional manager's wroth. This created a blame culture, where the centre manager would then try to identify which shift and section managers had failed to ensure there were no sacks left in the depot. However, when specific managers were tracked down, they usually thought up creative reasons why the problems occurred.

As well as the daily, on-time delivery target, the hubs also had cost targets. Every centre had to reduce the overall running costs by 5%. As the cost of temporary staff was such a large proportion of the total costs, this was an obvious target for cost-cutting.

Each day, David and Jim individually calculated the number of temporary staff that they needed for each shift for their departments. They used a specially built spreadsheet to make the necessary calculations. The spreadsheet used an hour-by-hour assessment of the workload over the forthcoming 24 hours. Typically, they would assess the number of staff they needed for each shift in a way that ensured that they always had enough staff to cope with the predicted peak periods of the shift. This meant that, for much of the shift, many staff would be waiting around with almost nothing to do.

Sue had repeatedly asked David and Jim to try to reduce the number of temporary staff that they were ordering from the agency. Their reply was always the same. If they reduced the number of temporary staff, then there would be more occasions where significant amounts of mail would be left undelivered each day. Sue was clearly reluctant to do anything that meant she would be a target for the ranting of the regional manager each morning.

However, the peaks and troughs of demand in the two departments rarely coincided. This meant there were often states where, staff in one department were under pressure, while staff in the other department would just be waiting for lorries to arrive. However, both David and Jim still resisted sharing temporary staff. The reason they gave was that they disliked having staff who might be tired from previously working in the other department. The unspoken reason was that neither David nor Jim was confident that they could get their shift and section managers to cooperate in sharing staff between them.

Typically, once a departmental shift manager had enough staff to cope with a period of high demand, they were reluctant in letting the staff move out of their section. They always feared that they would be unable to get them back when they needed extra staff urgently. That shortage of manpower could lead to them being reprimanded for poor performance.

In principle, Sue could use a single spreadsheet to calculate the total number of staff needed for the whole centre. In fact, her assessment was that, if she did, then she could reduce temporary staff costs by over 15%. This would easily enable her to meet her annual target of reducing running costs by 5%. However, she knew that if she limited the number of staff available to the departmental managers, they would always use it as an excuse when they failed to meet the 99.8% delivery target. Similarly, Sue was well aware she would not solve the shift problem simply by directing the shift managers to cooperate and share temporary staff hour by hour.

This may seem a trivial problem. Yet it is symptomatic of the chronic types of problems that many managers continually face. Both David and Jim were responsible for the on-time delivery performance of each of their departments. However, neither manager was responsible for the overall costs of running the centre. That was Sue's responsibility. Yet if all the managers, from both departments, actively cooperated to coordinate the number of staff available, they could easily meet the centre cost performance target. In fact, by sharing staff effectively, they would probably find it much easier to meet their on-time-delivery targets, even with reduced overall temporary staff numbers. This is because the ability to move staff between departments would help smooth out the peaks and troughs within the departments. In this scenario, the metaphorical batons that they need to pass between the two departments were the temporary staff. No matter how rational this argument was, David and Jim would not act like members of a relay team focused on reducing the overall performance measure of centre costs.

It is worth spending a few moments here to try to identify any similar examples, which you have experienced. In other words, imagine where you have seen or been a manager struggling to meet a target, simply because subordinates seem unwilling to share resources.

### The hub solution

When Sue described to me her problem of managers not sharing temporary staff, I explained the solution was easy. However, the first thing to understand was there were two aspects to the problem. To explain the first aspect, I described the example of the outward-bound course that we saw in chapter four. In that example, groups of three people used a single map to develop a route and monitor their progress in keeping to the planned route. You may remember that I asked whether an outward-bound group would develop into a team if only one person could use the map to develop the route and use it to monitor progress. In that example, most people say the scenario would stop the team from developing a collective thought bubble. However, to help managers see the problem in this type of case, I ask a different question. For example, let us re-consider the scenario in the outward-bound team-building course. Assume we changed the protocol again, away from each group of three people having to use a single map. We could change the protocol, so every individual had their own map to plan their own journey. Do you consider that small change in the protocol would encourage or discourage people from collaborating and forming teams?

Again, when I ask delegates at a master class this question, most reply that if everyone had their own map to use, it would encourage them to act as individuals competing against each other.

So, I explained to Sue the first problem was the two departmental managers were each using their own map. This was the Excel spreadsheet they were using to calculate the number of temporary staff they needed. This meant they were only accountable for their own map. I then explained the other problem. When developing their spreadsheets, they both focused on ensuring they always had enough staff to cover the peaks in demand. Neither was developing a map to minimise the cost of the unutilised temporary staff time or cost.

I explained there was a simple way to ensure that all the managers, from both departments, collaborated. That method was to engage them in a Leadership Game to progressively reduce the gap of unused resources. In this case, the gap was the total hub cost of unused temporary staff-hours.

However, before looking at that map, we needed to remember the number of undelivered sacks was also a critical issue. So, we also needed to represent that on the performance board. This meant that although the focus was to reduce the wasted temporary staff hours, this had to be achieved without adversely affecting the missed delivery performance.

As I described in the previous chapters, the way to measure delivery gaps in this type of situation is to graph the trend in upset customers. To do this, I asked Sue what the average number of parcels and letters were in a sack. Although she found this difficult to estimate, we agreed on a simple round number to use. That way, we could graph the number of upset customers each delayed sack would create. So this would be one of two graphs on the performance boards, which needed to be visible to everyone in the working area.

We now needed the two departmental managers to collaborate in reducing the overall cost of unused temporary staff hours. This meant they had to jointly produce and account for a single spreadsheet for the whole hub, showing the total cost of unused people-hours each day. The spreadsheet also needed to show how they planned to move people between departments during each shift, to ensure there was always enough staff, but with the minimum wasted staff hours. The challenge was for all the shift and section managers to develop the coordination protocols that would ensure that temporary staff were always available in the areas of most need.

Sue set up a spreadsheet that took the basic information from the two individual spreadsheets created by David and Jim. It automatically showed where surplus staff in one department could be utilised in the other department. It also calculated the total number of temporary staff-hours needed if staff were shared, with the total staff-hours needed separately for the two departments. The spreadsheet also showed the total cost of the unused staff hours.

Once Sue had completed the spreadsheet, she called David and Jim into a brief meeting. She reminded them the total running cost of the hub was too high, in comparison with other hubs. She showed them how the spreadsheet she had created used the information from their individual spreadsheets to calculate the total number of temporary staff needed for the hub for that day. It showed the hours where the hub was overstaffed and the calculated cost of that overstaffing. It clearly showed that they could reduce the total cost of temporary staff by 15% if the two departments collaborated in using temporary staff. However, Sue explained that she was not asking for immediate adherence to the more efficient staffing.

Sue told David and Jim that she expected all the managers from both departments to first agree how they could coordinate the use of temporary staff effectively. The aim would be to try to close the daily gap, between the current cost of temporary staff and the ideal level shown by her spreadsheet, as quickly as possible. She stated that this decrease in costs had to be achieved without adversely affecting the delivery performance of the centre. So, she wanted the shift and section managers to present their solutions on sharing staff, to David and Jim for their approval.

Sue said she wanted to see the daily graph showing the progress in reducing the over-staffing cost gap in the shortest possible period. Sue reiterated that she expected the collaboration to be achieved without any adverse effect on the delivery performance. She also explained the graph of upset customers. She expected both graphs to be displayed outside the shift manager's office and updated daily. She also expected section managers to sign off daily on their own copies of the Excel spreadsheets. In effect, this changed the rules of the game. Now, the managers of the two departments were all accountable for the effectiveness of the collaboration between departments.

In the meeting, David and Jim were relatively quiet and slightly shocked at what they considered as Sue's assertiveness in defining the new approach. They had been used to her leaving them largely to run their individual departments in their own way, with the occasional "nag" about costs. Neither manager showed any enthusiasm for the new approach. However, shortly after the meeting, they arranged for several joint meetings with the managers from both departments. They explained the new graphs and the shift and section managers had to get the buy-in for their proposals from both Jim and David. Jim and David again stressed to all the managers that they were responsible for developing the new coordination in a way that would not adversely affect delivery performance.

The nature of the shift patterns meant the whole process of consultations took about three days to complete. Then, to ensure a smooth transition, Jim and David agreed with their managers to progressively reduce the gap of excess staffing over about five days. At the end of that period, not only had the managers removed the overstaffing gap, but the delivery performance had improved, despite the decrease in overall staffing levels.

Sue was amazed. She had spent months trying to get the two managers to work together with almost no result. Almost immediately after her initial, short meeting, the situation had transformed. All that had happened in that meeting was that she made it clear that she was creating new rules of engagement.

The managers now had no choice but to ensure their managers were accountable for the map that showed their success in collaborating. This change created other benefits as well. Previously, each of the managers would often privately complain to Sue about the work of the other department. This stopped almost immediately.

It would be easy to assume the need to balance demand and resources only occurs when there is an obvious problem. However, as I mentioned earlier, commercial organizations that fail to balance these two factors consistently will eventually get into financial difficulties. Indeed, many of the most famous turnaround programmes have been preceded by a failure to address this problem.

"She is trying to remove unused resources"

## The story of Nissan

To demonstrate this point, we are to going to look at a case study, which I consider is one of the most astounding transformations of all time. It is not a transformation that I was in any way involved. However, it is still one that used similar principles to those of the Leadership Game. This was the turnaround of Nissan, the Japanese Car manufacturer, by Renault's Carlos Ghosn. At the time of writing, Carlos Ghosn has recently come into the news for all the wrong reasons. There seems to have been a particularly unpleasant boardroom power struggle in Nissan. One outcome of this has been that Ghosn has been imprisoned in Japan for, among other things, under-reporting his remuneration. However, irrespective of the outcome of those proceedings, one thing is beyond doubt. That is the amazing nature of the Nissan turnaround that Ghosn engineered years earlier.

Currently, the Renault-Nissan-Mitsubishi alliance is the largest manufacturer of cars. In that alliance, Nissan is currently the largest and most profitable partner. However, when the alliance was initially created, Nissan was almost bankrupt. To understand this transformation, we need to first look at Nissan's previous history.

Nissan was one of the Japanese manufacturing companies that started using the quality techniques introduced by Deming after the Second World War, as described in the previous chapter. In 1959, Nissan won the Deming Prize for quality in manufacturing. Later, Nissan focused on reducing the time to do everything from design to manufacture, using similar charting methods. This was presumably their way of reducing costs. However, at best, this was a way of reducing the direct labour costs of production. It did nothing to control the cost of unused resources. For this reason, it is not a robust way of reducing costs.

Nevertheless, Nissan was still sufficiently successful that they carried out a programme of building more factories across the world. Until the early 1990s, Nissan seemed to be enjoying unstoppable success. That success was widely acknowledged to be the result of the Japanese focus of quality. Yet despite their seeming success, over the following years Nissan, together with several other Japanese car manufacturers, had been building up a mountain of debt. The reason was mainly due to the lack of control over unused resources.

In the late 1990s, Renault was a French car manufacturer that had also recently struggled, after a failed merger with Volvo. Carlos Ghosn, then one of its senior executives, had managed to create a major turnaround of Renault. However, even though the Volvo merger attempt had been a disaster,

Renault's CEO, Louis Schweitzer, decided to create a strategic alliance with Nissan. Renault would take a 36% stake in Nissan in return for taking responsibility for five and a half billion dollars of Nissan's debt.

This bid had all the hallmarks of one of many, disastrous auto industry mergers. The Japanese culture was totally different from Western companies. Nissan had been struggling to make a profit for eight years. It was losing $1000 on every car sold in the US. Even after the Renault investment, Nissan had more than $11 billion in debt. If Nissan could not be turned around quickly, it would soon cease to exist. Ghosn knew that, as a non-Nissan and non-Japanese outsider, he had little chance of successfully dictating the changes that were needed. Yet a passive approach would just allow the death spiral to continue.

When Ghosn arrived at Nissan, he found "There was a culture of blame. If the company did poorly, it was always someone else's fault. Sales blamed Product Planning. Product planning blamed Engineering. Engineering blamed Finance. Tokyo blamed Europe and Europe blamed Tokyo." These are, of course, the very characteristics of an organization suffering from the Silo Mentality, which I mentioned at the beginning of this book. Nevertheless, within a year, Nissan's fortunes had dramatically turned around. The company was making a $2.4 billion profit.

Many authors have written books about Carlos Ghosn and this transformation in particular. Each author or ghost-writer describes their own version of what happened. Most descriptions give at least brief mention of the cross-functional teams that Ghosn favoured. However, the brief descriptions of these teams were just part of the detailed description of the journey spearheaded by Ghosn. These books, like so many others on leadership and transformation, aim to help aspiring leaders to learn the magic of acting like Ghosn. However, in January 2002, Ghosn published his own article. He explained that, yes, his secret of success was indeed using cross-functional teams (CFTs) to transform the organization. He had successfully developed his technique of using CFTs in previous turnarounds that he had headed.

While this may seem interesting, it would not appear to be the magic bullet that would help to create rapid transformations. After all, most organizations have had occasion to create cross-functional teams. However, few such teams are so successful that they would be identified as the key element in transforming organizations. Nevertheless, when we look at the transformation more carefully, we see the approach, which Ghosn had developed from his experience, was remarkably similar to that of the Leadership Game. In particular, Ghosn's approach was comparable with a set of Leadership Games focused on drastically reducing unused resources in the small number of critical pathways.

In effect, Ghosn had three urgent priorities. The first was to reduce the debt burden as fast as possible. The second was to return to profitable production in the short to medium term. The third was to ensure increased sales in the medium to long term. However, as well as understanding how to set up and use CFT's, Ghosn had one other advantage. He had all the benchmark costs for almost everything – from Renault's turnaround. In effect, these were a complete set of benchmarks needed for success. So both he and the teams could assess the cost gap between Nissan and Renault for every aspect of the business. It was this comparison that soon uncovered the fact that a significant part of Nissan's woes lay with the cost of unused resources. For example, many plants were running at barely above 50% capacity. Similarly, because of the Japanese approach called keiretsu, Nissan had more than $4billion invested in hundreds of other companies. In effect, this was cash not used to directly create value. In fact, Ghosn could see that, by disposing of non-core assets, Nissan could quickly halve its debt. However, he also knew the drastic changes needed, had to come from within the company, rather than from top-down orders. So, he set up nine cross-functional teams.

These were focused on:

- Business development
- Purchasing
- Manufacturing and Logistics
- Research and Development
- Sales and Marketing
- General and Administration
- Finance and Cost
- Parts complexity
- Organizational structure

In effect, these were nine connected Leadership Games. In brief, Ghosn gave the Manufacturing and Logistics CFT the goal of improving the utilisation of Japanese assembly plants from 53% to 82% in three years – (closing five plants). However, to ensure they closed the right plants, he included all the senior managers involved in the manufacturing and delivery pathway. These included executives from manufacturing, logistics, product planning and human resources.

Ghosn also quickly saw that Nissan's cost of parts was over 20% greater than Renault's. This was partly due to the number of different suppliers and parts. It was also partly due to the under-utilisation of Nissan's own parts plants. So he set up two different CFT's. The first focused on reducing the number of suppliers by 50% and costs by 20% over three years. Again, traditionally, this would be a project for the purchasing department.

However, this team consisted of executives from purchasing, engineering, manufacturing and finance. These were the executives who were involved in the parts pathway. The other CFT had to reduce the number of Japanese part plants from seven to four. It had to reduce the number of Japanese platforms from 24 to 15. Finally, it had to reduce the variations in parts (for example because of different engines) by 50%. Most departments of the organization were involved in this pathway. So, the CFT for this part of the parts pathway consisted of executives from product planning, sales and marketing, manufacturing, engineering, finance, purchasing.

However, this was not just a cost-cutting exercise. Nissan's models were all out-of-date. In other words, the new product pathway, from concept to delivery, was not effective. So, Ghosn gave this pathway the name of Business Development. He then gave that CFT the target of launching 22 new models within two years. The traditional approach would have been a sequential set of stages, starting with design and ending with manufacture. However, this CFT consisted of executives from product planning, engineering, manufacturing, sales and marketing. In other words, these were all the managers who would be in control of the various stages in the pathway to launch a model. The difference here is that all the managers in the pathway were controlling all the planned coordination along the whole pathway.

The other CFT's were all focused on the performance of other pathways in the same way. All teams were "given three months to review the company's operations and come up with recommendations for returning Nissan to profitability and for uncovering opportunities for future growth." Each CFT consisted of ten middle managers. However, "each team formed a set of sub-teams consisting of CFT members and other managers selected by the CFT. For example, the manufacturing team had four sub-teams for capacity, productivity, fixed costs and investments. In total, some 500 people worked in CFTs." In other words, there was a hierarchy of Leadership Games.

Within three months, Ghosn had a turnaround plan developed by Nissan's own executives. They were the teams that would have to carry out their own plans. In fact, the teams remained an integral part of Nissan's management structure. Even though the plans meant plant closures and staff layoffs, Ghosn considered that both he and his CFTs "had the trust of employees." This was because "We showed them respect and always careful to protect Nissan's identity and dignity as a company."

There are several points we can learn from this case study. Nissan had been trying to control costs by focusing on the direct costs of manufacture. As a proxy for direct costs, they had focused everyone on reducing the time taken to manufacture components and cars. In their earlier days, when all their factories had been working at full capacity, this had been a successful approach in both reducing costs and increasing capacity. However, as they opened additional factories worldwide, utilisation rates fell. So costs per car increased. Had they been continually monitoring the trend in the total cost of each car sold, the situation would have been very different. It would have become obvious, much earlier that they needed to make changes to ensure total costs per car remained competitive. In reality, as the managers expanded Nissan into other countries to meet the demand, there was no control of unused resources in Japan.

Most organizations have methods to try to control quality and service response time. Such organizations will also have a top-down approach to reducing overall costs. Yet few organizations have ways of consistently monitoring and reducing unused resources. Yet, if they regularly monitored unused resources, then organizations would rarely need dramatic turnarounds and mass redundancies.

This is a lesson we will review in the final chapter when we look at how all organizations could work to ensure future success. In other words, it is in everyone medium-term interest to continually help balance resources with demand. Without resources being consistently balanced to variable demand, sooner or later, organizations will get into the type of problem that needs major and painful surgery.

## Benchmark comparisons

As we saw, one of the advantages that Ghosn had was benchmarks for every part of Nissan's business. In some types of organization, information on external benchmarks of excellence is freely available. In such cases, it should always be used as the basis of the relevant Leadership Games. However, in vertically focused organizations, the typical internal response to external comparisons is often to justify the gap. These are likely to include justifications such as: "We are a small organization", "We are a large organization", "We work in a different area of the county" "We have different customers", "We have older equipment". These reasons may or may not contribute to a gap. However, what is important is the people, who can potentially affect the gap, start to monitor whether the gap is increasing or decreasing. Then, they need to account for any changes that could reduce the gap. Once people focus on the process of reducing the gaps and see their success, they will soon forget the excuses.

However, what happens when benchmark comparison data is not available? How can we start to identify the level of unused resource? For example, what could Nissan have to be doing in the previous years, without benchmark data? This is the question we look at in more detail in the next chapters of this book.

## Summary

In this chapter, we have looked at how we can use the Leadership Game to control a factor that is critical to the efficiency of delivering services. That is the control of unused resources. We have seen that, to preserve excellence in efficiency, resources need to be consistently balanced with demand, while unused resources in one service pathway need to be shared with other pathways. We have seen that failing to have a robust protocol for consistently delivering the most effective balance, is likely to take organizations down the pathway of progressive degradation and eventual demise.

# Chapter 11

## Mapping the big picture

### Review and overview

We have previously seen that pathway maps enable us to achieve long-term goals, even when we consistently focus on short-term goals. In the next and final chapter, we will look at the ultimate challenge: How would a new CEO, parachuted into a large organization, use the Leadership Game to transform that organization. However, in this chapter, we are going to see how we develop more sophisticated high-level maps of the way organizations can develop winning strategies. Those are the strategies that will help them achieve their long-term goals.

### Mapping the path to long-term success

So far, we have relied on simple pathway maps of organizations to align groups to organizational goals. We have used these maps as a basis for understanding the Leadership Game. However, relying solely on maps of horizontal pathways is not enough to map the path to achieving the longer-term success of organizations. We now need to start developing more sophisticated maps, which better identify the role of the external parties in achieving the desired success.

To develop the highest level organizational maps, we first have to answer some of the most basic questions about organizations. These include questions such as: How do organizations exist? Why do they exist? What is their purpose? What makes organizations successful? How can we align everyone to help in achieving that organizational success?

### How do organizations exist?

For organizations to exist, people have to contribute either their time and/or resources to the organization. This means organizations can only work if they have the necessary contributors of those resources. The contributors may include staff, customers, investors and suppliers, to name a few. These groups are often called primary stakeholders. However, each stakeholder may cease to willingly contribute their resources, if they no longer consider they are receiving overall value in return for their contribution.

For example, customers are likely to buy from other suppliers if they feel they can gain better value elsewhere. Staff may leave an organization if there are low rates of pay and little job satisfaction. Alternatively, disenchanted staff, customers or investors may remain with an organization because they prefer the security of what they know over the fear of the unknown.

### Why do organizations exist?

Therefore, organizations exist while they provide better collective value to stakeholders than those groups could achieve without contributing to the organization. Organizations achieve this by providing goods and services that benefit from the organization's specialist knowledge and economies of scale. On the smallest scale, an organization could consist of a single person. For example, a butcher, baker or grocer may all be organizations run by a single owner. Yet those single owners can succeed by specialising in providing a specific service to customers. However, to achieve success, they have to offer advantages over the competition. Such an advantage may be the location. For example, people may shop at a corner store, because it could be more convenient than travelling to a supermarket. On the other hand, the supermarket may provide greater value as it can sell at lower prices, because of the economies of scale. As we will see, normally, organizations become more successful by creating greater value. In other words, it is in the organization's self-interest to provide the greatest value to its stakeholders, at the least cost to itself. As Adam Smith, the great 18th Century Economist said: "It is not from the benevolence of the butcher, the brewer, or the baker that we expect our dinner, but from their regard to their own interest."

### The problem with value

The problem with the concept of value is that it is like beauty. It is in the eyes, or mind, of the beholder. So someone may help run a scout or guide group, even though there is no monetary reward. The value they receive for their contribution may be purely about the satisfaction they gain from the experience. They consider the value they receive is greater than the value of the resources (their time) they are committing. Yet someone else might consider that such use of their time would provide them with no value. In that case, they would not want to "pay the price" of providing their time to the organization.

So we have to accept that whenever we use the term value, we are implicitly implying the concept of current **perceived value**. In other words, organizations need to provide value as perceived by external assessors or stakeholders. However, many different people may be looking at the same picture, yet they may all have different assessments of its value. To complicate matters further, there are many conditions that would change an individual's perception of value. For example, someone may consider they are receiving good value for money at their local supermarket. However, a new supermarket may open in the locality, selling superior products at lower prices. Almost immediately, that individual will stop considering the original supermarket is providing good value. In this example, the benchmark standard, used by the customer to assess value, is not created by either the first supermarket or the customer. It is created by the alternatives available to the customer.

We will assume that most stakeholders can choose whether they commit their resources (time, money, etc.) to a particular organization. So we will assume that to be successful, an organization needs to be meeting or exceeding the value benchmarks set by the alternatives available to the stakeholders. Throughout the preceding chapters, we have just used the term "benchmarks" for the standards each pathway needs to meet. We can now start to see that we can identify benchmarks back from the standards the organization needs to meet to provide value to its stakeholders.

So, stakeholder systems included more than just the stakeholder. They include all the other systems that affect the stakeholder's perception of the overall value they receive from the organization. In other words, they include the systems setting the benchmarks by which the stakeholder assesses value. For example, customers may be external stakeholders. However, the customer system will include the organization's competitors. That is because the competitors are setting the customer's value benchmark.

### Mapping the stakeholder systems

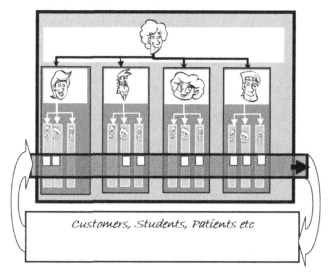

Customers, Students, Patients etc

So, as I identified earlier, this means the complete map of an organization cannot be limited to the internal workings of an organization. The full organizational map has to include the connections between the organization and its critical stakeholder systems. Those stakeholders provide resource inputs to the organization, as well as receiving benefits from the organization. So we can first map the whole organization system as in the diagram below:

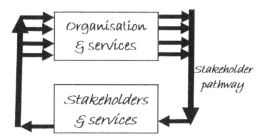

### What does the organization need from stakeholders?

Often, management theory focuses on what the organization should provide to stakeholders. For example, many approaches assume that success depends on improved customer service or better quality products. However, for the Leadership Game, it is far more useful to start at the reverse view. This view starts by asking, "What does the organization need *from* the stakeholders, to be successful?" For example, to be successful, the organization may need some or all the following services from its customers:

- Repeat orders from existing customers
- Maximum number of possible orders (that is sole supplier status)
- Customers prepared to pay a premium for higher value products or services
- Recommendations to other potential customers
- Orders from new customers

The more that customers value the organization's services, the more likely the organization will be able to get the services it needs from its customers. In other words, in general, the reason that organizations try to satisfy customers is because that is the way the organization is most likely to obtain what it needs from customers. So the information, which we need to group to provide a context, in the first stage of the GAME loop, includes what the organization needs from its stakeholders to be successful. That helps gives a purpose for everyone to collaborate to provide the maximum value to those stakeholders.

### What does the organization need to provide?

So everyone in the organization should understand that the organization needs services from customers. This helps staff and managers see why services have to meet the benchmarks standards. After all, customers will only provide those services, if they are gaining significantly higher value from the organization, in comparison to other sources. This means that we could ask all the groups in the organization to identify those interactions between the customer and organization that would affect the customer's perception. For example, for an airline, there may be many such interactions. These would include the booking process, check-in, promptness of departure and arrival, various aspects of cabin service, provision of information, as well as identifying the price of the flight.

### Moments of truth

These interactions have become known as "moments of truth". This is from the book written by Carl Janson. As a new chief executive, He transformed an ailing, national airline. The airline previously had a terrible reputation for the quality of service, lateness and reliability. The reputation was so bad that the only way they could attract passengers was by massively discounting the price of seats. The new chief executive arranged for all the staff to attend a training program that would rapidly turn around the fortunes of the organization. The program showed how it was possible for staff to change customer's perception of the airline, so travellers would consider the airline as their first choice, even if they had to pay full price.

The programme showed there were many "moments of truth" that could affect the passenger's perception of the value they received from the airline. Every connection a member of staff had with a passenger was a moment of truth. Every time a flight left on-time was a moment of truth. Every time a passenger heard someone else talking about the airline, was a moment of truth. So it was the responsibility of everyone in the organization to do everything in their power, to help create favourable moments of truth. These were the moments that helped develop travellers' views that this should always be their first choice of airline. Once the airline achieved that result, they could fill their flights with passengers paying full price for their seats. Once all the staff focused on that common goal, the reputation and the fortunes of the airline were transformed.

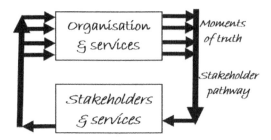

The point to remember is the organization based the programme on what the airline needed from its customers. It needed passengers to make the airline their first choice, even if they had to pay full price for their seats. We can apply the same principle to the context of every Leadership Game.

### Win-Win psychological contracts

The purpose here is to aim to ensure that every connection between the organization and its stakeholders helps create a win-win contract. As we saw in previous chapters, that contract is the psychological contract, rather than a legal one. For example, the relationship between a supermarket and its customers is likely to be strongest when there is a perceived win-win nature to that relationship. In that state, customers feel they win because they receive better value from that supermarket than they receive from competitors. The supermarket wins because it sells more items at more than it costs the supermarket to buy and process items. So groups could map a customer pathway and identify all the moments of truth along the pathway, which could affect the customer's perception.

### Value leverage

So, for organizations to thrive, they need to create outputs, which are perceived as a greater value than the value consumed by obtaining the necessary inputs. For example, in simple terms, commercial organizations can measure the value of their outputs by the value of their income. So to thrive, they need to ensure they have a greater income from the services they provide than the cost of resources used to achieve those sales. Typically, we call that difference the profit or contribution. However, as we will see in this and the final chapter, for the Leadership Game, there is another relationship. That relationship is more important than the simple difference between the totals of these two values. It is the value of inputs needed to produce a set value of outputs (e.g. the cost of producing a set income, or a set number of products). Or, to be more precise, it is the predictable trend of the ratio that is important.

For example, in the previous airline example, we can assume that over a relatively short period, the income from travellers increased as more travellers paid full price for their tickets. We can also assume the total costs, including staff costs, remained at roughly the same level. Thus there would be a reduction in both total costs and staff costs to every £1000 of income, even though the total staff cost remained the same. Described in yet another way, every £1 of staff cost would be creating more value, as measured by income, for the services provided. We are going to call this ratio, the **Value Leverage** of a resource. As the value of the consumed inputs increases per unit of output, the value leverage decreases. In effect, value leverage is a form of measure of cost-effectiveness. However, the trend of the cost per unit is only useful if we can assume that the quality is not affected. A reduction in cost does not improve the value leverage if it is achieved by reducing the quality of the product or service.

## Value leverage trends

The reason, the resource value leverage is of particular interest in Leadership Games, is because the trend of value leverage is a useful predictor of future success or failure. For example, consider the example of Nissan, described in the previous chapter. As the utilisation of Nissan's Japanese factories progressively decreased, the value leverage of the staff and property would have also decreased. In other words, Nissan could have been checking the value leverage trend, even without Renault's benchmarks used as a comparison. The trend of the resource value leverage for all factories would have been suggesting future problems several years in advance. The value leverage at full capacity could have been the benchmark that Nissan could have been aiming for. So in simple terms, we can say that:

**The future success of an organization is likely to depend on its ability to create the greatest perceived value at the least cost**

Again, this opens a whole new area of questions we can use to engage staff and managers in creating more performance boards. We could ask these questions after a group has identified "what does the organization NEED from customers, to ensure future success". Then we could ask "What could we do, which would encourage customers to provide those services to the organization?" As staff engaged in these questions, they would be grouping the information and creating the context, which would help them take control of performance.

## Re-enforcing psychological contracts

This approach can be a powerful start to the Leadership Game. This is because, from the perspective of a single member of staff, it may seem that he or she has little control over the success of their organization. This is particularly true if they view their responsibilities solely as carrying out the requested processes. After all, the only way to be more effective would be to continually work harder. However, this perception can rapidly change as soon as groups start checking the change in value produced by their collective efforts. This is what happens when they start assessing the effectiveness of their system as the external assessors. Yet, it is possible to further improve individuals' understanding of the effect they can have on the organization's success or failure. This occurs when they better understand the effects of psychological contracts and re-enforcing cycles.

For example, the whole point of moments of truth is that the effect goes far beyond a single transaction. So, a customer may feel they have good experiences from friendly and helpful staff when they visit their local supermarket. However, that experience will slightly strengthen the psychological bond the customer has towards the supermarket. As we have seen, we call that bond the psychological contract.

Progressively, the psychological contract or bond strengthens with repeated, favourable moments of truth. The more that happens, the more that customer is likely to keep returning to that supplier rather than competitors. As the contract strengthens with repeated experiences, the customer may even pay more for what they consider as a product or service that they could buy for less from other sources. They may even recommend the supplier to others. The supplier wins, not just by receiving more than the cost of the products and services. The supplier also wins by gaining both repeat customers and new customers. As even more customers recommend the supplier, the benefits may start to increase exponentially, because even more customers are recommending the supplier. So we call this a reinforcing cycle. The early events may only achieve small changes to the strength of the psychological contract. However, those changes bring about further changes. So each cycle achieves a greater change.

### Connected Virtuous cycles

When such cycles progressively build higher perceptions of value and stronger psychological contracts, we call them virtuous cycles. Such virtuous cycles, which affect the customer experience, can allow organizations to become successful within relatively short timescales. Similarly, as we have seen in previous chapters, engaging staff, in consistently finding and removing performance gaps, can provide enormous benefits in motivation and a general sense of achievement among those staff. It can reduce costs, allowing the organization to distribute more value to the stakeholders, including staff, customers and shareholders.

So the Leadership Game can create a virtuous cycle of increased motivation among managers and staff to increase the value received by clients or customers. In turn, that can create a virtuous cycle of more loyal customers who often recommend the organization. This increased value can further strengthen the virtuous cycle creating progressively faster organic growth. Such connected cycles are potentially so powerful they can form the foundation of a strategy to create a successful future.

### Vicious cycles

Not all cycles are virtuous. In fact, vicious cycles are far more common. Organizations may try to increase profit by reducing the quality of their products. Customers desert the organization, thus reducing profit. This creates a stronger driver to reduce costs further, which often speeds up the exodus of customers. That reduces profit even further. The problem is that, with both virtuous and vicious cycles, there is typically a time delay between the cause and observable effect. So, for example, reducing quality may, for a short period increase profitability. It may seem as though it is a highly successful strategy for a while. By the time customers start deserting the supplier, the cause of the problem may well have been forgotten.

A classic example of this is Marks and Spencer in the UK. This company was once the leading clothes retailer in the UK. The founders were passionate about the quality of the clothes sold. Their customers were renowned for their loyalty to "M & S". After the founders retired, the new managers found that they could greatly increase profits by sourcing the products from the cheapest global suppliers. However, by doing that, they lost control over the quality that they gained from being close to their previous UK suppliers.

For some years, the strategy was highly successful. Profits soared. The strength of the psychological contract meant that customers kept returning, even as the quality fell. Many of the external designers used by the company then complained the company was reducing costs further by just copying their designs, without paying royalties. So the best designers looked elsewhere for customers for their services. Still, profits continued to rise, far above that ever achieved by the founders of the company. Then, suddenly, customers started deserting the store. The company had lost control, not only of the quality of the goods provided by its suppliers but the quality of the design of the clothes that its customers were looking for.

Profits slumped. One manager even publicly blamed the profit slump on the fact that "The problem is there is no customer loyalty any more." Clearly, the manager thought that is was the company's right to expect loyalty from their customers. While Marks and Spencer is, at the time of writing, still a major clothes retailer in the UK, it will probably never reclaim its title of being the pre-eminent UK clothes retailer. It would seem that even now, managers have not learnt the lessons of a virtuous cycle.

### Understanding stakeholder systems

To fully understand any stakeholder system, we need to map the related systems that will affect the stakeholder's perception of value. So, as I have previously pointed out, the customer system would need to include the organization's competitors, who are setting the value benchmarks. Similarly, we could add a system called "economic environment" to the customer stakeholder system. Clearly, if there is an economic recession, this could affect the customers' ability to buy goods or services from the organization. For example, if the organization provided luxury goods, the customer may not consider those goods a great value for money. This would happen where the customer considered food and other basics were of greater value, considering the limited resources of the customer. Equally, if the organization specialised in supplying salads to the retail market, we would need to include a system called "weather" in the customer system.

It may appear that many of the systems affecting the customer's perception of value are outside the control of the organization. However, a closer inspection shows that this is not necessarily the case. For example, as we have already seen, if a competitor starts to produce higher quality services or products, that quality standard becomes the new benchmark standard. So, well before customers start deserting the company, an organization could predict the potential crisis. This could achieve this by monitoring the gaps between the organization's standards and the standards set by its competitors. If the negative gaps are increasing, it is likely to suggest a crisis is not far away. Thus the whole organization would need to be focused on addressing such gaps.

Equally, the weather may not be in the control of the organization. However, the weather may cause variation in demand for the organization's products. So the organization has to become robust enough to deal with that variation. Understanding these relationships can initially take some effort. However, that effort can pay handsome dividends. This is particularly true when it ensures that everyone in the organization is aware of how they all have a critical part to play in the success of the organization. That understanding is a useful part of the information "grouped" when playing the Leadership Game.

However, even just identifying "the customer" as a critical system may not provide enough detail to identify the critical success gaps. We may often need to identify other critical groups within the customer system to provide the right focus for our performance systems.

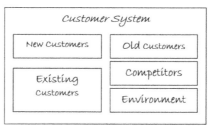

We may need to identify different systems for "current customers", "previous customers" and "potential new customers". This is because we may need different strategies for different types of customers. Even within a customer system, we may need to identify specific, critical systems within that customer system.

## Refurbishing case study

To show the reason for identifying this detail in our map, I am going to use another case study. This was a company that refurbished offices. I was asked by the directors to help them to cascade their new quality values throughout the organization. I thanked them for their invitation but explained that before I could start to help, I needed to understand exactly why they felt they needed to engage people in quality values.

They explained that until recently, they had been a very successful company. They had been very profitable and had been able to rapidly expand organically. However, recently, that had changed. They were now finding it much more difficult to win new contracts. Feedback suggested that a lack of focus on quality was the cause.

I explained that it was essential to fully understand the cause of the issues before trying to apply a cure. So I asked them to give me some background to the history of their organization. They explained that in their market, as in many other construction markets, they produced tenders quoted at cost price. The profit always came from changes and additions sought by the client while the project was in progress. Each major refurbishment had a dedicated project manager who received a bonus based on a percentage of profit.

I asked them what happened if a project manager did not make a profit. They replied that he or she would soon be dismissed. I then asked what happened if a project manager did not achieve the necessary quality standards. They explained that they would try to make clear to the project manager how important quality was because satisfied customers were essential to their business.

At this point in the discussion, one of the directors had a light bulb moment. They saw the organization had different motivators for profit and quality. Making a profit on a contract was critical to the project manager's bonus and future employment. However, achieving the quality standards was simply a "nice to have" factor. We will look in more detail at the unintended consequences of most external motivators in the final chapter. For the moment, it is important to realise that the Leadership Game creates intrinsic motivation. In general, it does not rely on extrinsic motivators. However, it does need that any external motivators are not adversely affecting whether people "play the game".

In this organization, the focus on profit was potential a contributory factor in the problems they were facing. However, the fact the bonus had always been in place, suggested the bonus alone could not explain why the company had changed from being successful in facing its current problems. After the early discussion with the small group of directors, they agreed that I should first have some informal discussions with all the directors, and some project managers. My aim was to try to identify what had changed in the last two years that could have caused the change in fortunes. During these discussions, I identified the history of the company was that it had been started by two founders. I shall call them John Cooper and Keith Plant, although these are not their real names. Both were still on the main board of directors. John Cooper was the Managing Director. However, he was soon to retire. The other directors were responsible for different regions and had all achieved previous success as project managers. Several of these area directors were competing for the post of Managing Director, which John was soon to leave.

John Cooper had previously taken an active interest in all major projects. Although, over the last eighteen months, he had been progressively withdrawing from his hands-on role in projects. Nevertheless, he was still universally disliked and feared by the other directors and project managers. They all considered him as a "loose cannon". This was because he would turn up unannounced on a site and start screaming at the project manager if he felt the site was not to the necessary standards. Somehow, he had the knack of immediately identifying those areas of the refurbishment that were not to the highest standards. These outbursts on these visits were known among project managers as being "Cooperised". Project Managers dreaded the thought of an inspection by John and did everything possible to avoid being Cooperised. Almost everyone was looking forward to John Cooper's imminent retirement.

Keith Plant, on the other hand, was popular, at least among the other directors and successful project managers. He was the commercial director of the organization. He judged directors on their ability to produce profits for the company. He would be a key player in choosing John's replacement. He believed in "empowerment" of the directors and project managers, as long as their projects and areas were highly profitable. It soon became clear to me that fear of Cooperisation had previously been the balancing motivation that ensured quality standards were achieved as well as profitability. As John had progressively withdrawn from inspecting the progress of projects, the easier it had been to increase short term profits by cutting corners and ignoring quality. However, I was not convinced that simply providing a balancing motivator, to improve quality, would necessarily allow the company to be as successful as it had previously been. There was another piece of the jigsaw that was still missing. Currently, the company was quoting for the same level of enquiries as they had before their decline in fortunes. The problem was that they were failing to win the tenders on an increasing number of those proposals.

So I arranged a session with the directors, to try to identify what might be causing the relatively rapid drop in successful bids. In the meeting, I handed the directors a set of pre-printed A4 sheets. These sheets had the headings for:

- Project contract date (approximate)
- Project Name
- Area Director
- Customer
- Names and roles of key decision makers
- Key reasons for the bid being accepted/rejected
- Competitors

John Cooper was on holiday, so could not attend the meeting. However, the purpose of the exercise was to allow all the directors to group the necessary information to develop a "bigger" picture of all projects, rather than just their own. So, in the session, I asked the directors to complete a sheet their most recent project quotes, whether the bid had been successful. Then each one, in turn, took their sheet and used Blue Tac to place the sheet on the wall. They then briefly described the key factors of the project. We continually rearranged the sheets to ensure they were in date order. Once all the early sheets were up, I asked them if any patterns were starting to emerge.

One pattern was the reason most often stated for rejection was "poor quality". The role "customer" was a stakeholder role that was on the sheet. However, there was little duplication of names of the customers. The other role that did occur on all sheets was "surveyor". Sometimes, the name of the same surveyor appeared on several project bids. This role was the surveyor employed by potential customers to both assess the detailed proposals and ensure the project was completed to the standard in the proposal.

I now asked the directors to create a new set of sheets for their previous most recent project proposals. They again started to individually put up details of their projects with a brief verbal description. This was rapidly repeated for several cycles. To my surprise, the sequence of accepted bids still did not seem to be based on repeat business from satisfied customers. This was because, once a customer had had an office block refurbished, it could be some time before they needed another refurbishment. However, as the next round of projects progressed, a clear pattern was emerging.

The surveyor's role continued to be a key figure in the acceptance process. Also, more of the same surveyor names were appearing on more of the sheets. The reasons the area directors had not seen this relationship before was the surveyor's projects were often in different areas, under different directors and for different customers. So as far as each director was concerned, each project had a different surveyor.

Also, the area directors had failed to appreciate the crucial role played by John Cooper, when he was taking an active role in all major projects. John knew the importance of the role of the customer's surveyor. This was because he was involved in all projects and so would immediately realise when the same surveyor was involved in a new contract. John had always repeated that it was important to keep the customer's surveyor happy. However, the importance of this fact was never fully understood by the project managers and other directors. Simply "telling them" had not changed their mental models. The key drivers of their mental models were making the most profit and avoiding Cooperisation.

In the past, surveyors had often made complaints to John Cooper, that a project manager was not taking their concerns seriously. When that happened, John would make sure he knew of all the issues that were concerning the surveyor. That way, John knew exactly where to look when he was on site. He would then Cooperise the project manager to make sure the manager immediately made the necessary improvements. The Surveyors knew that they could always contact John to get issues remedied quickly. This ensured that they felt "in-control" of the projects and were almost always satisfied with the result. It was this that made them recommend the company to their future customers. This was the key factor in preserving the virtuous cycle on which the company's previous success had been build.

As we have seen, a key aspect the Leadership Game is to be able to map the flows in an organization and the gaps in those flows. Vicious and Virtuous cycles are an important part of those flows. Managers and staff need to understand the critical gaps in such cycles, which are crucial to successfully achieving the desired future. Once they understand those points, they quickly see how small changes can bring about disproportionate consequences.

In this example, the changes were trivial. The first was that, on completion of the project, the customer's surveyor was asked to respond to a survey. The first question was "On a scale of 0-10, how likely are you to recommend us to your future clients?" The customer was also asked to fill in a satisfaction score sheet. These assessments would affect the Project Managers' bonuses. Previously the bonuses had been based solely on the profitability of the projects. Now, they would only be paid in full, if the surveyor's score and customer's score were 8 or above. In effect, these small changes replaced the need for Cooperisation to ensure the surveyor's enthusiasm for using the company in future projects. So in this example, the customer system involved more than just the customer, the competition and the environment. The surveyor was a critical stakeholder and so had to be included in the customer system.

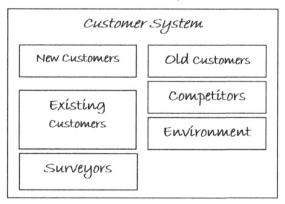

At first sight, this solution looks very different from the case studies in previous chapters. However, further investigation shows the likenesses. The large bonus ensured project managers were accountable for profit. Cooperisation, preserved quality standards, even though it was unpopular and contrary to almost any published ideas on "good" management.

So what was previously a virtuous cycle, had become a vicious cycle. The more surveyors became dissatisfied with the company's work, the more difficult it was to get new business. The solution was simple. It was to ensure the project managers were continually assessing the project as the external assessor. However, the directors only started to see who was the critical external assessor, once they had developed the "big picture" map of the pathway connections.

## Reward systems

There is another factor we can learn from this case study. That is the unintended consequences of external motivators and reward systems. From most of the previous case studies, it should be clear the Leadership Game does not rely on rewards to motivate groups to improve performance. The game inherently creates the motivation to collaborate. Indeed, reward systems for individuals can adversely affect the motivation to collaborate. In effect, they create the rules of a game that encourages competition. Even group rewards often create unintended consequences. I could fill a book with examples of such rewards. However, it will be enough to outline just a few examples to explain the point.

In one example, I found a reward system where everyone in the unit was given an extra half-day holiday if the unit beat the overall productivity measure of the previous month. The aim was to consistently improve productivity. However, all that happened was that one month, the unit would exceed the previous month's productivity level. The next month, when everyone took their extra leave, productivity would be terrible. However, that made it an easy target to beat on the following month. So productivity for the year fell.

In another example, one of my delegates explained that, as

far as he was concerned, having graphs of performance did not work. He explained that he was responsible for a large fleet of delivery drivers and vans. He had sent every driver on a course to learn how to drive in a way that minimised fuel consumption. To provide an extra incentive, each group of drivers had a notice board with graphs of their individual fuel consumption performance. He explained the graphs certainly had a motivational effect. All the drivers started competing to see who could use the **most** fuel per journey. He had set up the graphs to create competition. This has nothing to do with the approach of the Leadership Game. It is using graphs from a vertical perspective.

Another problem caused by reward systems is that they often focus on a single, easily measurable, performance indicator. That indicator will be either quality or availability or cost (efficiency). So people will focus on improving that one performance indicator, to gain the reward. However, they are likely to achieve that standard at the expense of the criteria that are not being measured. For example, if people are rewarded for the number of parts they produce, they may stop focusing on the quality they are producing.

Of course, in many organizations reward systems are an integral part of the wages package. To ensure that these do not adversely affect the success of the Leadership Games, we need to remember just one point, which we identified previously. People should always be able to win, just by playing the Leadership Game. They only lose by not playing. It is the latter part of that rule that is important. In other words, people should not be able to receive rewards by not playing the game. We will look at the practical application of this in the final chapter. For the moment, we need to return to creating high-level maps of the organization.

## Customers, recipients and demand systems

When we are building such high-level maps, we need to understand the clear differences between various types of stakeholders. For example, there is often confusion between the customer systems and the systems that represent the recipients of the organization's services. In the Leadership Game, the customer system is the system that pays for the organization's services. The recipient system is the system that directly receives the services. In the supermarket example, these are both the same. However, there are many examples where they are not the same.

For example, in the UK, there is a probation service. The purpose of the service is to work with offenders, who have been released from prison, to try to stop them reoffending. At one of my master classes, a delegate from the probation service approached me to discuss a problem he had. He explained the service was trying to implement Total Quality Management. Their major problem was trying to measure the quality of the interactions with their "clients", who were the offenders. They were trying to measure quality by creating a feedback questionnaire from the offenders. However, they were struggling to identify suitable questions.

I asked him "Who are the customers for your organization's services?" Thinking it was a silly question, he politely explained that they did not have customers, they had clients. These were the offenders. To make my point, I asked him "Who pays for the services you provide?" Slightly exasperated, he explained the obvious. The government paid for the services and thus indirectly the taxpayer. I explained that in that case, the government and taxpayer are the customers for the service because they are the ones paying for the service. I continued to ask "What does the customer expect, in return for paying for the service?" He replied the government would expect the reoffending rate would be lower, because of the interventions of the probation service. I then asked whether he agreed the customer's assessment, of the quality of the service they were paying for, would be the degree to which reoffending was reduced. He agreed but said "Yes, but the reoffending rate is not a quality measure. It is just one of the many Key Performance Indicators we have."

I explained that "quality" meant "fit for purpose". The entity passing through the service pathway was the offender. At the end of that pathway, the measure of whether the offender had become fit-for-purpose would be whether he or she could work in society without reoffending. So, the reoffending rate was the same as the defect rate in, for example, manufacturing.

This is the type of misunderstanding that occurs when people try to implement initiatives developed in other industries. Without a clear model of the stakeholders and contracts, people cannot translate the model into one that is relevant to their own organization. In a psychological contract, the people paying for a service expect the service provided to meet certain standards that provide the value needed. The service has to be "fit for that purpose". The degree to which it is achieving that purpose is a measure of quality from the customer's viewpoint.

### Demand systems

This does not mean the quality of service relates only to customers, or the stakeholder paying for the service. For example, in the UK, there is a system of further education for 16 to 18 year-olds. The education is paid for by the government and the taxpayer. However, further education is not compulsory. So students can choose whether or not they enrol for further education. They can choose which college of further education to attend. Equally, they can choose whether to complete their studies or to drop out of the system. So, although they are not paying for the service, it is the students who are the critical demand stakeholder.

This means that colleges need to develop and preserve strong psychological contracts with their students. The more perceived value provided to the student, the stronger the psychological contract is likely to become. The higher the perceived value, the more likely prospective students will want to enrol with the college. The stronger the contract, the more likely students are to stay with the college potentially, achieving higher levels of qualifications. So the quality of services provided to students is likely to be critical to the future success of the college.

Besides, in simple terms, colleges are paid by the government for the number of students attending. The government regulator OFSTED assesses the quality of the colleges' services. A report stating the college is failing could lead to the closure of the college. A report, stating the college is "Outstanding", is likely to encourage prospective students to enrol. So OFSTED is also a critical stakeholder affecting the level of demand. It is a stakeholder that could be a part of the marketing strategy of the college to enrol more students. Yet few college managers or lecturers perceive OFSTED in this manner. Managers and lecturers often see inspections as something to dread and with unpredictable results.

### The challenge of multiple, stakeholders

Another challenge faced by many managers, particularly in public services, is that they have to meet the demands of multiple stakeholders. For example, in local government, a project may affect local residents, council tenants and various councillors representing different areas and political persuasions. The same type of problem occurs when developing new IT systems, or for any new project. Often, it is very difficult to get people to define exactly what they want before a project starts. However, the same people will soon complain if the completed project does not meet their standards.

In this environment, it is usually worth spending time before the project starts to classify the success criteria and their benchmarks. At first, most managers find, even the prospect of doing this very scary. Yet it is usually possible to get some form of consensus fairly quickly. In effect, we use the same approach as described in many of the case studies. Ideally, we get the various stakeholders in the same room. We ask them to imagine what the outcome from hell would look like, writing each standard on a sticky note. We then get the group to categorise their ideas as previously described. We then ask them to do the same for the outcome from utopia.

Once these have also been categorised, we start the next stage. Each success criteria will have both a standard from hell and a standard from utopia. So each hell standard is given a number. Then, for each hell criteria, the group then try to identify if there is an existing utopia description, which describes the other extreme of the same criteria. In effect, they are building up a set of success criteria, with hell and utopia descriptions for each. Depending on the nature of the group, one or more people have to be accountable for each criterion. They need to take the information and formalise it in a way that will get the buy-in from the entire group. Such presentations need to define the criterion, what good and bad look like, and how they could achieve success for that criterion.

While this may take several iterations, it is usually better to spend the time to address differences at the beginning of the project, rather than after it is too late. Once you finally have a list of success criteria, with clear hell and utopia descriptions, the description can be used to guide the whole project team in understanding what is, and what is not acceptable. They may not be able to reach the utopian standard. However, they should be able to agree on the benchmarks that are needed for the project to be a success. In principle, there may be champions for each criterion. Those champions are responsible for consistently assessing ideas and progress as external assessors of that criterion.

The point here is we can take the same approach, whether the challenge is to transform an organization or to develop a new IT system. The more specific information about the success criteria at the highest level challenge, the easier it is to align the various Leadership Games and teams involved in the related sub-projects.

## Mapping the whole journey

We can now start to bring together all these various aspects of mapping, to enable us to develop a set of high-level maps of the organization. We achieve this by mapping the answers to a series of questions. These high-level maps should provide anyone with a clear view of where the organization is going and what it needs to do to get there.

So we can start by mapping the answers to the following questions:

- Where have we come from?

- Where are we now?

- Where do we want to be?

The answers to these three questions enable us to map our journey.

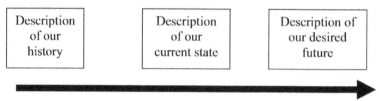

As we will see in the next two chapters, having a description of the desired future is not always as simple as it may sound. However, for the moment, we will assume that the organization does have a clear goal. So, to see what changes we need to make, to achieve that goal, we need to map the answers to another set of questions

### What Business are we in?

We need to start with a description of the services that we currently provide, or will provide in the future: Often, organizations describe this in part of their mission statement. For example, the aircraft manufacturer Airbus has the mission statement:

"Airbus is an international pioneer in the aerospace industry. We are a leader in designing, manufacturing and delivering aerospace products, services and solutions to customers on a global scale. We aim for a better-connected, safer and more prosperous world."

So their high-level service is "designing, manufacturing and delivering aerospace products, services and solutions". That could immediately be split into service pathways for every different product, service or solution.

### *What is the critical expertise required for our business?*

For high-level mapping, we should also define the critical expertise needed, if it is not obvious from the service description. For example, although it is rarely stated, banks are in the business of managing risk. Whenever they provide loans to lenders, there is always a potential risk of default. Such defaults will affect the security of the money provided by investors and lenders.

The financial crash of 2007 was primarily caused because banks ignored risk. This was because senior executives thought they were just in the business of making short-term profits. They often removed the risk assessment from their service pathways, to increase revenue. The consequences, of "forgetting" the critical expertise of the business they were in, were catastrophic. As we will see in the following chapters, the consequences, of an aircraft manufacturer forgetting the expertise of providing aircraft capable of safe air travel, are also catastrophic.

### *What inputs do we need to provide our services?*

Clearly, many organizations will need a set of inputs that will include:

- Revenue to finance the operations
- Demand/orders for services
- Skilled and motivated staff
- Materials

### *Which stakeholders will provide those inputs?*

This list will typically include:

- Customers
- Investors

- Suppliers
- Staff

## What services do we need from each stakeholder?

The services an organization needs from external stakeholders obviously include such items as orders and payment from customers and investment from investors. These are the services from the external stakeholder that will supply the inputs required by the organization.

## What do we need to supply to the stakeholders?

In other words, we should map the services that we need to supply to each of the stakeholders, so they supply the services needed by the organization. As explained earlier, everyone in the organization needs to understand the reason organizations supply services is to ensure the organization continues to receive the inputs it needs to survive and thrive.

## Who are the other groups in the stakeholder systems?

We need to know who the other organizations are that are setting the benchmark standards for the services. These are the standards we need to meet or exceed if the stakeholders are to provide us with the services we need. We have seen the groups that are likely to set these standards are competitors and inspection bodies. Again, it is important that everyone in the organization understands the service benchmarks are set externally. If we do to meet or exceed these standards, the critical stakeholders will get their services from elsewhere. The organization could cease to receive the inputs it needs to survive.

## What are the service benchmarks of excellence?

Where possible, we need to find out what standards are being set by groups like competitors. That is why supermarket chains consistently monitor the prices of competitive supermarkets.

### Grouping the information

The reason we need to map the answers to these questions is that is part of the high-level group of information that everyone in the organization needs to understand to have a "big" picture of the organization. Once developed, such maps should ideally be simple enough to only take a few minutes to present. Similarly, anyone in the organization should be able to present or account for them. The more people account for the high-level maps, the more that group of information becomes established in people's minds.

## Summary

We saw in previous chapters that engaging people in Leadership Games starts with grouping all the relevant, higher level information. Ideally, this information should give people a clear view of the various stakeholder systems and how they relate to organizational success. By itself, this will not create change. However, when all Leadership Games are based on this same high-level map, it enables people to feel an integral part of the organizational challenge. It gives them a common language by which they can relate their various actions. We have also seen in this chapter that understanding the reinforcing cycles, which involve critical stakeholder systems, can greatly assist managers in targeting their efforts. Finally, we saw how it was possible to map the big picture of the organization.

# Chapter 12

## Creating the persistent dual structure

### Review and overview

In chapter one, I explained that despite its drawbacks, the vertical structure was still the most successful of all management approaches. This was because it was simple, powerful and structural. We can consider the management hierarchy as focused on coordinating the resources needed to deliver services. Those services may be internal or external. Often, the management structure has a second duty of improving performance. It typically focuses on improving people's performance by cascading performance targets. However, simply improving individual performance does not necessarily translate into overall performance improvement. Unfortunately, as we have seen, the vertical structure also encourages silo mentality. That often makes it slow and difficult to engage individuals in collaborating to improve organizational performance.

We have seen the horizontal approach of the Leadership Game is also simple, fast and powerful. It has two parts. On the one hand, there is the GAME board of the pathway system performance. This shows the evidence of success in removing a system capability gap. On the other hand, there is a group of peers currently working in the silos of the horizontal service pathway. This is the group that has the potential to remove the capability gap. To transform silo mentality into a culture of high-performance teams, all we need to do is to bring these two parts together. We can achieve that by ensuring each group is responsible for playing the game. The fail-safe, which ensures success, is that the group are responsible for accounting for the evidence on the game board.

However, if this approach is to match the success of the vertical hierarchy, it needs to have a persistent, horizontal structure of responsibilities. This becomes even more important for large, complex organizations. The vertical and horizontal structures have to work in unison, in the same way as they do in a relay team. So, in the final two chapters, we will see how to install persistent, horizontal structures. We will see how this can enable even large organizations to rapidly and consistently adapt and improve.

Although we will look at transforming whole organizations, we can use the same approach at any level. In other words, a divisional director or a section manager could set up a persistent twin structure, just within their local area of authority. So the principles could be equally applicable to all levels of management.

## Is it worth the effort?

However, before we examine how to embed the horizontal structure into all or part of an organization, we need to satisfy ourselves that it is worth the effort. After all, we have seen how powerful the Leadership Game is in addressing all types of issues as they arise. We have also seen how simple it is to use. So we could only use the Leadership Game whenever we needed it. The problem with using ad-hoc Leadership Games is that we have to set up each game individually. Unfortunately, it often takes a crisis to motivate managers to trigger the use of the Leadership Game. In other words, it is used to solve issues after they have caused problems. It is not being used to naturally adapt and improve in a way that will prevent such problems occurring. Nor is it being used to consistently make the changes needed for future success. Yet these are the characteristics we need if we are to overcome the weaknesses of the vertical structure.

In effect, vertical focused organizations are built to deliver the products or services needed today. They are not designed to naturally and consistently adapt to the changing environment in which they operate. Nor are they built to inherently absorb and use all the best ideas. They are not designed to continually improve to meet the demand for even higher standards of services. Indeed, they are not even designed to align the whole organization to a common goal. So, inevitably, vertical organizations go through cycles. They may become successful. Then as other organizations use more effective ways of delivering value, they start to become less successful. Gradually they start to decline.

We have seen how managers can then suffer from "boiled frog syndrome". This is where the variation in the performance figures masks the adverse trends. So managers see no reason to change. We have seen how they will often reject information from above or outside, which may show the problem. The downhill slide often continues, until either the organization fails or faces such a crisis that a new leader takes over and transforms the organization. And so the cycle starts to repeat.

Indeed, even when vertical based organizations seem to be performing successfully, downfall can sometimes be abrupt. This is because managers are often making decisions based on past performance information. We have compared this to driving a car by only looking through the rear-view mirror. In those circumstances, they often seem blissfully unaware of clearly predictable crises in front of them.

In comparison, the horizontal structure is specifically focused on continually bringing about effective change. It is focused on consistently optimising organizational capability to meet the benchmarks that are critical to its success. It also continually aims to predict and avoid preventable issues. Also, the structure of Leadership Games helps ensure that all the players are accounting for the way they are helping the organization achieve the common goal. So there is an overwhelming case for combining the permanent vertical structure with a persistent horizontal structure.

### The common goal

We have seen that horizontal structures align the relevant groups to a common goal. So obviously, if we are to achieve that at an organizational level, there first has to be a persistent, organizational goal. Unfortunately, as I mentioned in the previous chapter, identifying a long-term goal is not as simple as it might seem. In theory, if there is a vision statement, that should describe where the organization needs to be in the future. However, there are many different, conflicting definitions and uses of vision and mission statements. Sometimes a vision statement will describe the desired future state of the organization. This could be in terms of "to become number one". Alternatively, it could describe a future state of the desired environment created by the organization. This could be in terms of "A world without hunger". In practice, particularly in commercial organizations, such vision and mission statements are often not related to the direction the chief executive is guiding the organization. There are several reasons for this.

One reason is that some years ago, it was noticed that many successful organizations had vision and mission statements. Many business authors saw this as a key factor in aligning organizations to a common goal. Often they quoted from Alice in Wonderland. In those excerpts, Alice is at a crossroads. A Cheshire cat is looking from a nearby tree. Alice asks "I was just wondering if you could help me find my way." The Cheshire cat replied: "Well, that depends on where you want to get to." Alice says it doesn't matter. So the cat replied, "Then it really doesn't matter which way you go."

The benefit of having a vision seemed obvious. So many vertical based organizations decided to copy the idea of having a vision statement. Executives crafted vision statements and displayed them on notices all over the organization. Yet, predictably, this had little effect on aligning the organization. Anyway, we have seen the main purpose of having a long-term goal is to help to plan a route. In chapter four, we saw that, once we have a route with milestones along the way, everyone can continually use the information to help in constantly making short-term decisions. So, it is pointless to have a vision, which is not actively used to plan a route or to consistently check whether the short-term decisions are consistent with the mission and vision statements.

Even worse, vision and mission statements often conflict with the real direction of the organization. Jason, a colleague of mine, explained one such example to me. The chief executive had asked him to help align the organization. When Jason asked if the company had vision and mission statements, the chief executive explained that he had told his senior management team to craft suitable statements. Jason expressed concern because he knew all the top executives had to own these statements. However, the chief executive explained that he would fully "buy into" the vision that his team was developing. The final versions described a utopian, environmentally friendly organization mission and future vision. So Jason ran his first session with all the senior executives. He went through the vision and mission statements, phrase by phrase. He explained that each phrase describes one of the aspects guiding how the organization should operate and where it needed to be. So, for each phrase, he engaged the group in identifying how to measure their progress towards achieving that state. However, as the session progressed, it became clear the chief executive was becoming more and more irritated. Finally, he exploded. He stood up and said "Let's be clear. The job of this group is to increase profitability. This is a total waste of time." He then walked out.

The important point here is that, if there is to be a vision, it needs to be a genuine description of where senior executives are consistently focusing the organization. However, even then, there is another problem with vision statements. This occurs when senior executives just follow leadership tips from management gurus, without understanding the psychology. For example, Jack Welch was a well known chief executive of General Electric. He published his view that leadership starts when you show people "where you are going, what your dream is, where you are going to be". So he said it was important for any chief executive to rewrite the organization's vision. In principle, this may seem perfectly reasonable. After all, if the chief executive develops the vision, then presumably he or she genuinely owns that vision. The problem with this approach was highlighted by one of my delegates. She explained that in the previous two years, her organization had had three different chief executives. Each one had started their tenure by re-writing the vision statement. The delegate asked me how you could align the organization when the vision changes every few months. Clearly, if the goal is constantly changing, it is going to be very difficult to align the organization to a common goal. So, in the cases where there is not a stable long term organizational goal, how can we align everyone to a common goal?

Fortunately, there is an alternative solution to overcoming the problem of long-term goals. To understand that solution, let us start by again mapping the high-level organizational pathway, which we looked at in the previous chapter.

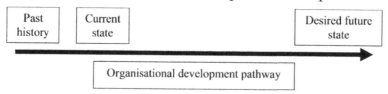

This path seems to need a definition of the long-term goal. However, the time we take to achieve that goal depends on more than just the effectiveness of the route or pathway to our final destination. It also depends on our capability to travel along that pathway as effectively as possible. The higher the capability to travel along the route, the faster we are likely to arrive at our chosen destination. In other words, our priority is to ensure the organization can transform and adapt as effectively as possible. This means that an early milestone on that journey is to have the capability to rapidly develop all critical services, so they meet the benchmark standards needed for future success.

The way we can achieve this is to develop a persistent structure for Leadership Games. We can focus those games on "achieving services of excellence." That could be a constant, common goal, almost irrespective of the long-term goal.

However, there could be an informal, generic long-term goal. This could simply be "To become one of the best organizations (or division, department or section) in our class".

So, for the moment, we will focus just on the pathway from the current organizational state, to the state with a permanent horizontal structure of Leadership Games. This is the state that enables the organization to travel the pathway to any desired future, in the shortest possible time. Therefore our first challenge is to understand how we create that structure.

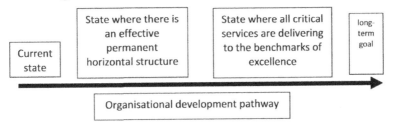

## *Explicit dual structure and responsibilities*

As I have mentioned several times, when managers set performance targets in vertical organizations, it implicitly implies that everyone has two responsibilities. If we are to integrate a horizontal approach, we now need to make that implicit dual responsibility explicit.

The vertical structure is created by the relationship between functional managers and subordinates. In simple terms, the "rule" of that structure is that subordinates are responsible for carrying out the actions requested by their manager. So, in this structure, subordinates help provide services by carrying out those requests. Yet a subordinate can then also be a manager with his or her own subordinates. It is these relationships that create the vertical structure.

However, the persistent horizontal structure is created by a different set of relationships. It is created by the relationship between project teams and project boards. In other words, a project team may act as a project board for the subsidiary projects involved in the overall project. As we have seen, for simple challenges, the project board may only consist of a single manager. Nevertheless, each project team has to get the buy-in from the project board for their proposals and progress.

So at the top of the vertical structure, each member of the top team is a subordinate of the chief executive. Each member is individually responsible for carrying out the actions needed to deliver the services within their function. However, in the horizontal structure, the members of the top team become the project board for all the component improvement challenges. They will also collectively account to the chief executive as a team, for the evidence showing how effective the organization is at developing services of excellence. So the top of the horizontal structure is made from the permanent roles of the top team. To understand how we could use this in practice, we will look at the example of a pharmaceutical company.

## The pharmaceutical company

In simple terms, this organization carried out all the tests and trials to enable a drug to gain the regulatory approval necessary to come to the market. The company derived much of its income from a percentage of the royalties on the sales of the drugs that gained approval. However, many of the drugs tested never made it through all the approval stages. The organization consisted of two main divisions. These were the business development division and the technical division. The technical division managed the projects, which carried out all the tests and trials needed for approval. The business development division carried out two separate functions. The first function was to find companies that had developed promising drugs, but could not carry out all the necessary trials to bring the product to market. The second function was to market any of the drugs that received final approval from the regulatory agency.

The two divisions did not work well together. People in business development were continually complaining the approval process was always much longer than predicted. The technical people were always complaining that members of the business development never carried out sufficient due diligence checks before passing the drug to technical staff for approval. In other words, many of the drugs had not even passed early tests needed to show they had a reasonable chance of success. So the chief executive asked the two divisional directors to jointly oversee the changes needed to make the company more effective. In effect, the two directors became the project board of the challenge of improving the performance of the overall service pathway. In simple terms, they identified four benchmarks by which to assess the effectiveness of the service pathway. These were the accuracy of the estimated values of:

- (Quality) Certainty of the drug being approved
- (Availability) Time for the approval process
- (Cost) Cost of the approval process
- (Value to the organization) Revenue in the first three years of approval

So the challenge was to constantly improve the accuracy of the predictions of these four benchmark values. They started by developing a map of the sequence of stages from first identification to final marketing. They changed the protocol so that as soon as business development identified a potential drug, it was allocated to a two-member product team. The team always consisted of one member of staff from each division. At each connection between the stages, each team had to present their four graphs of how their estimates were changing as time progressed. They also had to present the evidence of the reasons for the change in assessments.

Also, each month, the product teams had to present, to their colleagues and directors, the evidence of what they had learnt from the process. If a drug failed a test, they had to identify any improvements that could have rejected the drug earlier in the pathway. They also had to present any other proposals for improving the process, to ensure their predictions were more accurate in future. The better the accuracy of their predictions, the less likely they were to waste resources in future on testing drugs that stood little chance of approval or lacked market potential.

If the proposals gained the buy-in from those present, the directors formalised and documented the proposed changes in the protocols. They then presented those proposals to the chief executive. These presentations included their assessment of how the changes would improve the success rate, together with the predicted decrease in costs and approval time for the drugs. Although this is a simple example, which only involved two groups, it shows how the permanent vertical and horizontal structures can easily compliment each other.

## Connecting vertical and horizontal structures

However, we need a general rule that allows us to develop much more complex horizontal structures, which interconnect with the vertical structure. So, let us start with a simple vertical structure of one manager and four subordinates in a single unit. In the vertical structure, the manager coordinates her subordinates to provide three different services.

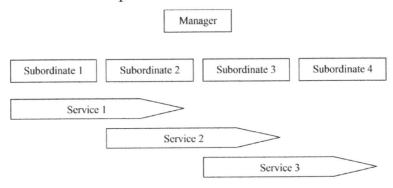

In effect, the manager is also the leader or project board for the performance of each of those service pathways. As shown in the diagram, each service pathway involves a team of two subordinates. Each pathway will consist of a set of process units joined by connection units. In the scenario from utopia, each team will know the critical quality, availability and cost benchmarks of each of the services in which they are involved. They will know the performance gaps for each criterion. Each service pathway will have a set of internal issues relating to one or more process or connection units. Each issue will contribute to one or more service performance gaps. So, for example, in the factory case study, tags and colour matching were two different issues in the service pathway producing plastic pellets used for moulding. Individually, each issue was contributing to all three of the performance gaps in quality, availability and cost of the service pathway.

So each challenge will involve a specific set of issues. Each issue can cause a specific set of performance gaps. In other words, each service pathway will have a related set of challenges. Those challenges will need prioritising. There will be a Leadership Game or performance board for each current challenge. Each challenge will have a performance team of people involved in carrying out the relevant processes in the service delivery pathway. Each team will frequently meet to agree on their individual actions in improving the performance. However, each team will also be regularly presenting their proposals and progress to the leader or project board of each challenge.

Therefore, even in this small unit, there is an incredible amount of complexity. Yet that complexity is created by repeating simplicity. Those simple principles, which apply within a unit, also apply across units. For example, consider an issue that needed to be resolved across functions. That would mean the service pathway involved would involve two or more units. In that scenario, the project board would involve the managers of those separate management units. The project team would include representatives of the groups most able to address the issue.

Clearly, this complexity is best dealt with at the level it involves. In other words, each individual should be able to account for their personal roles in their local service pathways and challenges. They should also be able to account for the relationship between this local information and the high-level service pathways and challenges. We have also seen that if they collectively account for the plan and progress of their challenges, they will automatically collaborate to improve service performance. So, in simple terms:

*When everyone is consistently accounting for the success of their individual and collective roles, the complexity looks after itself*

This suggests that to address the complexity of organizations, all we need is a simple system that ensures everyone is individually and collectively accounting for their progress. To understand how that system works, first consider the vertical structure as a set of connected triangles, with each manager at the top of the triangle.

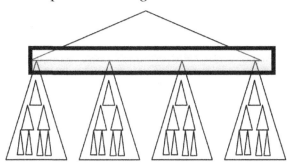

In the horizontal structure, the top team is the project board for all improvement challenges. Although, they will also act as the team, collectively accounting to the chief executive for the plans and successful progress of the performance improvement challenges. Each board member can ensure there is upward accountability within their own function. So each board member can account to the rest of the board for their function's part in high-level challenges.

At first sight, this just looks like a different way to draw the vertical organization. However, the triangles represent upwards, collective accountability of teams to their managers. It does not represent the downward delegation of managers to individual subordinates. So, given that we are starting with a vertical organization, it can be useful to initially use that structure to set up local horizontal structures.

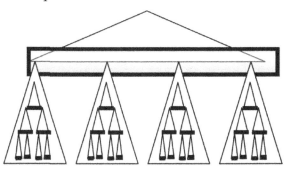

Then, where there are cross-functional projects, the two or

three board members act as the project board for that challenge. They also act as the project team accounting to the rest of the top team project board for their progress. Again, although it sounds complicated, it is easy to control at a local level. So, at each level, subordinates form a project board for the lower level challenges.

Although the previous diagram only shows the functional project boards, in principle, you could overlay the diagram with all the cross-functional project boards. Even the group of front-line, non-managerial subordinates form a project board for the lower level challenges. For example, consider the legal case study in the first chapter. The whole legal team met each morning. In effect, each member of the team was accountable to the project board for that day's challenges. The department manager only acted as the project board when the team needed higher-level approval, which they considered was outside their authority. That was when they needed to arrange changes with the local court.

### Mapping complex organizations

To understand how this can work in practice, we need to apply it to a real example. However, rather than describing another case study, we are going to use a different approach. We are going to consider and work through a complex scenario. So, I am going to ask you to imagine that you were appointed to the post of chief executive of a large, complex company. Working through an imaginary example can be a powerful way of developing our skills. It can release us from being trapped by the seeming barriers we face every day. However, most importantly, it will show us that to build a horizontal structure, we need to "think differently". Many horizontal measures of performance are significantly different from traditional vertical measures. The way people behave in the horizontal structure is also different from the behaviours many managers have experienced in the vertical structures of their current organizations. However, most importantly, the types of questions you need to ask are different from the questions or answers that are relevant to vertical structures.

Obviously, the skill to ask the right questions develops as you run more Leadership Games. However, mentally playing through scenarios is also a powerful way of developing that skill. As you imagine how the various stages will play out, you can predict the points where you may find initial resistance to "playing the game". You can then develop potential solutions to such stoppers.

So, to make the scenario realistic, we will use a real company, which is in the news at the time of writing this chapter in early June 2019. The example we are going to use is that of Boeing. The only knowledge I have of the aircraft industry is from managers and accident investigators who have attended my master classes. None of these has been from Boeing. However, there is a considerable amount of up-to-date information about Boeing in the public domain. The reason Boeing has been in the news is that currently all Boeing 737 MAX aircraft have been grounded worldwide for the last three months. This followed two fatal crashes within five months. So the following scenario is built from that public information, rather than from any intimate knowledge of the company. We are going to use the scenario to look at several aspects of the Leadership Game.

Therefore, in this chapter, we will use the example of Boeing to see how we could create a dual structure in any large and complex organization. Then, in the final chapter, we will use the scenario to compare the results of our scenario and the path that Boeing has followed. Finally, we will use the

Leadership Game principles to predict that, if Boeing does not radically change soon, it is creating a substantial risk to its future survival.

## The story of Boeing

Currently, Boeing employs over 150,000 people across the globe. One of its main divisions is Boeing Commercial Airplanes. That division employs more than 70,000 people worldwide. There are more than 10,000 Boeing commercial jetliners in service. Boeing claims that their planes fly passengers and freight more efficiently than competing models in the market. Currently, more than 5,700 Boeing aircraft are on order.

However, the scenario I would like you to consider is one where you take the post of chief executive of the airplane business in late 2016. This would be two years before the first 737 MAX crash. Then, Boeing had not even delivered any 737 MAX aircraft. So you would have no reason to assume there would be a problem with that design. Boeing has an aspiration to be the "Best in Aerospace". So we will use that as the mission. We will assume that Boeing Commercial Airplanes is a vertical organization. We will also assume that to improve organizational performance as rapidly as possible, your priority is to transform the organization to have a dual structure.

However, given the company employs over 70,000 people, where do you start? At first, it could look like mission impossible. So, it is worth looking at a brief outline of how you could approach this type of situation. This process should help you see how you can apply the same principles to your situation. As we progress through the scenario, it will be useful for you to imagine being in each of the stages described. Identify how people might react and identify changes, which you consider would improve the process from your own experiences. Then try to identify how you would approach a similar situation in your organization.

So, as the new chief executive, you need to initially concentrate on the first part of the development pathway. This is that part that results in having an organization with an effective dual structure. However, to plan the pathway, you need a clear picture of what the short-term future from hell and utopia would look like. Once we have that, we can identify the milestones that we have to pass, at each stage of the pathway.

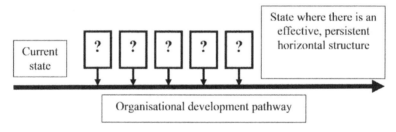

### Hell and utopia for dual structures

For this explanation, we will say the "state from hell" would be a vertical organization with extreme silo mentality throughout. The utopian state, which we are aiming for, is for an effective dual structure throughout the organization. We could test this by asking anyone in the organization to describe their role. If that person were completely fulfilling their responsibility in the horizontal structure, they would be able to take anyone to a board or screen and use the relevant maps to account for the following:

- What the organization does, what it is trying to achieve, and its current challenges
- The service pathways in which the person is

involved

- The performance improvement challenges in which that person is currently involved, as well as any other previous challenges

- How those improvement projects are helping the organization achieve its goals?

- Being able to fluently account for those aspects would be a good indication of how their thought bubble was directing their behaviour.

## *Testing and rolling out the dual structure*

Often managers, in vertical organizations, find it scary to even think about trying to achieve this state in their organizations. Yet, the earlier pharmaceutical example shows how simple it can be to achieve. Similarly, we will see how easy it is to implement, even in an organization as complex as Boeing. So, we will assume that in 2016, you have no reason to believe that Boeing has any hidden issues, which could suddenly derail your plans. Thus, you begin your project with two parallel strands. First, you need to start developing the capability to test and roll out the dual structure of the Leadership Games. Then you need a way of focusing those Games on a longer-term goal.

This chapter is mainly going to focus on how you could ensure the dual structure is being successfully cascaded throughout the organization as rapidly as possible. At first, that dual structure will simply focus on improving local and cross-functional service standards. In the next and final chapter, we will see how you would rapidly focus those Leadership Games on all the issues that were critical to the future success of the organization. In particular, we will see how you would have uncovered the safety time bomb that was going to have such disastrous consequences.

### The invisible leader and catalyst team

However, the first step you will have to take is to engage an "invisible leader". This will typically be the member of the board who will build and develop the initial catalyst team. You may remember from previous chapters that a catalyst team is a small team that has developed the skills to engage groups in Leadership Game challenges. The catalyst team might first consist of a facilitator, a performance information specialist and a project manager. It should be able to grow or shrink as needed. The invisible leader would be a suitable executive. This would be one who has a role that is analogous to the corporate services manager in the Metropolitan Police case study. Boeing has a board of twenty people. One of those is the Vice President of Total Quality. So that might be your invisible leader.

As a matter of urgency, the invisible leader needs to engage the catalyst team to identify some local problem areas. These would be areas where they could work with the managers to engage teams to rapidly address the issues. It does not matter what the issues are. The point of the exercise would be to develop the capability of the catalyst team and invisible leader as quickly as possible.

For example, news reports at that time highlighted problems with the North Charleston factory. It had problems affecting the delivery, cost and quality of the Dreamliner aircraft produced in the factory. The quality problems in the factory were such that Qatar Airways had stopped accepting aircraft delivered from North Charleston in 2014. The airline only accepted Dreamliners made at the plant in Everett. In the same year, workers at the North Charleston plant were told to watch a video of the airline's chief executive chiding them for production delays. However, the problems at the factory had persisted.

So, the catalyst team may well use some issues in this factory to start developing the trial roll-out of the Leadership Games. They could start with any of the approaches we have seen in the previous case studies. Those would include the approaches used in the safety and housekeeping case study. They could also use the week from hell approach, or tracking down the issues affecting quality, delivery and cost, in the same way that the tags and colour matching problems were solved. The catalyst team should be able to achieve several successes fairly quickly. This would provide the necessary evidence of the success of the approach.

### High-level map

The catalyst team would also develop a high-level map of the organization, as well as a central store for all the maps and other information. As always, they would achieve this by cycling around the GAME loop. However, to better understand how that works, we are going to look at a slightly more sophisticated version of the GAME loop. Previously, we have looked at the sequence of the four stages, through which each piece of information passes. However, a more realistic diagram would show that all four stages are continually receiving and returning information from a central data store.

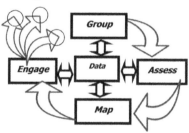

In practice, this central data may just be a sub-directory on a network disc. That subdirectory may have further subdirectories for information gained for different service pathways. So for example, maps, which are created in the mapping stage of one cycle, are returned to the central store to be used by the group stage of the next cycle. In this way, the central data store builds up a progressively more detailed set of information on each cycle.

So, the catalyst team would start by creating the map of the stakeholder systems, which we saw in chapter eleven. The map would include the services that connect those systems with the organization. This information would be held in the central data store. The team would then map the virtuous cycles, which needed developing to achieve the aim of increasing market share. Once the top team agreed on this, it would form part of an induction package for the Leadership Game. That way, eventually, everyone in the organization would be able to account for the big picture of the organization.

### Leadership Game training for managers

Similarly, the catalyst team could develop a first stage training pack or session, which was suitable for all managers. This would show managers how to run the simple "week from hell" sticky note exercise for their direct reports. Managers would need to learn the "rules of the game". These would include teams making regular presentations of the evidence of their proposed plans and progress. Teams always needed to gain the buy-in from the manager or project board. The teams needed to appreciate that proposals are likely to be rejected if they aim to improve one value criteria by detracting from another. Those involved would need to realise the aim of the Leadership Games was for improvement projects to be self-financing where possible. All this could be condensed into a standard training package for managers being introduced to their first Leadership Game. Such training could be rolled out quickly, whenever needed. However, just training managers will not, in itself change behaviours.

### The motivation to develop leadership skills

In chapter one, we identified the manager of a relay team played both the role of manager and the role of team leader. So in effect, managers are developing their leadership skills when they start using the Leadership Game to engage their teams in improving performance. The more effective they become as leaders, the less time they need to spend on crisis management. However, by definition, managers in vertical organizations are likely to spend most of their time in the management role.

This means they will not necessarily be motivated to hone their leadership skills unless they are facing a crisis. They are more likely to be motivated to stay in their comfort zone of managing people. So just developing the training packages to implement Leadership Games is not enough. After training sessions, managers will just default to their established behaviours. This means that you need a simple way to ensure all managers are using Leadership Games to improve performance and develop their leadership skills.

There are, of course, many different ways of achieving this. The best way will depend on the circumstances. Probably the fastest and simplest way is to use an approach which uses a combination of the vertical and horizontal structures. This approach uses a standard performance sheet for all managers to use. That sheet would act as the performance board of the "developing leadership skills" Leadership Game. That sheet would have a small number of graphs. The first is "number of direct subordinates not currently in performance teams".

Managers could then be given a vertical target of engaging all their subordinates in effective Leadership Games within a month of receiving the first training. The evidence of their progress would be on their performance sheet. Managers could account for those sheets at their monthly one-to-ones with their immediate manager. If managers were still being given other vertical targets, such as reducing costs, there would need to be a protocol on how they should achieve that target. That protocol could be that they had to provide evidence on the performance sheet, about how they had engaged their direct reports in addressing the overall cost-reduction target.

The performance sheet could be gradually developed into something more sophisticated, which would further develop managers' leadership skills. There could be graphs showing how many services did not currently have champions. The sheet could also include the number of services that still did not have a complete set of agreed benchmark standards. Then, the performance sheet could be developed even further. It could include a graph and list of all the internal issues identified but not yet being addressed. It could have a similar list for all cross-functional issues that still needed teams, some of whom were outside the manager's area of authority.

Indeed, the power of this last type of list is easy to miss. Traditionally, in vertical organizations, when managers have problems, they often consider them as being caused by other departments. In a vertical structure, they may well consider that the only solution is to complain to their superior. However, this problem could easily be removed with a simple protocol. If one manager enters the need for a cross-functional team to address an issue, there should be a way to ensure the issue automatically appears on the list of the other manager. So, in effect, both managers now have to account for a cross-functional team to address the issue, without having to refer the issue to superiors.

Similarly, the leadership performance sheet could be enhanced to include another graph. This would be for the number of cross-functional teams or project boards the manager was involved with as a member. So every manager would have to account for their level of collaboration with peers. Overall, this level of sophisticated performance sheet shows how the vertical and horizontal structures can progressively dovetail together. Each manager would have to account to his or her superior for their progress in developing leadership skills. In principle, this system, together with leadership training, should ensure rapid change. This is because it would ensure that everyone in the organization was engaged in the dual structure of Leadership Games in a relatively short timescale.

### The common goal

I am going to assume that, as the new chief executive, you have a challenging strategic goal in mind. For this scenario, it could be "to achieve a ten per cent increase in market share of orders". So you will need to engage your top team as the project board for that challenge. However, to achieve that goal, the top team needs first to identify the major, high-level barriers that are stopping the company from achieving that goal. For each challenge, the top team will need to set up a project board. That board will then be responsible for setting up the necessary project teams who will collectively address the challenge.

### Team size

Your first stage in this process is to get Boeing's board to agree that list of critical issues. One problem is the size and make-up of the board. We will assume that you have a board of twenty dominant individuals. Each member will be used to being in-control of their own empires and areas of responsibility. As they have only ever experienced the vertical structure, we will assume there is a high degree of silo mentality. Anyway, twenty is too many to form an effective team. Sports teams are usually between two and fifteen people. Research into high-performance teams in organizations suggests the best size is between four and fifteen. So your first challenge is to understand how you can even start getting such a group to collaborate.

One approach could be to split the group into, for example, four teams of five. Each team could then use a separate break-out room for the challenge of agreeing on the major stoppers to success. The psychological dynamics of this arrangement are completely different to twenty people in a single room. Each group is small enough to start acting as a team. Each team will consider that other teams will be completing the task. So any team not developing a list would feel they are "losing".

### Identifying the stoppers

Each room could have a facilitator. Facilitators could use a sticky note exercise to involve everyone. Alternatively, they could use the traditional method of asking for ideas and ensuring the team write them on a flip chart. With such small groups, it is far more difficult for any one person to refuse to be involved. The groups could then bring back the four flip charts into the main room for amalgamation. However, there are many other ways of achieving this result. It is not important how it is achieved. What is important is that everyone on the top team takes the first steps in developing collective ownership of the cross-functional challenge. This is clearly different from just being given individual targets for their separate functions.

### Identifying accountability

Once all the top team had agreed on the list of critical issues, the next step would be to ensure each challenge had a project board. In these circumstances, you would probably arrange for everyone to have a sheet of sticky labels with their name on. You then ask everyone to check the list of challenges. Ask them to consider if they have an interest in each challenge being a success. Alternatively, consider if they believe their division could assist in making it a success. If either is true, they should put their name against the challenge.

The responsibility of the names on the challenges is to ensure they have nominated and engaged all the necessary members of the project board for that challenge. Each project board needs to be in place, and able to account for their early plans, before the next meeting of the top team. In this way, this simple approach should start to focus everyone on removing all the known, cross-functional issues.

In principle, once you were at this stage, you would have started the process that should rapidly cascade the dual structure through the organization. You would have also got agreement on the major issues that needed to be addressed to achieve a strategic goal. In effect, you would also have a project board responsible for guiding and accounting for the progress towards the goal.

Of course, this is only a simplified outline of how you could arrive at this point. However, from my experience, it is not that far away from what would be needed in similar circumstances. So it shows that you could make great progress in a relatively short time. However, despite the progress, it is far from certain that anyone would have identified safety as a major issue. Indeed, we are going to assume that safety was not on the list of issues. So in the final chapter, we are going to look at the next stage in focusing the whole company on the small number of issues that matter the most.

## Summary

In this chapter, we have seen the basic approach to creating a dual structure, which can cascade high-level challenges throughout an organization. We have also seen how to set up a fail-safe system to monitor the robustness of the cascading throughout the organization. In the final chapter, we continue with the Boeing example to see how to ensure there are no nasty surprises that could derail the project.

# The final chapter

## Creating the future from utopia

### Review and overview

In the previous chapter, we used Boeing as the basis for understanding how we could use the principles of the Leadership Game to create persistent dual responsibilities throughout an organization, However, before we return to the Boeing scenario, we need to see how to focus that second structure on the issues most critical to success.

We will see that we achieve this with a structure of upwards fail-safe systems for each of the critical success benchmarks. Once we understand the principle, we will return to the 2016 Boeing scenario to see how that approach would have predicted the safety time bomb that exploded two years later. We will then replay the scenario in 2019 to assess Boeing's future chances of failure.

### Creating the future

Management gurus often use a quote from Abraham Lincoln. "The best way to predict the future is to create it". While it is a motivating phrase, it often seems easier said than done. Yet, if we look at it from the horizontal perspective, there is a clear path to creating the organization's future. As we have seen, the success of organizations depends on the ability to provide a set of critical services to standards that meet a set of critical benchmarks. So an organization's ability, to create its future success, depends on its ability to develop the right set of service pathways, which meet the standards needed for that success.

For example, consider an organization providing the best possible services at the lowest cost. Such an organization is likely to be far more successful than the competitors providing lower grade services at higher costs. So the way to create the desired future is to start by identifying the critical services and benchmarks. These are the benchmarks that will determine the organization's future. Once these are defined, it is relatively simple to identify the issues that are stopping us from achieving the necessary levels of service. Then, all we have to do to create the ideal future is address those issues

So, we can say that:

*An organization's ability to create a successful future depends on its ability to develop its critical service pathways, to the benchmarks standards of excellence needed for success.*

This principle holds true for both internal and external services. This means the organization "from utopia" is not just an organization that has been successful until now. It is an organization that has the permanent ability to ensure its critical services consistently adapt to meet or exceed the benchmarks needed for a successful future.

### A good start but something missing

So in the previous chapter, we started the scenario where you were the new chief executive of Boeing in 2016, before the launch of the MAX. You have already made a good start. You have engaged one member of the top team to develop a catalyst team. The top team have identified the high-level set of issues, which could stop the company from achieving your challenge. You have project boards for those challenges. Every member of the top team is cascading the leadership game throughout their functions. So in a relatively short time, everyone in the organization should be focusing on improving their own local services.

One problem is that we have not yet identified the benchmark standards needed to create a successful future. In particular, we have assumed a worst case scenario where no one, in the top team in 2016, has identified any safety issues. Because, we have not identified the critical benchmarks, we have not even started to consider how to ensure the top team is controlling the progress to achieving those standards. Yet these are the standards that are critical to success. However, ensuring senior executives are in control of the critical standards is not as simple as it might appear. To better understand the scale of the problem, we are going to briefly leave the Boeing scenario. We are first going to consider the simpler example of a company supplying aircraft engines to Boeing.

### The Aero-engine supplier

Imagine the supplier of aero-engines is supplying engines as a service. In other words, instead of just selling the engines, in effect, they sell a fixed-price rental service of fully maintained engines to airlines. So the supplier is more likely to be successful if the engines are reliable and rarely break down. On the other hand, the supplier will be in trouble if the engines are unreliable and continually need extra maintenance. This is because the engine supplier will have to bear the recurring cost of repair. This means the quality issue of engine reliability would be fundamental to the future success of the organization. So it would seem obvious for this quality issue to be one of the highest concerns for the board and chief executive.

### Others-in-control of critical benchmarks

Yet often the quality of products and services is not considered as an issue that is the direct concern of the chief executive or the board. They are likely to see such issues as technical matters, which relate to several different delegated responsibilities. So, in the aero engine example, reliability depends on several areas. These include design, testing, manufacture and maintenance. Different divisional executives are responsible for these functions. Indeed, managers may re-delegate such responsibilities several times until they reach the relevant front-line staff. These would be the ones who carry out the actions that could affect reliability.

To make matters worse, each engine may consist of several thousand different parts. A failure in the design or manufacture of any one part could cause engine failure. For example, a failure of a single rotor blade could destroy many other blades causing total engine failure. Even worse, it is not just the separate parts that could fail. It is the connections between the parts that could fail. Each of these aspects could be the responsibility of different people in the organization.

So chief executives often only focus on what they are measured on, and what they consider is within their direct control. Typically, that revolves around what is probably the second most successful management tool. That is the profit and loss, and balance sheet. In simple terms, this is the accounting tool that shows the difference between inward revenue and outward costs. So chief executives often consider their main focus is on increasing revenue and reducing costs.

Thus we have a situation where, on the one hand, a quality issue, such as reliability, is critical to the organization's success. This means it should be a critical responsibility of the chief executive. Yet, on the other hand, the many different people, who control quality, could be several tiers of management below the chief executive. So from that perspective, the chief executive is bound to be others-in-control of quality.

In an organization based solely on a vertical structure, this problem can be difficult to overcome. Even if someone on the executive board has sole responsibility for quality, they would have little direct authority or influence over the actions of front-line staff. Even if that person had hundreds of inspectors, it still does not solve the problem. We have already seen that separating inspection, from the control of processes, ensures the people in the service pathways become others-in-control of quality.

This problem is not just applicable to manufacturers. It probably applies to most commercial, vertical-based organizations. For example, the chief executive of a fashion company probably delegates responsibility for the design and manufacture of the clothes to different executives. In turn, those executives delegate to their subordinates. So the chief executive is likely to be others-in-control of the quality of the design and the quality of manufacture. Yet these quality aspects are critical to the future success of the company.

The fact that the chief executive is likely to be "others-in-control" of quality causes another major problem. The easiest short-term way to reduce costs is often to reduce various aspects of quality or fitness for purpose. The fall in cost is often immediate. However, the effects of reducing fitness are often delayed. In other words, it may take months or years before previously, loyal customers decide to change suppliers because of a drop in quality.

The most effective way to solve the problem is to have a dual structure focusing on the quality, availability and costs of service pathways. If the product or service is not fit for purpose, then the organization is unlikely to survive. So, to be able to create its own future, an organization must have fail-safe systems at the highest level for quality, availability and cost of its critical services.

Those fail-safe systems need to feed up from the relevant, lower-level control systems. The structure needs to ensure that top executives are clearly in control of the fitness of their services to create the ideal future. Clearly, this is not a normal part of vertical structures. Nor is it a normal form of information reporting. So we will need to start thinking differently to see how we create such systems.

### The golden thread through performance systems

To understand how to develop such systems, we need to answer three questions. The first question is "What are the benchmarks that are critical to success?" We obviously cannot create fail-safe systems until we define the benchmarks we need to reach. The second question is "who are the teams that are accounting for any gaps in the fail-safe systems?" Those are the teams that will answer the third question: "What are the golden threads that connect all the relevant performance systems to the fail-safe systems? To see how we can achieve this in practice, we will return to our 2016 Boeing scenario

## Return to Boeing 2016

In our Boeing 2016 scenario, you now need to urgently create the fail-safe systems for all the criteria that are critical to Boeing's future success. Your invisible leader was the VP of Total Quality. So we will assume that he set up a sub-group, within the top team, to act as the fail-safe quality team. In effect, this is the team that will work with the catalyst team to set up a fail-safe system to ensure that the value perceived by the customer is always improving.

## Accountability for the fail-safe system

However, a general benchmark of quality is too complex to monitor with a single measure. It needs to be split into its high-level components. So, the first challenge, for the quality team, is to identify the proposed set of component benchmarks.

This is not as simple as it may appear. In theory, the team could achieve this by having discussions with the salespeople. They would try to identify the criteria, which are important to customers' buying decisions on the company's product or services. However, in practice, this approach will not always identify the full list. This is because people often take some criteria for granted.

For example, safety is the type of criteria that can often be taken for granted when all manufacturers have a good safety record. Under those circumstances, safety is no longer a distinguishing characteristic. It may only appear on a list when trying to identify the characteristics of the product or supplier, which a customer would definitely avoid. In other words, a customer would not buy a fleet of aircraft, if the model or supplier had a bad reputation for safety.

So, often, the most powerful approach is the one I outlined in chapter eleven. This is to identify the criteria for the product from hell and the supplier from hell. In other words, identify the characteristics that would create the opposite reputation to the one needed. To do this, you start by identifying the criteria that would ensure customers would not buy a particular product from a particular supplier. Then repeat the exercise for the product and supplier from utopia. Between these two lists, you should be able to set up a small list of criteria with hell and utopia descriptions.

### Identifying the critical benchmarks

We will assume the quality fail-safe team include the executive responsible for sales and marketing. The team may also talk to several salespeople and even a representative from a customer. From these conversations, they distil the information to a small set of benchmarks, which are critical to customers' buying decisions.

One such benchmark is obviously the selling price of the product or service. However, we are going to assume the selling price is related to Boeing's overall cost of production. So that is controlled by a cost-efficiency fail-safe team. This means that initially, the team is just trying to focus on the quality criteria that affect the customers' decisions. We will assume the team identify a relatively small list.

The first criterion, they identify as important to airlines, is the running costs of the aircraft per traveller. They also identify this consists of three main parts. The first is the fuel consumption per mile. The second is the maintenance cost. The third part is crew flexibility across all the planes in the airline's fleet. Ideally, airlines would like their crews to be able to fly all the different planes in the fleet, without expensive extra training.

The second main criterion is quality. This is made up from reliability and safety. Clearly, reliability is important because, if planes need unscheduled maintenance, it increases running costs as well as creating delays in flights. Also, if an aircraft had a bad safety record, passengers would fly with that airline.

In principle, each top-level criterion would have a team accounting for the development of the fail-safe team. Each team would identify the path of the golden thread that links all the relevant lower level benchmarks with the high-level benchmark. However, we will just use the safety criteria as an example of how all the other golden threads can be traced.

### The fail-safe benchmark team as external assessors

Clearly, the aim for the safety benchmark is zero accidents. The way to minimise future accidents is to consistently aim to remove the causes of accidents. Yet even a cursory investigation shows over half of aircraft accidents are blamed on pilot error. So it is easy for Boeing's executives to be others-in-control of the accident rate. However, a closer examination of those accidents shows that most pilot errors happen when something unusual and unexpected happens. Under those conditions, pilots have to suddenly take manual control.

For example, the unexpected event could be a sensor failure causing the autopilot to suddenly switch off. There may also be conflicting information on the displays. Thus, there are potentially three ways to reduce the chances caused by this type of error. The first is to reduce the probability of unexpected system failures. The second is to give pilots better guidance on what action to take. The third is to train pilots to be better at dealing with unexpected events. Potentially, the benefit of effectively addressing all three issues would be to halve the probability of a serious accident. So you need a team need to look at all three aspects.

This safety fail-safe team also needs to be able to assess as external assessors. To ensure that ability, it is important that at least some of the team are free from any conflict of interests. For example, consider a manager who was responsible for the operations in the vertical system. That manager may well have a target of reducing costs. That could potentially mean that the manager would resist any investigation into aspects related to safety within the pathway he or she was controlling. So the team should probably include at least one or two pilots. This could be one test pilot and one pilot with experience of flying planes built by a competitor.

So we will assume the safety fail-safe team has been set up and that they start by looking at how to avoid system failures. As always, they do this by continuing to loop around the GAME loop. So they start by grouping all the information needed to create the benchmark of excellence. That would include the current internal best practice standards, as well as any known competitor standards. It would also include any regulator standards and information logged by pilots on in-flight incidents. All that information needs to be grouped into benchmark frames, in the same way that KLoEs were grouped in the housing example. So let us consider how this would be achieved.

### The safety benchmark

Almost all large, commercial passenger aircraft have the same best-practice approach to safety. That is redundancy. So, although only one pilot is in control at any one time, you will see a pilot on each side of the plane in any cockpit. Each pilot has a separate set of controls and visual information. Each set of visual information comes from a separate set of external sensors on each side of the plane. So there are two, separate sets of control systems. These systems are kept as different as possible, so a single cause cannot affect both systems at the same time. For example, pilots are not allowed to eat the same meal before a flight, in case they both get food poisoning. Sometimes sensors on the opposite sides of the plane are made by different manufacturers.

In the same way, there need to be clear, contingency routines. In other words, if some part of the current control system fails, there needs to be a standard way of engaging the contingency system. For example, consider the scenarios where one sensor fails and starts to give an inconsistent reading to the pilot in control. Under those circumstances, that pilot can look over to the other side for a comparative reading. Occasionally there is a third sensor. This is connected so that if one sensor fails, the system can automatically identify which sensor is wrong and swaps to a fully working sensor.

On the latest aircraft, a similar approach is used on flight computers. There are three autopilot computers. All three function independently and contain three different processors manufactured by different companies. Even if all three computers fail, there is still the contingency of the first pilot taking control. If that system fails, the second pilot is yet another level of contingency.

Despite this level of redundancy, every effort should be made to prevent the failure of any part of any single system, to minimise the probability of an overall control system failure. There should also be the highest number of possible contingency systems. However, equally important, for every system, there should be an effective way of sensing a system failure and then triggering an effective contingency.

This arrangement provides the utopian standard for every part of all aircraft control systems. However, not all aircraft systems will meet all the utopian standards because they will have older designs. So an average system would be less than utopia. A system from hell would be one where that was a clear lack of prevention of failure. It would have no inherent contingency system and no way of showing or identifying whether it had failed. It would have no clear way of transferring to a higher level contingency system.

So, we can now start using this information to build the necessary frames of reference for safety systems. We could use a scale of minus five to plus five. Minus four would be hell, while utopia would be plus four. Zero would be the minimum acceptable level of redundancy. Any system is only as strong as its weakest link. So, if any part of the critical in-flight systems was below zero, the safety fail-safe system should immediately flag the top team. Indeed, the fail-safe should create a major alert on any aspect, of any single component system, which was anywhere near minus four.

Before looking at all the control systems for all the Boeing models, the safety team would need to prioritise their work. They are likely to prioritise any recently designed or changed control systems or systems that had not been proved by several years of service. At this stage, the MAX version of the 737 had not yet been launched. So we can assume that any changes to the control systems would be some of the first to be assessed against the best practice benchmark standards. So it would soon become obvious the 737 MAX had a new system called the MCAS. To understand the importance of this system, we need to briefly look at the history of the 737 MAX.

### *The history of the 737 Max*

The narrow-bodied passenger airline industry is dominated by just two players, Boeing and Airbus. The basic 737 aircraft first launched in 1967 and has a good safety record. There are multiple versions of the plane. So, one of the major benefits for airlines is that all the variants have the same cockpit controls. That gives the airlines the maximum flexibility of their aircrews, with the minimum amount of retraining time. Airbus has an equivalent range of aircraft called the A320 family. Back in 2010, a new range of bigger engines was developed, which used fifteen per cent less fuel. This was potentially a big saving for airlines. So there was a big demand for the new engine. As the Airbus 320 family had high wings, these bigger engines would fit the old airframes. However, because the 737 had much lower wings, the larger and more fuel-efficient engines would not fit the old airframes. Originally, Boeing decided they would have to design and build a new aircraft. But that could potentially take many years, during which they could lose customers.

Then, technicians found a way to mount the larger diameter engines on the 737. However, the engines had to be placed father forward and higher on the wings. That meant the centre line of the engine's thrust had changed. So, if the pilot applied too much power, the plane could easily lift the nose into a dangerous position. To overcome this, Boeing developed a computer system named MCAS. This system used information from an external blade shaped sensor on one side of the nose of the plane. This sensor gauged the "angle of attack" (AoA) of the airflow to identify if the plane was tilting dangerously upwards. In that state, the computer system would automatically correct the pitch of the plane, by altering the large horizontal wings on the tail of the plane. Because the system was designed to stop pilot error, it was designed to remain in control even if the pilot switched off the normal autopilot.

## *Assessing the safety of the MCAS*

Given the information publicly available in 2019, after the two air crashes, we can make a reasonable prediction of the results of a safety analysis undertaken in 2016, before the launch of the MAX. In effect, we can look at the safety standards needed for any system and assess each stage of the service development pathway to see if it meets the necessary benchmark standards.

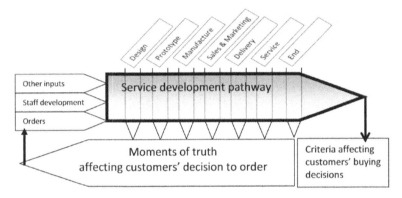

We will soon see that even a simple comparison of the MCAS system with the safety benchmarks would have immediately shown major problems. For example, let us assume the safety team started at the design function. On the scale of redundancy for the sensors, the MCAS would have a score or minus four. This was because the MCAS system only used information from one of the two AoA sensors fitted to the 737. These sensors were known to be prone to failure. If that single sensor failed, the MCAS system could not only fail but immediately put the plane into a dangerous dive.

On a benchmark for how easily the pilot could switch off the MCAS system, it would also score minus four. This was because pilots were not even going to be informed of the presence of the MCAS system. However, on further analysis, the team would probably give it a minus six (worse than hell!). This was because, if the pilot switched off the normal autopilot, they would assume that they had full manual control. Yet, even when the pilot thought he or she had full manual control, the MCAS would keep re-engaging every twenty seconds. However, the pilots would have no knowledge or experience to address the fault. So if the MCAS was receiving a faulty signal from the sensor, it could keep tipping the nose down, overpowering the pilot's control.

So now let us assume the team applied a similar test to the prototype testing function. On the benchmark for the standard of testing of the MCAS system, it again would score minus four. This was because it appears that no one had ever tested it, even in a simulator, for what would happen to the flight if the sensor information was wrong. The development team had just assumed the sensor would never fail, even though there was plenty of evidence to the contrary.

There are many other safety benchmarks, which relate to contingency, prevention and redundancy, at which the team would look. Amazingly, the MCAS system badly fails on almost every one of them. Yet even a failure on any single aspect could have such catastrophic consequences, that it should have triggered warning signals to the chief executive the new model was potentially unsafe. Yet, as far as we know, because there was only a vertical structure, the board had never even discussed the question of safety. So what could have caused such a massive failure in the development of the 737 MAX?

### The root cause?

Clearly, it would be dangerous to just fix individual problems without first identifying the cause. This is because, until you identify the cause, you cannot assess whether it has also caused problems in other parts of the design of the MAX. Indeed, in the worst case scenario, the problem could have spread to the design of other models. There is still not enough information in the public domain to be certain of the cause. Nevertheless, it has all the hallmarks of extreme silo mentality and others-in-control of safety throughout the MCAS software design team. Yet it is inconceivable the normal software design process, which developed software for so many great Boeing models, could be that bad. So, the likelihood is the problem started back in 2010.

It was at that time the board originally decided that Boeing would need to design a new plane to meet the Airbus challenge. Possibly, their technical teams had decided that it was not possible to safely add the new, larger and lower fuel consumption engines to the 737 airframe. However, the predicted delay in bringing a new, competitive model to the market met great resistance from Boeing's current customer base. In particular, American Airlines threatened to move its whole fleet over to Airbus. So there was huge pressure on the board to find a way of using the new engines on the existing airframe.

It seems likely that at that point a dedicated team was set up, specifically to solve the 737 problems. It also seems likely that a senior executive set up the team under the control of a business manager, rather than a technical expert. While I have no inside knowledge, whether this is what happened, all the symptoms point to this scenario. The symptoms also point to the fact the MAX development team was kept isolated from the normal development and testing staff. This is because, in 2019, we found that test pilots had been specifically kept away from the final testing of the MCAS system. One reason for this isolation seems to be that a key selling point of the 737MAX was that it needed little extra training for pilots with 737 experience. Indeed, the only extra training provided would be some relatively trivial online training package taking less than a couple of hours. So there seems to be a conscious decision to "hide" any mention of the MCAS. Someone appears to have removed all reference to MCAS, even from the manuals. The evidence that suggests this was a deliberate act, rather than an oversight is the acronym MCAS does still appear in the glossary of terms in the manual. Understanding the scope and motivation of such a team would be critical. For example, if the team was responsible for all the MAX development, then it is possible other areas could be equally flawed. Indeed, the whole aerodynamic analysis would be in question.

It is important to remind ourselves why we are using the Boeing scenario. We are using it to see how the dual structure of the Leadership Game enables the organization to create a successful future. To achieve that future, it is essential to identify and remove the issues that could stop or hinder progress to the desired outcome. In this scenario, each high-level benchmark has a team acting as the fail-safe system. Although we have only looked at the safety benchmark team, the teams for the other benchmarks would take the same approach. The reason we used the 2016 scenario is that everyone has 20/20 hindsight. In other words, in mid-2019, it would be obvious to trace back the problems with the MCAS system, because it had already caused two fatal crashes. However, in 2016, it is unlikely that a new chief executive would have become aware of any potential safety problems with the 737MAX unless they set up a dual structure.

Remember, Boeing employs over 70,000 people and had a good safety record. Indeed, it is likely that the first sign of problems would not have become obvious to a new CEO until after the first crash in 2018. This could even be the case if the Leadership Games were just being used for solving issues identified by managers, as needed. The issues, which were critical to the company's future, could only be found by a formal introduction of the dual structure. Also, that structure needed to be focused on the high-level benchmarks needed to create the desired successful future.

## The 2019 approach

We are now going to change the scenario. We are no longer going to assume you became the CEO of Boeing in 2016. Instead, we will use the scenario where you become the new CEO in mid-2019, while all the MAX aircraft are still grounded. We can use this example to compare your Leadership Game approach with the vertical approach, which current Boeing executives are using.

By now, it has become common knowledge that Boeing had offered an optional extra warning light at $80,000. This is a warning light, which should have signalled the two AoA sensors were giving conflicting readings. In theory, such a light could have helped pilots in both crashes to identify the problem. In practice, it would not have altered anything. There were several reasons for this. The first was that neither planes involved had the optional extra fitted. Second, even if it had been fitted, a bug in the MCAS system stopped the light from activating. The third reason was that a single light does not identify which sensor is not working. Indeed, as far as we know, if the single sensor used by the MCAS system was the faulty one, the software had no way of identifying that fact. Nor was it able to switch to use the other AoA sensor. Indeed, even if the light had been fitted and was working, the pilots still had no knowledge of how to disable the MCAS system. In other words, even with the light, the MCAS system was still scoring minus-four on the hell to utopia scale.

Despite all these factors, Boeing's publicly stated strategy seems to revolve around just three elements. The first is to add AoA disagree lights to all MAX planes. The second is to correct the software bug that failed to trigger the light, even when the light was fitted. The third is to improve the manuals and IPad training package to cover the MCAS system. Currently, it appears that Boeing has now updated MCAS software and the pilot training material. Boeing has presented these for approval to the US regulatory body, the FAA. So let us first use the analysis approach of the Leadership Game to assess whether this is an effective approach to create the maximum certainty of a successful future.

The approach of the Leadership Game is to move away from the future from hell and towards the future from utopia. The future from hell would occur if both passengers and airlines lost faith in the safety of the 737MAX. Let us assume the critical point to trigger that state is somewhere between three and four serious incidents within a two-year period. If that assessment is correct, Boeing is already halfway down the road to hell! If there are any future incidents, even if they are unrelated to the MCAS system, it could have a dramatic impact on public perception of the safety of the MAX. In that scenario, what could the future from hell look like?

In June 2019, there are less than four hundred MAX aircraft. Within two years, there could be nearer two thousand in operation. So, imagine the chaos if two thousand 737MAXs had to be grounded for a prolonged period. It is possible there would not be enough spare aircraft to replace them. Travelling would be completely disrupted. Some airlines and leasing companies would probably go bust. In the worst case scenario, that could be the trigger for a domino effect. That could even result in another financial crisis, affecting other banks and causing a worldwide recession. The claims against Boeing would almost certainly mean that it would have to be rescued. This may seem absurdly pessimistic. However, it is not impossible. So let us consider what set of circumstances would change this imaginary scenario into a reality.

### Perfect storm

The problem with trying to predict any irregular incident, such as a fatal accident, is that such incidents often only occur when there is a "perfect storm". This is where a combination of different factors all occur at the same time. To understand this, we can consider the analogy of continually throwing twenty dice from a cup. Each dice represents either a weakness in a system or a condition that could exploit that weakness. A perfect storm may be represented by ten or more of the dice showing a six. So, for example, this could represent ten different things going wrong during a flight, which, when combined, would lead to a crash. You cannot predict when a perfect storm is going to happen. It could happen on the next throw. It may not happen for a year of throwing the dice. All we can predict is the probability of a perfect storm. However, we can predict what factors will increase or decrease the probability of a perfect storm.

For example, consider the scenario where five of the dice are slightly unbalanced. We will assume that fault is such that they show a six on every other throw. This obviously greatly increases the chance of a perfect storm. On the other hand, if the defect meant that those dice rarely land showing a six, it would decrease the probability of a perfect storm. The implication is the rarer a system weakness can occur, the less probability of a perfect storm.

Similarly, consider the scenario where three people are throwing sets of twenty dice. The probability of any one of them throwing a perfect storm remains unchanged. However, the probability of a perfect storm, between all players, is three times greater than if only one person is throwing dice. So if there are currently 300 of a particular aircraft currently flying, then when 900 are flying, the probability of any single aircraft having an accident remains unchanged. However, the probability of an accident in the fleet increases three fold. In other words, as the number of planes in service increases, the probability of an incident, involving that model, also increases. The only way to counter this increasing probability of an accident is to minimise the number of systems weakness that could contribute to a perfect storm. This means that, unless Boeing focuses on removing every possible system weakness, its future is in the hands of the rolls of the dice. They could be lucky. But that is not the way to create a successful future.

So how does this approach vary from the Leadership Game approach, which you could use, if you took over the role of CEO in June 2019? You know that Boeing is already halfway down the pathway of the future from hell. You know there is a high probability that other MAX safety problems remain unidentified. You also know the probability of a perfect storm increases with the number of MAX aircraft in service. You also know there are over five thousand MAX aircraft on order. So, even being able to meet Boeing's previously high safety standards may not be enough to ensure a successful future. To create such a future, Boeing has to remove every system weakness that could potentially lead to a perfect storm. That includes the weaknesses that Boeing executives currently consider as others-in-control. Yet finding those weaknesses seems to be more challenging than finding a few needles in a field full of haystacks. They could be anywhere among the seventy thousand employees or the millions of parts involved in the aircraft. They could be in the thousands of suppliers, or the hundreds of thousands of their employees. They could be in the tens of thousands of pilots employed by the airlines. In addition, they could be in the thousands of the airlines' maintenance engineers. So where could you even start?

### Project perfect storm

From the perspective of a Leadership Game, the solution is always easy. The fact there is a real crisis makes it even easier. It is always easier to align people to a common goal when there is a real crisis. And in June 2019, Boeing is facing a genuine crisis. In effect, its future depends on its ability to prevent a perfect storm. As the new chief executive, you could even call the challenge "Project perfect storm". In this project, everyone needs to account for how they are contributing to the success of that project. The aim would always be to develop the fastest and most cost-effective way to find and remove every potential issue, which could contribute to creating an in-flight perfect storm.

Under these conditions, it is relatively easy to rapidly develop a culture that is intolerant of anything that could lead to an aircraft accident. That way, you could soon have seventy thousand people focused on finding the needles in the various haystacks. So we need to look at how you could set up the Leadership Game for project perfect storm. It would aim to eliminate avoidable accidents. But where would you start?

### Lesson from the safety audit

To understand how simple it would be to align the whole organization in these conditions, we need to go back and consider what happened in the safety audit. In effect, all the fail-safe safety team did was to focus on the Group part of the GAME loop. They built a frame of reference with a utopian standard of best practice for the control systems. That enabled anyone to easily assess the current standard of those systems. The normal roll out of Leadership Games already has one fail-safe system, which monitors the number of people not yet engaged in Leadership Games. All you need now is a way of ensuring the gaps in all the Leadership Games are consistently assessed against the defined standards of excellence.

For example, in the previous chapter, we looked at the scene where the invisible leader was the Vice President of Total Quality. With The Leadership Game, the challenge for that role is simply to ensure that all performance boards are using the standards needed by Total Quality. So a top-level fail-safe system for Total Quality would be the trend of the number of critical standards not yet under control. This would be the amalgamated total from the managers' performance boards. In other words, the top-level fail-safe systems only need to monitor that teams are using the Total Quality standards on the performance boards.

The difference with project perfect storm is the priority would be first check the Total Quality standard used to assess the critical cockpit systems. If there were a Total Quality focus on all the cockpit systems, then that would automatically minimise the likelihood of a sudden failure of the autopilot and sensor systems. It is essential to absorb the sheer power of what has just been described. With the Leadership Game, there is no longer any need for setting up separate initiatives such as Total Quality. All that we need to ensure is that the fail-safe systems use the standards, which are inherent in such initiatives.

### Better than best practice

However, reducing sudden systems failure was only one of the three solutions, which we need to minimise the possibility of pilot error, causing a crash. The second was to give pilots better guidance on what action to take in the event of a system failure. The third was to train pilots to be better at dealing with unexpected events. The reason we are going to look at these now is that neither can be addressed by using the current best practice or current standards of excellence. Both of these solutions need standards that are even higher than the current best. So we will start by looking at the information given to pilots when a system failure occurs.

### Pilot information

For example, consider the current solution to let pilots know the two AoA sensors disagree. The solution is a light, which comes on to show a problem. This may be currently considered as an acceptable solution. However, a single light does not tell the pilot which sensor is faulty, or how it is affecting the various autopilot systems. It does not even give the pilot the different readings, as there are no AoA dials on the dashboard. If the MCAS system is only using one sensor, it does not allow the pilot to switch the MCAS to the other sensor. Indeed, using a single lamp is comparable to a solution from a previous century designed by Heath Robinson or Rube Goldberg. It does not take much thought to imagine a standard that uses a solution from the twenty-first century.

For example, let us define the standard from utopia for information given to the pilot when there is a failure of a sensor or autopilot. We might define it as: "All information, which is needed for either pilot to safely take immediate control, is always displayed clearly and unambiguously". One possible solution could be small touch screens the size of a typical sat nav. If there was a sensor disparity, the screen could display the different sensor readings and allow the pilot to disengage one. It could even suggest a course of action. Such a screen could also display any relevant information on the whole range of possible system failures. There may be many reasons why aircraft designers could not use this solution. However, by identifying an imaginary solution from utopia helps people to more practical solutions, which can provide similar benefits.

### Pilot skills

The same approach needs to be taken in developing pilot skills to deal with the unexpected. It is almost certain the MAX will only be re-certified if pilots have the training to ensure they can control the plane with the MCAS system switched off. So, in principle, that training will ensure pilots can safely fly the aircraft, even after switching off the MCAS system. Such training is clearly essential. However, on its own, it is not enough to meet the standard from utopia. We might define that as "all pilots having consistently certified skills to instantly address any set of conditions that could lead to a perfect storm."

To meet that standard, we need a protocol that is additional to the occasional pilot simulator training. Again, we need a twenty-first-century method of developing instant responses to a constant stream of unpredictable challenges. And again, it does not take much imagination to realise that virtual-reality video games are an ideal way for pilots to develop such extra skills. Further, it would not be that difficult for Boeing to develop such training games. Indeed, Boeing could use a similar approach to minimise the possibility of human error with maintenance engineers. The point here is that, just by defining the standards from utopia, the Leadership Game can engage people to go even beyond current standards of excellence.

## Boeing's future

So, the Leadership Game approach, which you could use as the new chief executive in 2019, is very different from Boeing's actual approach. Perhaps the roll of the dice will be in Boeing's favour. Perhaps pilots and worldwide regulatory authorities will force Boeing to meet much higher standards. In either case, it does not seem as though Boeing executive are the ones who are creating Boeing's future.

However, the purpose of this exercise was not to judge Boeing executives. Nor was it to try and predict Boeing's future. The purpose was for you to assess the difference between vertical and dual structure organizations. It is for you to consider which type of organization is more effective at creating its future.

## Applying the principles

It would be easy to assume the Boeing scenario is not relevant to other types of organization. However, it is very relevant. It shows the power of the GAME loop. The safety issues could be quickly identified because there was a frame of reference for the safety criteria. This was the Group stage of the GAME loop. That frame showed utopia as having massive redundancy and effective contingency control. It was the comparison of the actual state, against the utopian state, which immediately identified Boeing's weaknesses.

This principle is applicable to all the criteria, which are critical to an organization's future. Yet it is a principle that many managers would often prefer to avoid. Indeed, some people have argued that this is a differentiating factor between management and leadership. Management aims to maintain the status quo by solving today's problems. Leadership aims to engage people in collaborating to close the gap between utopia and the current performance. With the latter approach, success is continually achieved, every time the gap reduces. So, success can be achieved every day, rather than just on reaching an arbitrary target set by a superior. This principle is fundamental to the Leadership Game.

So, to help you take the Leadership Game to an advanced level, I am currently working on a set of tools, which will be made available on the website at:

https://www.perceptiondynamics.info/members-area/

## Conclusion

I started this book, saying that change and performance improvement could be fast and fun. I explained the Leadership Game could transform silo mentality to a culture of high-performance teams. By now, I hope you can see exactly how easy it is to bring about change. However, this book has gone much further than the promise made in the first chapter. It has shown how any manager can become a leader and create the future they want. This is as true for first-line manager as it is for a chief executive.

Remember, if you would like to learn more about the Leadership Game, you can do so by becoming a Leadership Game member on the website. That site will be continually updated with more information on the approach, as well as providing a forum for you to discuss your issues with experts and other practitioners. There will also be information about consultancy available to help in setting up Leadership Games.

In conclusion, I wish you every success in using the

Leadership Game and making your life much more fun and effective. Thank you for reading this book.


All the best


Ian Robson

# About the author

Ian Robson has spent 25 years as a consultant, helping organizations to remove silo mentality and radically improve performance. Those organizations range from small enterprises to national and multinational businesses. They include many well known public and private sector organizations. Thousand of senior executives have attended his public master classes. Ian has also built up several companies from start-up to sale.

# Acknowledgements

I would like to thank Chris Knight for his great work in setting up so many successful Leadership Games.

Made in the USA
Columbia, SC
01 May 2020